ONE WEEK

FEB 20

MANCHESTER
UNIVERSITY PRESS

Politics Today

Series editor: Bill Jones

Local government today

Third edition

J. A. Chandler

Manchester University Press
Manchester and New York

distributed exclusively in the USA by Palgrave

First edition published 1991 by Manchester University Press
Second edition 1996
This edition published by Manchester University Press
Oxford Road, Manchester M13 9NR, UK
and Room 400, 175 Fifth Avenue, New York, NY 10010, USA
www.manchesteruniversitypress.co.uk

Distributed exclusively in the USA by
Palgrave, 175 Fifth Avenue, New York,
NY 10010, USA

Distributed exclusively in Canada by
UBC Press, University of British Columbia, 2029 West Mall,
Vancouver, BC, Canada V6T 1Z2

British Library Cataloguing-in-Publication Data
A catalogue record for this book is available from the British Library

Library of Congress Cataloging-in-Publication Data applied for

ISBN 0 7190 6035 4 *hardback*
     0 7190 6036 2 *paperback*

First published 2001

10 09 08 07 06 05 04 03 02 01   10 9 8 7 6 5 4 3 2 1

Typeset in Photina
by Servis Filmsetting Ltd, Manchester
Printed in Great Britain
by Biddles Ltd, Guildford and King's Lynn

Contents

v

Figures, maps and tables

Figures

Maps

Tables

Preface and acknowledgements

Local government ought to be seen as a far more important institution than is often suggested by the popular press and the systems, poor as they are, for ensuring civic education in Britain. Local government is important not only because of the many services it provides to the citizens of Britain, but also its capacity, which is far from fully realised, to contribute to a more democratic, free and humane society.

This book is intended to explain the structure and processes of local government in Britain to undergraduate, BTEC and 'A' and 'AS' level students of politics, public sector studies or business and economics. The study also develops a challenging critique and interpretation of the role of local government in Britain today and how the system evolved into its present state. Thus the study aims to provide an understanding of the value and potential of the system of local government in Britain.

There have been many changes to the system of local government in Britain since the second edition was published in 1996. Many of these changes have been a result of the constitutional radicalism of the Blair Government. They include the formation of the Scottish Parliament and Welsh Assembly, the regional development agencies, the Greater London Authority and English Regional Development Agencies. Structurally, the 2000 Local Government Act has revolutionised the way in which local authorities make decisions and ushered in the probability of directly elected mayors as significant political figures in Britain. Managerially, the implementation of Best Value will also have major repercussions on the process of local management. This edition will therefore chart the development of the local government systems up to the end of the first Blair Administration.

The British local government system should not, however, be viewed as particularly typical of the local government structures of other major liberal democracies. When considered in a comparative perspective, British local government has some rather strange features, most of all illustrated in the size of its units, its lack of smaller community-based structures and the centralisation of the system. This study places the system in comparative perspective through a series of inserted boxed paragraphs which, if read separately, will also provide a basic introduction to the structure of local government in the larger countries of the European Union and the United States.

Thanks are due to colleagues who have provided help and encouragement towards the completion of this volume. In particular, Michael Hunt, David Morris, Daniela Nepote, Barry Owen, Robert Jones, John Kingdom, Ralph Spence and Ann Wall in various ways provided assistance for this project. I have also received welcome assistance to enquiries from many local authorities and connected organisation, but especially Barnsley and Sheffield Metropolitan District Councils and the Local Government Association.

Thanks are also due to my wife Krys for allowing space and time to complete the work and also comments she has made on drafts of the chapters.

Abbreviations

AMF	*Association des Maires de France*
BIC	Business in the Community
CCLGF	Consultative Council on Local Government Finance
CCT	compulsory competitive tendering
CIPFA	Chartered Institute for Public Finance and Accountancy
CND	Campaign for Nuclear Disarmament
COSHE	Confederation of Health Service Employees
CoSLA	Confederation of Scottish Local Authorities
DTLR	Department of Transport, Local Government and the Regions
DfES	Department for Education and Skills
ESRC	Economic and Social Research Council
FBI	Federal Bureau of Investigation
GCSE	General Certificate of Secondary Education
GLC	The Greater London Council
GMB	General Municipal and Boilermakers Union
IDeA	Improvement and Development Agency
INLOGOV	Institute for Local Government Studies
JP	Justice of the Peace
LEA	Local Education Authority
LGA	Local Government Association
MBA	Master of Business Administration
MDC	Metropolitan District Council
MHLG	Ministry of Housing and Local Government
MP	Member of Parliament
MSF	Manufacturing, Science and Finance
NALGO	National Association of Local Government Officers
NEC	National Executive Commitee
NHS	National Health Service
NPM	new public management
NSPCC	National Society for the Prevention of Cruelty to Children

NUPE	National Union of Public Employees
NVQ	National Vocational Qualification
OFSTED	Office for Standards in Education
PFI	Private Finance Initiative
RDA	Regional Development Agency
SOLACE	Society for Local Authority Chief Executives
SRB	Single Regeneration Budget
SSA	Standard Spending Assessment
TGWU	Transport and General Workers Union
TUC	Trades Union Congress
UCATT	Union of Construction and Allied Trades and Technicians
UDCs	Urban Development Corporations
UNISON	UNISON (It is not an abbreviation)

1

The local government system: an introduction

Local government is a unique and valuable institution. It is the only organisation subject to election by all registered voters of Britain other than the national Parliament. As such, it should have an authority in the governance of the Nation second only to Parliament.

What is local government?

In Britain, local government refers to the authorities and dependent agencies that are established by Parliament to provide a range of specified services and represent the general interests of a specific area under the direction of a locally elected council. The web of public and private agencies that supply the needs of communities is however far wider than just the local authority. In recent years many authors have observed that Britain is subject to local governance, rather than simply local government, in order to emphasise that local authorities do not have a unique role in supplying the needs of their communities. The government of a locality will, for example, be subject for certain purposes to health trusts, regional development authorities, colleges of further and higher education or housing associations. Private as well as public agencies are also involved in the provision of collective services through legislation empowering private companies to sell essential services such as water, gas and electricity.

Local government should nevertheless be valued in a democracy more highly than the numerous other bodies that also shape aspects of urban and rural life. It differs from other agencies that supply local services in two important respects.

1 Local authorities supply a large range of services rather than, as in the case of many *ad hoc* agencies or quangos, a small number of specific tasks. They are therefore capable of co-ordinating many separate functions and determining a strategy for the well-being and development of a community as a whole.

2 Local authorities are the only agency representing communities in Britain whose councillors are chosen by elections open to all adult citizens of that community. Thus, local authorities not only provide many services, they also can claim to represent the views and aspirations of their communities.

The constitutional status of local government

Local government can trace its origins to Anglo-Saxon times before England, let alone Britain, had coalesced into a unified State. Nevertheless, throughout the twentieth century, governments have operated on a principle, supported in the courts, that local government only exists by grace and favour of the state. A government enquiry into political parties and local government in 1986 typically states that

> It would be wrong to assume that constitutional convention amounts to or derives from any natural right for local government to exist. It is a convention based on, and subject to, the contribution that local government can bring to good government. It follows from this that there is no validity in the assertion that local authorities have a 'local mandate' by which they derive their authority from their electorate placing them above the law. (Widdicombe 1986, Para. 3.6: 46).

Local government in Britain exists by virtue of Acts of Parliament. The structures, functions, funding and many of the processes of local authorities are determined by law. Councils can only undertake actions that are justified by law. If a local authority operates outside this framework, it may be held by the courts to be acting *ultra vires* and obliged to stop its unlawful action. Devolution of power by the British Parliament located in Westminster to Scotland has however complicated this framework, since the Scottish Assembly now has the powers to legislate for the structure and functions of local government in Scotland.

In most Western liberal democracies local, as opposed to federal, government is organised through ordinary legislation rather than constitutional arrangements. In some federal systems, such as the United States, it is the states and not the national government that determine the structure and powers of local authorities.

The range and functions of local government

All areas of Britain are divided into local authorities and there are in total over 10,000 local governments. The great majority are, however, legally classified as 'minor authorities'. These are the parish, town and community councils which

Table 1.1 *Tiers of local government in larger liberal democracies*

	Region/Federal	Upper/county tier	Lower communal tier
France	Region	Département	Commune
Germany	Land	Gemienden Stadtkries	Kries or none
Italy	Region	Province	Commune
Spain	Region	Province	Municipios
United States	State	County	City or township
Sweden	None	County	City

have little or no responsibility for providing services. The number of principal authorities that have significant functions is only 467.

The design for the principal structures of local government is based on single-tier and two-tier structures. Where a single-tier authority is established there is but one principal local authority covering that particular area. If a two-tier system is present, the tasks administered by local government are divided between a smaller district authority and a larger county in which there will be several districts. The two tiers are not, however, in an organisational hierarchy so that the smaller 'lower' tier of government is not subject to control by the larger 'upper' tier as both are given a separate range of functions.

In comparison with larger liberal democracies Britain is unusual in having many single-tier authorities and, so far, no three-tier local government structures. Table 1.1 illustrates the tiers of sub-national government in a number of liberal democracies, although there are some variations in some of the countries listed. For example, some large cities and especially capital cities such as Washington are effectively single-tier structures.

Two-tier structures are only present in England and, apart from London, cover predominantly rural areas. There are 34 counties and 238 districts associated with this system. Following the Greater London Act of 1999 that came into force in July 2000, London is governed for certain purposes by the Greater London Authority and for others by 32 London Boroughs plus the separate City of London. Unitary local governments in England exist in large conurbations that were in 1972 designated metropolitan areas. Although they initially had a two-tier structure, the 6 metropolitan counties were abolished in 1985 leaving local government in these areas divided under the control of 36 metropolitan districts. In the first half of the 1990s, a further restructuring of the system established in some larger towns and a few counties 46 single tier, unitary local governments. The arrangement is illustrated in Map 1.1.

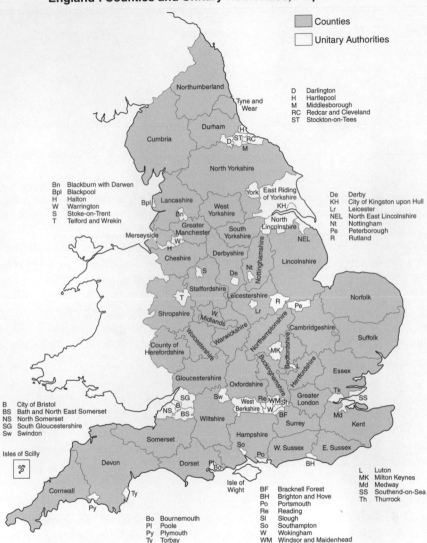

England[1]: Counties and Unitary Authorities, 1 April 1998

Counties

Unitary Authorities

D   Darlington
H   Hartlepool
M   Middlesborough
RC   Redcar and Cleveland
ST   Stockton-on-Tees

Bn   Blackburn with Darwen
Bpl   Blackpool
H   Halton
W   Warrington
S   Stoke-on-Trent
T   Telford and Wrekin

De   Derby
KH   City of Kingston upon Hull
Lr   Leicester
NEL   North East Lincolnshire
Nt   Nottingham
Pe   Peterborough
R   Rutland

B   City of Bristol
BS   Bath and North East Somerset
NS   North Somerset
SG   South Gloucestershire
Sw   Swindon

Isles of Scilly

L   Luton
MK   Milton Keynes
Md   Medway
SS   Southend-on-Sea
Th   Thurrock

BF   Bracknell Forest
BH   Brighton and Hove
Po   Portsmouth
Re   Reading
Sl   Slough
So   Southampton
W   Wokingham
WM   Windsor and Maidenhead

Bo   Bournemouth
Pl   Poole
Py   Plymouth
Ty   Torbay

1 Local Government Structure

Map 1.1   *Counties and Unitary Local Authorities in England*

Source: Office of National Statistics (1999), *Britain 2000*, London, HMSO.

Map 1.2 *Unitary Local Authorities in Scotland*

Source: Office of National Statistics (1999), *Britain 2000*, London, HMSO.

Since 1996, Scotland and Wales have been divided into 22 and 32 unitary authorities respectively. The pattern of their systems is illustrated in Maps 1.2 and 1.3.

The functions of unitary authorities are broadly similar and cover all the tasks listed in Table 1.2 which has grouped London Boroughs, metropolitan districts, English unitary districts and Scottish districts as unitary authorities.

Joint boards

There are some differences between the authorities in respect to police and fire services. In London the police and fire services are administered by the

Bd	Bridgend
BG	Blaenau Gwent
Ca	Cardiff
Cy	Caerphilly
Mon	Monmouthshire
MT	Merthyr Tydfil
N	Newport
NPT	Neath Port Talbot
RCT	Rhondda, Cynon, Taff
T	Torfaen
VG	The Vale of Glamorgan

Map 1.3 *Local Authorities in Wales*

Source: Office of National Statistics (1999), *Britain 2000*, London, HMSO.

Greater London Authority, although prior to its creation they were directly
under the authority of central government, which assigned them to Home
Office supervision. In the other unitary authorities, these services are
administered by joint boards that cover several neighbouring unitary
authorities. Although some counties are single police authorities, this
service may be shared between two or more counties. Joint boards to operate
local bus services were also established in metropolitan areas with the abolition of the metropolitan county councils. Following deregulation and privatisation of most bus services, these boards now largely have a planning
function.

Table 1.2 *Function of local authorities*

Function	County	District	Unitary	Joint board or London authority
Education	*		*	
Housing		*	*	
Social services	*		*	
Police	*			*
Fire and civil defence	*			*
Highways	*	*	*	
Transport	*			*
Museums and art galleries	*	*	*	
Libraries	*		*	
Planning		*	*	
Strategic planning	*		*	
Economic development	*	*	*	
Recreation, parks, sports facilities	*	*	*	
Refuse collection and street cleansing		*	*	
Weights and measures	*		*	
Food and health inspection	*		*	
Cemeteries		*		
Markets		*		

Minor authorities

The evolution of local government in Britain has led to a peculiarly disjointed distribution of minor authorities in Britain. The many minor authorities in England are parish or town councils, but in Scotland and Wales they are community councils. They cover predominantly rural areas and small towns and are only occasionally present in cities. A parish in England can apply to the Department of Transport, Local Government and the Regions (DTLR) to become a town council. This status allows its chairman to be dignified as mayor of the community, but conveys no other significant duties. This structure is summarised in Table 1.3.

The functions of parishes are discretionary and many are only local forums for the discussion of local problems. Parishes can, however, provide for the recreation, and cultural and economic development of their communities. A few

Table 1.3 *Minor authorities*

Area	Minor authorities
London	No parishes
Metropolitan districts	A few parishes or town councils in more rural areas
English unitary authorities	Parish and town councils in more rural areas
Two-tier areas	Predominantly parish or town councils
Scotland and Wales	Community councils in rural areas

parishes, generally larger town councils, have taken up these duties and provide sports facilities, parks, museums and arts festivals or installed closed circuit surveillance cameras in town centres. Parishes also have the right to be consulted on planning issues affecting their areas and may be involved in street lighting. In general, most parish and community councils wish simply to raise local issues with larger more powerful local authorities, but potentially they have a greater capacity to affect their areas than is often realised.

Why local government?

There have been numerous government enquiries into local government and its functions during the twentieth century and also much academic and political writing on this vital institution. It is possible to identify from this literature a muddled but generally consistent set of arguments that are used to justify the role of local government within the British administrative system.

Taking some of the administrative load

One of the widely accepted justifications for local government is that, within any large nation, it is important to ensure that the central government is not overloaded with responsibility for a vast array of policies and public services that are necessary for public well-being. The Layfield Report (1976) observed that

> If all public services were provided directly by the government and Ministers were formally accountable to Parliament for all local decisions, the machinery of government would become even more overloaded. (Para. 15: 53)

Ensuring effective service delivery at local level

The nineteenth century liberal philosopher John Stuart Mill, whose ideas perhaps encapsulate the thinking that lies behind our liberal democracy better than any other writer, argued that local government has the capacity to ensure that local residents put their local understanding to use in designing local policies and services. Central government bureaucrats, however wise and learned, cannot, for example, be as knowledgeable on the best site for a school in Inverness or Chorlton-cum-Hardy as the elected representatives of the people who live in those areas.

> It is but a small portion of the public business of a country which can be well done, or even safely attempted, by the central authorities. (Mill 1975: 364)

Or, as stated more recently, local government can ensure

> economy in resource utilisation in a society which cannot afford to waste national standards unrelated to local perceptions of need. (Jones and Stewart 1983: 10)

Facilitating democracy

Justifications for local government based solely on the institutions' capacity to deliver efficient services or take some of the administrative load from central government do not in themselves require elected, as opposed to appointed, councils to achieve these tasks. Securing more efficient government and relieving administrative overload can be and, for many tasks, is secured by quangos such as the health trusts or privatised businesses such as water companies. Local government as the only institution of the state elected by all citizens over the age of eighteen must be justified by additional arguments.

Jones and Stewart considered an essential value of local government is its capacity for enhancing

> democracy and self government in a society which cannot afford to entrust control over bureaucracy to twenty one Ministers and 650 MPs. (1983: 10)

Herman Finer argued that

> local governments . . . are safeguards against the tyranny of the wholesale herd, levelling, standardizing and conventional, hating and destroying original individuals and groups. (1945: 4)

Government reports have all endorsed the importance of local government for securing democracy in Britain. Widdicombe (1986) divides this contribution into the areas of participation, responsiveness and pluralism (Para. 3.11: 47). An effective democracy requires that many of its citizens participate in the political system. Local government ensures that there is a much greater opportunity for people to be involved as councillors in making the decisions that affect their communities and also greater opportunities to affect the decisions of councillors through activity in local parties and interest groups. It was also argued by J.S. Mill (1975) that participation in local government can be an important means of ensuring that citizens and politicians gain a mature education in the values required to establish a stable democracy.

An effective democracy must also respond effectively to the many requirements of its members. It is more likely that different needs expressed by geographical communities can be satisfied by locally democratic governments that are subject to influence by these varying demands. L.J. Sharpe argues that

> Communities not only vary in the mixture of needs and therefore service they require in an objective sense, but there is often disagreement within the community as to what the mixture should be . . . Understandably, no central government has the tenacity, the energy or the time to cope with the reconciliation of these conflicts . . . (1970: 168)

Arguably, the most important role of local government within a democracy is to facilitate a pluralist system. The pluralist theory of democracy developed by theorists such as R.A. Dahl (1961; 1971), maintains that power should be spread throughout society and no single organisation can be completely dominant. Where power is concentrated in governments, the principle of election can ensure that those who lead governments must respond to the demands of the many interests in society if they are to win elections and remain in office. Local governments are, therefore, important for spreading power and also establishing authoritative organisations concerned with local issues whose leaders will be sensitive to the demands of local groups.

Inconsistencies and omissions

Whilst the justifications made for local government in Britain are rarely subject to criticism, it must be questioned whether these arguments are sufficiently robust as a defence of local institutions in Britain. The arguments favouring local government tend to be instrumental. The institution is valued as it lightens the load of central government, improves and co-ordinates service delivery or enhances democracy in Britain. What is omitted from such justifications are arguments that value local government as important in itself rather than because it enhances the well-being of the Nation as a whole.

British justifications for local government lack any reference to the importance of local government in upholding basic human rights and values. In many countries, communities are seen to have a right to express their views and to retain their integrity. Britain only adhered to the European Charter of Local Self Government under the Blair Government. This document establishes a right for local authorities to regulate and manage a substantial share of public affairs under their own responsibility and in the interests of the local population. (Article 3.1)

It also considers that, as the preamble to the Charter observes,

the right of citizens to participate in the conduct of public affairs is one of the democratic principles shared by all member States of the Council of Europe

and that

it is at the local level that this right can be most directly exercised.

British justifications for local government are also oblivious of a fundamental argument about local government, which in Europe is found in the idea of subsidiarity, the principle that power ought to be passed down to the smallest political unit within a society capable of undertaking a required public function. The subsidiarity principle entails that if district authorities can, for example, manage the housing issues of a community, they should be empowered to undertake that function rather than national or regional governments.

Alexis de Tocqueville (1946), the early nineteenth century French theorist who analysed the politics of the United States, provided a powerful liberal justification for this principle. He followed liberal ideals that individuals should have as much freedom as possible, but accepted that people must on occasion provide services collectively for themselves. He observed that if each individual could participate directly in the policy process necessary for securing these collective services they would have greater freedom to shape that policy. The larger the community devising a policy the greater the number of opinions that must be weighed in the decision-making process and, as a consequence, each individual will have potentially less power and freedom to influence decisions. Thus, individual freedom is enhanced where decisions are made by direct participation in the smallest governments capable of efficiently providing a necessary communal service.

de Tocqueville found such a bastion of liberty in the small townships of New England where, as in some towns today, all the citizens of a town meet regularly to decide their local policies. Whilst direct democracy exists in only a few local authorities in the United States, there remains a strong ethos in the Nation that local communities are an expression of local independence and hence, compared with Britain, local people are very resistant to changing local government boundaries.

The consequences of conceptual muddle

The failure of British justifications for local government to establish clear ethical grounds for its status has enabled a parallel development of ideas on the structure and role of the institution that are largely incompatible with the arguments favouring the system as a means of facilitating greater democracy. In particular, a belief in providing opportunities for political participation seems to be difficult to reconcile with a strongly held assumption among observers of British Government that local authorities should be relatively large in size in order to be efficient and effective providers of services. This issue, discussed in more detail in Chapter 2, has created in Britain fewer and larger local authorities with consequently reduced opportunities for direct participation in local government than in any other nation of the European Union or the United States.

The widely held belief that local government has no right to exist except as a consequence of central legislation is also particularly difficult to reconcile with the idea of local democracy. Justifications for local government in Britain never enquire how it is possible to guarantee that local government can enjoy powers separate from those of central government and influence central government on behalf of local citizens within a regime that permits central government, by a simple majority in Parliament, to alter its power and status. In practice, central government appear to value central control far more than local democracy. Following recommendations of the Widdicombe Report which paradoxically had justified local government on grounds of its capacity to enhance pluralism within the Nation, the 1986 Local Government Act forbids local authorities from politically campaigning against central government. Such an Act denies local authorities the right, fundamental to pluralist democracy, that individuals and communities should have the capacity to influence central government.

The relatively weak justification for local government provided by government reports may be seen as both a cause and a symptom of the current hard life and times of local authorities. As will be shown in the next chapter, the boundaries and functions of local government in Britain have been in a continuous state of change over the last thirty years. The extent to which local government has discretion to pursue its preferred policies is also more restricted than in the vast majority of other liberal democracies. Although local authorities in Britain are not simply agents of central government that must only do what they are told, they are given discretion only in so far as this does not undermine the interests of whatever government is in power. Without a firm justification for local government that is accepted widely among local political interests, there is little to motivate a strong defence of the institution against continual moulding and manipulation of the system to suit national rather than local interests.

Further reading

There are a considerable number of general textbooks on local government in Britain that would provide an overview of the system. Care must, however, be taken to refer to later editions of these studies, since change to the system has been so extensive in the last decade that any study before 1990 will describe aspects of the system that are no longer in force. Among the studies which are as sufficiently up to date as is possible and widely recommended are Wilson and Game (1998), Byrne (2000), Elcock (1991) and Kingdom (1991). It is also worth referring to the latest edition of Dunleavy *et al.* (1998) *Developments in British Politics*, which contains a chapter on local government. Putting local government in a wider context of local governance beyond the centre are Gray (1994), Rhodes (1988) and Greenwood and Wilson (1989).

Introductory textbooks need to be highly descriptive in order to help those unfamiliar with the system, and can often provide little interpretation of how local government has developed, or relate the system to wider political theories. There are texts that assume more prior knowledge and have more space for greater depth. These works, that can be recommended as studies that will take you further than just a description of the system, include Stoker (1991), Hampton (1991) and more recently the study of diversity in local government by Stewart (2000).

Justifications for local government became a concern among writers in the mid-1980s and there are a number of studies that touch on this area. Widdicombe (1986) is a good example of the 'official' view, but more reflective are Jones and Stewart (1983) and more recently material produced by the Commission for Local Democracy and especially studies by Phillips (1994) and Stoker (1994). The Commission's material is re-edited in Pratchett and Wilson (1996) and there is also valuable material in King and Stoker (1996).

Web sites

Accessing material on local government through the internet is an important means of ensuring that you can obtain the most recent information on legislative changes to the system. The most useful entry is through the government's web pages on www.open.gov.uk. From this site you can through the index find material published by individual government Departments. The DTLR web pages are most relevant for local government and can be directly accessed on www.local.dtlr.gov.uk. You can also access from the open.gov index the web pages of individual local authorities. These differ greatly in quality, but generally the larger metropolitan districts and the Greater London Authority have extensive details on their activities. Some information on the Scottish system of local government can be obtained from the web site for the Scottish Executive www.scotland.gov.uk.

Other sites with some information are hosted by the Local Government

Information Unit at www.lgiu.gov.uk and the Local Authorities Association www.lga.gov.uk, although some parts of these sites are restricted to members. The Improvement and Development Agency (IDeA), which was formerly the Local Government Management Board, provides information and research findings at www.idea.gov.uk. A further information site is www.laria.gov.uk. of the Local Authorities Research and Information Association.

2

Structure and territory

Britain may lay claim to a world record for the population size of the effective lower tier of elected local government. As Table 2.1 indicates, in other liberal democracies the lower tier of local units of government serve a much smaller number of citizens.

France has some 36,000 communes, many of which have populations of less than a thousand. Sweden, which has comparatively large units, has only 3 municipalities with populations of over 200,000 and 66 with fewer than 10,000 inhabitants (Gustafsson 1988 32). Despite a considerable reduction in its lower tier authorities, Germany still has nearly 9,000 such structures. In the United States there is considerable variation in the number and size of city and county governments. Illinois at one extreme has 6,500 units of local government compared with less than 20 for Hawaii. In most states, many cities have less than 1,000 inhabitants, but the largest cities such as New York and Los Angeles administer populations of several million.

The evolution of the system

Until the 1830s local government in Britain had evolved along a path that was broadly followed by many other countries. The lowest tier was the parish, comprising communities ranging from small towns to collections of hamlets that were given rights and duties relating to the provision of basic services such as maintaining roads or apprehending petty criminals. In an age when religious and temporal government were not clearly separated, the parish was also a territorial division for the church.

Parishes were an organic unit of government, established by developing communities in accord with local needs, that subsequently gelled into a traditionally accepted structure. They were not, therefore, a product of systematic central planning or control. Most parishes are very ancient and some can trace

Table 2.1 *Average population of lower tiers of local government systems*

Britain	
Metropolitan and non-metropolitan districts and unitary authorities	139,300
France	
Communes	1,500
Germany	
Gemienden	9,000
Sweden	
Municipality	29,200

back their ancestry to Anglo-Saxon origins. Their boundaries emerged through a gradual process of land settlement and church building, which reflected local rather than central needs. Parishes often formed the focus for the loyalties and consciousness of place and belonging for their inhabitants.

As befits organisations representing the interests and needs of a community, most parishes were initially governed as democracies. Residents of the community would meet at regular intervals, often in the church vestry, and reach decisions through consensus or majority vote. They appointed officers who usually served the parish on a voluntary basis. By the eighteenth century, many of these once democratic participative parish governments had decayed into oligarchic systems dominated by wealthy families and particularly by the local landowner, the squire and that other local luminary, the parson or rector of the parish.

In most of Europe the lowest tier communities have, larger administrative areas created and sustained by central government superimposed on them. In Britain, since Anglo-Saxon times these took the form of the counties, although for many centuries there existed in some areas intermediate groups between the counties and the parishes called hundreds. As a sub-division of government, the county was intended to consolidate central power, originally of the monarch, so that they could sub-divide territory into areas to be managed on their behalf by a trusted lieutenant. The trusted aide of the King or Queen was originally the sheriff, an office much despised in the legend of Robin Hood. Gradually most of the powers of the sheriff were transferred to a Lord Lieutenant. This office, which was firmly established by the reign of Elizabeth I, was normally held by an aristocrat with large estates in the county.

By the eighteenth century, the Lord Lieutenant was an influential member of the governing elite, undertaking responsibilities for keeping the civil peace in the county on behalf of central government. Since they were usually members of the nobility, they had a seat in the House of Lords and therefore had influence over legislation and government. One of the Lord Lieutenant's most important functions was to keep the Home Secretary informed of political dissent from the lower classes by marshalling networks of spies in the pay of government. Below the Lord Lieutenant were Justices of the Peace (JPs), usually gentleman farmers, who presided over local magistrates' courts and the county court of quarter sessions. From this lofty position they dealt summary justice to the agrarian felon and poacher.

Parishes, as locally based political units, were not to be trusted by large landowners or central government. They were subjected to central surveillance and by the eighteenth century their deliberations were shadowed by the JPs. As the major function of county government was political repression and law enforcement, the administration of county matters became closely linked with the legal system. The parish councils had to report each year to the quarter sessions on their financial stewardship, so that their many activities could be checked by their betters.

Outside the structure of county and parish, a number of larger towns, which had at some time in their history commercial importance or royal favour, enjoyed independent status through the award of a Royal Charter that established them as a borough. This power usually included the right to send one or two worthies to Parliament. Once achieved, a Charter was rarely rescinded even though a formerly flourishing town might diminish in wealth or disappear altogether, as was the case of Dunwich, which as a result of coastal erosion was by 1800 largely under the North Sea.

Although these towns were self-governing and not directly subject to supervision by JPs, they were usually far from being free islands of democratic radicalism. For the most part their councillors were selected, as opposed to elected, from

In many European States and in the United States the second tier of local government, equivalent to the county in Britain, was traditionally viewed as the unit that supervised and co-ordinated the smaller community-based first-tier units. Thus, in France the department, which was until the 1980s controlled by an appointed civil servant, the prefect, supervised the activities of the communes and could suspend their mayor or council if they were thought to be acting improperly. Similar arrangements existed in Spain and Italy although reforms in these Mediterranean countries have now reduced the powers of the prefect or provincial governor and created elected councils, which select a president to run the activities of the department or province, leaving the prefect to take a more managerial than policy-making role. In the United States the county, although always subject to an elected council, was seen as a body representing state rather than local interests.

historically important trades in the town or simply through co-option by a coterie of self-perpetuating councillors who spent little on city development and more on town halls and big dinners. By the eighteenth century these councils were often viewed as a national disgrace even by the standards of the time (Fraser 1979).

The growth of towns and decline of the parish

During the nineteenth century British local government diverged in its structure from its European neighbours through a process that marginalised the parishes, replacing them with authorities whose territories were delineated according to a centrally imposed rationale based on efficiency rather than community. The motivating force behind this change was the philosophy of liberalism that justified the industrialisation of Britain.

> The 10,000 parishes in Britain, whilst having far fewer powers than the 36,000 French communes, are, in geographical terms, the English equivalent of these structures. Britain, unlike most European countries and the United States has effectively disempowered the community-based level of government.

The growth of industry from the late eighteenth century caused serious strains within the local government system. In the periphery of London and the expanding industrialising towns, the existing parishes had to cope with a newly arrived population, who had no roots in or loyalty to their new place of residence. In some of these towns local government effectively collapsed as JPs and parish worthies could not cope with the new conditions.

It was not until the political breakthrough of liberalism in 1832 that progress to a new system based on liberal principles could be sustained. The Electoral Reform Act of 1832 was not a triumph for democracy, but a concession wrung from the landowning oligarchy, which obliged them to share power with the capital-rich industrialists and men of commerce. The Act broke up a traditionally established structure of electoral usage that secured places in Parliament for landowners and replaced it with a more uniformly organised system of constituencies whose electors qualified for the vote by virtue of propertied wealth held in either land or buildings. The liberal triumph opened the path for the capitalists to participate in the government of the cities that they had largely created and sustained. The subsequent Municipal Corporations Act of 1835 allowed larger cities to become boroughs governed by representative councils and laid down rules for the formation of new municipalities. The Act not only created new boroughs, but permitted restructuring in larger towns with debased Royal Charters. Within the new boroughs, rate payers, in effect property owners, could elect a council to manage the environmental concerns of the community and police its lawless streets.

Not all towns immediately leapt at the opportunity afforded by the 1835 Act. New local authorities cost money if they were to effectively improve living conditions. Rate payers then, as now, were initially reluctant to participate. The established, largely Tory, councillors who were the beneficiaries of the older systems of government often allied with shopkeepers and innkeepers to oppose what they saw as control by newly arrived grasping and ruthless capitalists (Fraser 1979). However, by the 1850s most large cities had a borough council and more far-sighted local businessmen saw that local control could be developed so as to greatly benefit their commercial interests as well as making their cities centres of magnificence. Through the zeal and genuine local sentiment of local industrialists, city governments reached a zenith of power and influence in the late nineteenth century and built as their cathedrals the gothic town halls that are among the largest public constructions of that age.

The demise of the parish

Whilst municipal government flourished, the liberal values that had created the Victorian town hall moved like a juggernaut to roll over the parish as a unit of government in rural areas. The rural parish was seen by liberals as a bastion of Tory influence. Its most costly function was to administer poor relief, which required rate payers to provide for the basic sustenance of impecunious parishioners. By the nineteenth century the institution was subject to fierce criticism from liberals and also many Tories who were convinced that such welfare fostered idleness. The system was also impossible to administer in the new industrial cities and served as a brake on labour mobility. The 1834 Poor Law Amendment Act established a uniform system for alleviating poverty, which was to be administered by new single-purpose authorities, the Poor Law Unions. The members of the Unions were elected by local taxpayers but were subject to tight, centrally determined controls and inspection by Poor Law Commissioners. The system effectively bypassed parishes and removed their most important function.

Although many conservatives opposed the new poor law structures, the system set a precedent to be followed by later governments caught up in the process of coming to terms with the growth in population and the social demands of industrialisation. In 1848 an *ad hoc* network of health authorities was established to eradicate the scourge of deadly epidemic disease through water purification and sewage systems. In 1862 some parishes were grouped together to form highways boards and in 1870 the introduction of compulsory education led to the formation of *ad hoc* school boards. By the 1880s local government consisted of a complex amalgam of structures that included some 300 multi-purpose urban governments and in other areas a bewildering patchwork of agencies operating alongside the older parish and county governments.

Rationalisation of this complex system began with the democratisation of

Table 2.2 *Local government in Britain 1930–74*

Area	First tier	Second tier
Cities	County borough	n/a
Larger towns	County	Borough
Smaller towns	County	Urban districts
Rural areas	County	Rural district

county government in the wake of electoral reform at the national level. The 1888 Local Government Act established elected county councils and removed the powers of JPs and Lord Lieutenants over most aspects of local administration. The Act also gave some of the larger cities the accolade of a county borough, confirming their status as unitary authorities. Proposals in the Bill to rationalise the *ad hoc* boards were withdrawn, partly due to the complexity of the legislation on counties. This was later achieved through the 1894 Local Government Act, which created multi-purpose rural and urban district councils based on the boundaries of the health boards. Once the framework of elected county, county borough, borough and district councils was in place, many of the *ad hoc* agencies created to bypass the parish and county were merged with the new structures, although the Poor Law Unions remained until 1929 as a separate entity.

By 1914 the parish was therefore a vestigial unit of government with few significant powers. Local government was the responsibility of much larger territorial units and much of the ethos of communal government that still exists in much of Europe had evaporated. The structure of the system is outlined in Table 2.2.

From large to huge authorities

Despite its recent formation, demands to remould the structures created in the late nineteenth century into yet larger units appeared soon after the First World War. Early advocates for larger authorities included politically influential Fabian thinkers such as the Webbs (1920) and G.D.H. Cole (1947). By 1945 there was virtual unanimity among politicians and academics that the structure was outdated. W.A. Robson, one of the most distinguished authorities on local government in the 1940s and 1950s observed that

> For more than thirty years the organisation of local government has been growing obsolete and is now hopelessly out of date. Far larger units of administration than those afforded by counties and county boroughs are needed for such services as town and country planning, technical education, sewerage disposal, electricity and gas supply. (1954:35)

Cities had burst out of their nineteenth century boundaries to create urban conurbations governed by several independent local authorities. In such circumstances, argued the reformers, it was impossible to plan for cities as a whole without involving the agreement and co-ordination of several councils. Small local authorities were also argued to be inefficient as they could not employ economies of scale or serve special minority needs. The system could not, moreover, attract and retain well-qualified specialist officers or interest the most competent people of the community to become councillors. These problems were fuelled by internecine strife between the counties and the county boroughs. Expanding cities with serious housing problems could only buy cheap land on which to build new estates in neighbouring rural local authorities that had no wish to give up land to meet urban overspill. By the 1940s several county boroughs were campaigning for the extension of their borders to take in their suburban and semi-rural hinterlands. In addition, some larger boroughs were petitioning for county borough status, which would provide them with new powers at the expense of the counties.

Restructuring London

Reformist zeal remained unappeased until 1957 when Henry Brooke, who had formerly been an opposition leader on London County Council, became Minister of Housing and Local Government. His special interest in London led him to establish a Royal Commission to study the structure of local government in the region in the light of the repeated requests from a number of larger authorities for county borough status. The recommendations of the Herbert Report (1960) were, apart from a few details, accepted by the Government. The subsequent London Government Act of 1963 abolished the County Councils of London and Middlesex and drastically reduced the number of lower tier authorities from over 100 to create 32 large London Boroughs. The City of London which covers approximately a square mile of Britain's financial centre was however, not included in the reform and allowed to retain its separate identity and practices that date from medieval times. London as a whole was represented by a unique strategic authority, the Greater London Council (GLC), which had some powers such as the provision of housing, not normally assigned to county councils, but not some other county functions, principally police and education. The prestige of the education department of the abolished London County Council prompted the Government to retain this body as the separate Inner London Education Authority.

The 1970s restructuring

The Government chose to deal with criticism of the system in the rest of the country by the piecemeal procedure of re-establishing a Local Government Boundaries Commission. A body to recommend new boundaries for local authorities had been formed by the Attlee Government in the late 1940s, but had made little headway. A new Commission established in 1958 made several recommendations to increase the size of some local authorities. Indeed, its success sparked off a major reform of local government structure in the 1970s through a roundabout route.

The Labour Minister for Housing and Local Government Richard Crossman was confronted soon after his Party's narrow electoral victory by fears from some backbench Members of Parliament (MPs) that changes to local government boundaries in Lancashire would be followed by a reordering of parliamentary constituencies in the county that would disadvantage the Labour Party. Crossman, a man not disinclined to father constitutional reforms, realised he could stave off this unpleasant difficulty by postponing boundary changes with the creation of a Royal Commission to enquire into the local government structure as a whole (Crossman 1975). The Prime Minister, Harold Wilson, readily perceived the electoral value of such a plan and sanctioned the formation of a Royal Commission to consider the structure of local government in England apart from the recently recast system in London. The enquiry is popularly referred to as the Redcliffe-Maud Commission as its chairman was the recently ennobled John Maud, who had chaired an earlier enquiry into local government management referred to as the Maud Report (1967). A parallel Commission, under the chairmanship of a lawyer, Lord Wheatley, was formed to consider local government in Scotland. The newly created Welsh Office jealously guarded for itself the right to undertake a review of local government in its principality.

The membership of the Redcliffe-Maud Commission was carefully balanced to represent the interests of the counties and larger county boroughs and the Conservative and Labour Parties. No thought was given to the interests of smaller communities so that the Commission was stacked against any solution other than the creation of fewer and larger local authorities. In conformity with orthodox academic and political thought, the Commission argued that 'the movement of opinion in favour of large authorities is impressive' (1969, Para. 110: 33). It proposed that most of England should be divided into 59 single–tier districts, based as much as possible around a major urban centre, which would have populations ranging from just over a million to 200,000 inhabitants. Three conurbations, the West Midlands, Merseyside and Greater Manchester were to have a different arrangement built around a two-tier metropolitan county and district structure. The Wheatley Commission on Scottish local government agreed with Redcliffe-Maud on the need for larger authorities, but adopted a two-tier region/district format, whilst the Welsh Office similarly advocated a two-tier structure for the principality of enlarged counties and districts.

The findings of the Commissions were accepted by the Labour Government, with a few modifications, but legislation to adopt the structure was shelved when the Government fell in 1970. The Conservative administration of Edward Heath picked up the principle of reform, but not the single-tier structure proposed for England. Partly due to pressure from Conservative 'knights of the shire' and to fears that many rural areas would become Labour controlled under the previously proposed arrangements, the Government decided on a two-tier system of counties and districts. They also increased the number of metropolitan areas to six with the addition of South and West Yorkshire and Tyne and Wear, but drew the boundaries of these areas much more tightly around conurbations to isolate Labour-held territory from Tory hinterland. The proposals for Scotland and Wales were more to the taste of the Conservatives and were adopted with few changes.

Drawing the new political map

Although the arrangement of local government boundaries established by the 1972 Local Government Act was not as radical as the Redcliffe-Maud proposals, a number of major changes were made to the counties with the abolition of several smaller units Rutland, Westmorland, and the divisions of Lincolnshire and the merger of Hereford and Worcestershire into a single county. New counties such as Avon were created. In addition to these major changes, adjustments, that are often still resented, were made to county boundaries such as apportioning some areas of Yorkshire into Lancashire (Bradford 1988). In Wales thirteen counties were merged into eight larger units which had little cultural identity. Predominantly English-speaking Pembroke was, for example, joined with the more Welsh-speaking counties of Cardigan and Carmarthen to create Dyfed, a wholly new name to most Welsh people let alone the English. Glamorgan, the most populous county was, on the other hand, split into three separate counties in a desperate struggle to ensure, irrespective of geographical size and cultural diversity, that each Welsh county had roughly similar populations. In Scotland, the traditional counties were swept away altogether to be replaced by nine Regions, including Strathclyde which encompassed a population of 2.3 million.

Although the county structure was severely mauled, the community element of the local government structure, in as much as this was represented by the boroughs and urban and rural districts, was wholly destroyed. In England the district map was almost entirely a new creation drawn up largely by Whitehall on the advice of a Boundary Commission established by the 1972 Act, which kept firmly to government guidelines that districts should generally have a population range between 75,000 and 100,000 with no area of less than 40,000 inhabitants (Wood 197: 162). For the most part, they adopted the Redcliffe-Maud procedure of joining together existing local government units and only in relatively few cases split existing authorities. Consultation took place with the local authority associations on matters of principle, but there was little attempt to stimulate grass roots discussion on boundaries. Not surprisingly, their findings initiated numerous local protests from offended councils who were about to lose their identity. The Commission received 28,000, written comments, largely adverse (Wood 1976: 164).

Despite a few concessions, the new districts had little rationale in terms of community. In Wales and Scotland a sense of tradition could be said to have been preserved by making many of the old redundant counties into districts. However, such action has little bearing on the values of community life. In England many of the districts were assigned names that were anonymous new creations, which did not convey any geographical meaning let alone sense of place.

Dissatisfaction with the new districts was widespread but localised. The local press in some areas showed signs of parochial resentments and, on occasion, spectacular protest might reach the smaller columns of the national press. A number of councillors representing Morecambe Bay publicly established themselves as a group seeking the division of the seaside town from Lancaster City Council; inhabitants of Newmarket strongly petitioned to be included in Cambridgeshire rather than Suffolk; Penistone Town Council passed a symbolic declaration of independence from Barnsley Metropolitan District. Such protest may underlie even greater popular resentment. A survey of the former Urban District of Stocksbridge, which in 1974 was incorporated into Sheffield Metropolitan District, showed that two-thirds of respondents considered that the existing arrangements for local government were unsatisfactory (Ashworth and Chandler 1981).

Few other liberal democracies have engaged in such root and branch restructuring of their local government systems, but relied on occasional piecemeal change. During this period West Germany and Sweden reduced the number of lower tier authorities, but not to the extent of Britain. In France there have been but a few mergers of communes and in Italy small communes are increasingly tending to co-operate and effectively merge on a voluntary basis. In the United States it is generally the practice that the citizens of any area subject to proposals that change their local government area are asked to approve the idea through a local referendum. In most cases citizens reject the changes.

Restructuring once again

The Thatcher Government had no immediate thoughts of again changing local government boundaries, but soon came to regret the creation of the GLC and the metropolitan Counties. Official criticisms rested largely on the cost of their administration and the belief that their removal would save money. In reality their abolition was largely due to the fact that they were predominantly Labour controlled and some were highly critical of the Government. The GLC particularly exhausted Tory patience. The idea to abolish these troublesome authorities had been considered but rejected by a cabinet committee in 1981, but when the committee failed to find a popular alternative to the existing method for collecting local taxes in time for inclusion in the manifesto for the 1983 election, a sudden inspiration from Mrs Thatcher led to the unearthing of the abolition policy. The decision was, therefore, as much born out of the need to be seen to be actively restructuring local government than from any well-considered desire for reform (Chandler 1988). Once the policy was enshrined in the manifesto, a bandwagon was on the roll. Despite popular feeling, parties normally manage to honour their commitments however misconceived they may be. The legislation proved to be the most troublesome issue of the 1983–87 Government, but despite widespread opposition, promoted, in part, by skilled public relations led by Ken Livingstone, the Bill to remove the GLC and metropolitan counties became law in 1985 and the authorities ceased to exist on 1 April 1986.

Although the metropolitan counties disappeared as multi-functional units of elected government, they still exist in a very attenuated form, since the abolition legislation set up *ad hoc* authorities in each metropolitan county to deal with police services, fire and civil defence and public transport. The membership of joint boards includes councillors nominated from the participating authorities although, in the case of police authorities, the membership includes a number of representatives of local magistrates and nominees of the Home Secretary.

The new structure of local government

Despite restructuring in 1974 and 1985, there were powerful elements within the Conservative Government who still considered that the local government system needed further drastic change. In 1990, following the fall of Mrs Thatcher, Michael Heseltine returned to the post of Secretary of State for the Environment and began preparing White Papers to redesign both the external and internal structures of local government. Whilst his suggested reforms of the management of local government made little progress, the White Paper on the structure of local government published in 1991 began a process that has once again redrawn the local government map.

The 1991 White Paper suggested that a unitary structure was probably the best system for organising local government and that a Local Government Commission should be established to make recommendations on a new pattern for local government based on this idea. Parallel studies of local government structure in Wales and Scotland were also undertaken by the Welsh and Scottish Offices. The Local Government Commission for England was established in 1992 under the chairmanship of Sir John Banham, previously Secretary General of the CBI and a former Director of the Audit Commission. It was given the task of reviewing the boundaries of local authorities in the non-metropolitan authorities of England and recommending how these could be changed into a more efficient and yet also popularly acceptable pattern. The Secretary of State for the Environment had the responsibility for making a final decision on the suggestions and placing the proposed solution before Parliament in the form of a statutory order rather than an Act of Parliament, thus decreasing the length of time the arrangements needed to be subject to parliamentary debate and scrutiny. The Commission decided that the task of redrawing local government boundaries in England was not to be determined on the basis of underlying principles, but pragmatically through studies conducted by commissioners on the needs of particular areas of the country and the views of local interests. A county or a group of counties were assigned to two commissioners who received the views of local authorities, groups and individuals in the area and then put forward a report suggesting possible new structures. The views of commissioners diverged sharply and some teams favoured the Heseltine suggestion of unitary authorities whilst others recommended a two-tier structure.

By the time the Commission began to publish its highly controversial reports, Michael Heseltine had left the Department of the Environment and his successors, Michael Howard and then John Gummer, seemed far less enthusiastic about a wholesale rationalisation of the system. Gummer was prepared to accept two-tier recommendations from the Commission, but also insisted on a greater number of single-tier urban authorities than were proposed. John Banham rebuffed by the Government resigned from the Chair of the Commission in March 1995 to be replaced by Sir David Cooksey, a businessman.

The structure of local government for England, outlined in Chapter 1, is therefore built up from an amalgam of different ideas and interests. There has been some consensus that counties such as Avon, Humberside and Cleveland created by the Redcliffe-Maud Report should disappear and that some cities such as Derby, Nottingham, Peterborough and Leicester should become unitary authorities and, therefore, resemble the unitary metropolitan districts. In some sectors there was, however, little or no coherence in the Commission's recommendations which removed, for example, the county of Berkshire dividing it into four unitary authorities, whilst retaining two-tier status in many similar areas such as Surrey or Hertfordshire.

The reorganisation of local government in Scotland and Wales has been subject to a much more rapid and less controversial process. The Secretary of State for Wales, following consultations with local authorities in the principality, drew up proposals to abolish the county councils set up by the 1972 Local Government Act and transform the majority of districts into unitary authorities. In effect, this has led to many areas that were county councils prior to 1974 receiving, once again, their former powers as a county, whilst retaining their district authority powers which they gained from the abolition of these smaller areas in 1974. In Scotland, the Secretary of State established a similar arrangement by abolishing the regions created in 1972 and transferring their powers to the existing districts to create a pattern of unitary authorities. The new arrangements for Scotland and Wales came into effect in April 1996.

The regions

The Government of Tony Blair has, despite an enthusiasm for structural change, so far not thought it necessary to restructure yet again the boundaries of existing local authorities. However, the Government came to power with a promise to establish regional government in Scotland, regional administration in Wales, planning regions for England and a strategic authority for the London conurbation. The development of regions within Britain is not, of course, a new idea and the Blair Government is responding to a long history of unification and separatist pressure that has marked England's relationship with the United Kingdom as a whole. Scotland became a part of Britain subject to government from Westminster in 1707 through the Act of Union, an arrangement in which the Scottish aristocracy were accepted into the House of Lords and effectively became part of the establishment that governed Britain as a whole. The system of devolved government to the landed elite in England enabled the Scottish nobility to control their territories with the freedom given to their English peers and this also ensured Scotland retained separate systems of public administration that included the legal system, education and local government structures.

Opposition to Scottish integration into Britain emerged in the early nineteenth century, stimulated by Irish separatism and also the growth of a partly invented Scottish nationalist culture by romantic educated Scots such as the novelist Sir Walter Scott. This movement led in 1885 to a recognition of the identity of Scotland through the creation of a separate Department of State, the Scottish Office, to deal with Scottish issues and a Scottish Grand Committee in Parliament, where Scottish MPs could review legislation that affected the province (Kellas 1968: 120–37).

Wales, in contrast to Scotland, had never established a strong landowning class to rival the English aristocracy and by the sixteenth century had become under the Tudors subject to the same administrative system as England in return for having Welsh representatives in the English Parliament. The growth of Welsh nationalism as a political force in the 1960s, however, prompted the Labour Government of Harold Wilson to create a Welsh Office mirroring the Scottish Office, but with rather fewer powers.

The continued growth of nationalist parties in Scotland and Wales since the 1950s prompted the Wilson/Callaghan Government to seriously propose a measure of devolution to these provinces and in 1979 a referendum was held on devolution in both provinces, but a majority of those voting in Wales opposed the measure. In Scotland a majority of those voting supported devolution, but the legislation required an absolute majority of all Scottish electors to put devolution into effect and this was not achieved. The Thatcher and Major Governments had no interest in devolution, a stance that partly ensured the virtual disappearance of the Conservative Party as a political force in these areas, whilst concern to keep support in Wales and Scotland remained an important issue for the Labour Party.

The formation of the Scottish Parliament and the Welsh Assembly mark an important change in the political structure of Britain and may mark the beginning of a more decentralised and possibly a federal Britain. The devolved governments in Scotland and Wales are not directly an issue for this book since they cannot be seen as local government structures. Their powers are determined by the Acts of 1998 that established the devolved governments. Unlike a fully federal system, the arrangement may be amended by a majority vote in the British Houses of Parliament.

> The Constitution of the United States can only be amended to affect the powers of the fifty states with the consent of the majority of state governments, whilst in Germany the federal system, based on sixteen Land governments, can only be restructured by the agreement of the upper house of the German legislature which is composed of representatives of the Länder. Several European countries such as Spain and Italy have, however, developed regional governments which are being given increasing numbers of powers and would, politically, be very difficult for the central government to abolish, given local political support for such structures.

The Scottish Parliament and Executive has, unlike any British local authority, the power to put forward legislation on a range of issues which substitutes for any laws relating to England and Wales. Among these powers is the capacity to make arrangements for the local government system in Scotland. Thus, the Scottish Parliament led by its Executive and First Minister is capable of restructuring its system of local government without reference to Whitehall and Westminster. The Scottish Parliament also has discretion on how local government in the province should be funded and structured and within the limits of the Parliament's powers, it has the ability to determine exactly what the Scottish authorities should do. So far, however, the Scottish Parliament seems relatively content with the structure of the system bequeathed to it by the Scottish Office and retains the pattern of thirty-two single tier-districts that came into being in 1996.

The Welsh Assembly has fewer powers than the Scottish Parliament and has the capacity to make only secondary legislation, which in effect is a power to modify broad framework laws made by the British Parliament in a process analogous to the development of statutory instruments. The Welsh Assembly is not capable of establishing legislation that is incompatible with law made in Westminster. The Assembly and Welsh Executive are, nevertheless, delegated considerable powers to implement policy on a wide range of domestic issues and also to propose policy changes within the framework of existing legislation. In practice Welsh local government was structured through the Welsh Office and in the new devolved arrangement it is expected that authority to structure the Welsh system of local government will lie with the Welsh Assembly and

Executive. However, issues such as funding may still rest heavily with London. Activities devolved to the Welsh and Scottish Governments are:

- Local government
- Health
- Education
- Transport
- Housing
- Planning
- Economic development
- Environment
- Agriculture
- Arts and sport

English regionalism

Pressure to develop regions in England derive far more than the progress towards Scottish and Welsh Regions from considerations on good local government practice as opposed to resolving nationalist pressures. The view that there should be a further regional tier of local government in England was expressed in the 1940s by Fabian writers and in particular by G.D.H. Cole (1947), who saw regions as a means for decentralising power concerning major public enterprises such as gas and electricity distribution or higher education to units of government large enough to efficiently handle these services but still responsive to a local population, rather than the national government. Further impetus was given to regionalism through the growth of economic planning as means of resurrecting declining economies and, by the 1960s, these pressures had led to the emergence of numerous *ad hoc* single-purpose regional administrations in England dealing with the supply of utilities such as gas and electricity, the collection of statistics and economic planning (Hogwood and Lindley 1982). None of the many regional bodies that were created had consistent boundaries and the system created considerable confusion and lack of clarity as to the exact geographical pattern of any English region. The untidy growth of regional bodies had sufficient recognition by the 1960s to prompt the Redcliffe-Maud Commission to advocate non-elected planning regions for Britain. This proposal was ignored by the Heath Government but accession to the Common Market added further pressures to develop regional government, since the European Union directs its aid to the more economically deprived parts of Europe through funding to regions.

Devolution to Scotland and Wales has been linked by many, but by no means all, members of the Blair Government to a more extensive programme of regional decentralisation that would also apply to England. However, whilst there is now substantial support in central government for such a development,

REGIONAL DEVELOPMENT AGENCY

SCOTLAND

ONE NORTH EAST

NORTH WEST DEVELOPMENT AGENCY

YORKSHIRE FORWARD

EAST MIDLANDS DEVELOPMENT AGENCY

WALES

ADVANTAGE WEST MIDLANDS

EAST OF ENGLAND DEVELOPMENT AGENCY

LONDON

SOUTH EAST OF ENGLAND DEVELOPMENT AGENCY

SOUTH WEST OF ENGLAND DEVELOPMENT AGENCY

Map 2.1 *Regional Development Agencies in England*

the idea is not universally popular and steps toward a regional tier of government in England are slow and faltering. Before the 1997 election, as a compromise between differing currents of opinion among its leaders, New Labour promised to create regional structures that would, at least in the first five years of the Government, fall short of elected assemblies. The 1998 Regional Development Agencies Act created Regional Development Agencies (RDAs) which mapped on to the areas covered by the Regional Government Offices created by John Major in 1994 as shown in Map 2.1. The RDAs are broadly responsible for promoting the economic development of their areas and this also includes promotion of business efficiency, employment, skill enhancement and sustainable development.

The agencies, appointed by the Government, include four representatives from local authorities, but have a majority of business members. In addition to the agencies, the Act created regional chambers which have greater local authority and voluntary group representation and have to be consulted on the strategies of the RDAs. The Government may use the chambers as the basis for establishing an elected legislature to control the RDA as the region's executive, if full-scale regionalism as a further tier of government becomes a reality. The regional structures have so far been established as a complement to local authority action in these areas and are not at present seen as organisations that will take over powers now held by local governments. It remains to be seen whether New Labour will make room for proposing the development of elected English regions in its second term of office.

The Greater London Authority

The formation of an elected regional government in London through the creation of the Greater London Assembly and Executive by the 1999 Greater London Act is a development that responds as much to the need to restore a strategic level of government to London following the abolition of the GLC rather than an extension of the debate on the need to establish regions throughout England. Following the abolition of the GLC, Britain was unique in not having a strategic authority to co-ordinate the capital city.

> All large liberal democracies establish a strategic authority to govern their capital city. In some cases, as in Sweden, this is a local authority constituted little differently from other local governments in the country but in many regimes special arrangements apply to the capital. Washington, for example, is not within any state but has a special federal district status that makes it a unique institution within the United States.

The new Greater London Authority covers the area of the former GLC but does not exactly replicate its functions and duties. It is possible that the new Assembly and Mayor of London may be a blueprint for later regional structures in England, but it is doubtful whether any other English regions would be given all the tasks established for the Greater London Authority, which include a significant role in the supervision of the Metropolitan Police, formerly under Home Office control. The powers of the Greater London Authority which are listed below are predominantly concerned with strategic issues such as transport and economic development that require integration between the various

London Boroughs.

- Transport
- Planning
- Economic development
- Policing
- Fire and emergency planning
- Culture
- Health

The Greater London Authority, therefore, provides some large-scale strategic services, but unlike the old GLC does not have powers, for example over housing, that are also held by the London Boroughs.

Conclusion

The preceding history of local government structures shows a steady progress towards marginalising small community-based units of government and the concomitant development of large authorities which can scarcely be termed local. The trend is but one element of a process whereby local authorities in Britain have become much less community based and yet more subject to central restraint and guidance than the systems of other liberal democracies. This tendency stems largely from the development of attitudes towards local authorities that place them as servants, or more appropriately, stewards, of the centre. This centralist ethos does not pay much, if any, regard to values such as community representation and local democracy. Some indication of this indifference has already been discussed at the end of Chapter 1 and a further analysis of the underlying attitudes that shape the present structures and development of local government is provided in later chapters in this study.

Further reading

There are no extensive recent histories of local government. The most useful text that is widely available is Keith-Lucas and Richards (1978) and much is also covered in the misleadingly titled study by Sheldrake (1992). The post-Second World War developments have been chronicled by Young and Rao (1997). The socio-economic development of the modern system is skilfully analysed by Redlich and Hirst (1970) in an extensive study first published in 1903. Bulpitt (1983), whilst not a history, nevertheless provides a valuable insight into the development of sub-national government in Britain.

Studies of the geography, boundaries and community basis of local government in Britain, are, for reasons that should be evident from the chapter, rather thin. There are, however, a reasonable number of studies on the concept of community such as Plant (1974) or Bell and Newby (1971). Among writers who apply the question of community to local government, Hampton (1970) provides a thoughtful analysis and the Redcliffe-Maud Report (1969), especially the research volume material on community and parish councils, repays further study. A study of the changes in structure in the 1990s is provided by Steve Leach (1998).

The unusual nature of the British local government system cannot be fully appreciated without some familiarity with the local government systems of other countries. Recommended comparative studies include Chandler (1993), Batley and Stoker (1991), Page (1987) and Bowman and Hampton (1983). A clear but detailed analysis of local government in the United States is provided by Dye (1988) whilst the French and British system is iconoclastically compared by Ashford (1981) but given that this is not a quick read, Lagroye and Wright (1979) is an approachable source. Wollmann and Schroter (2000) have edited a useful comparative study of local government reform in Germany and Britain.

3

The functions of local authorities

The Local Government Act 2000 has substantially refocused the role local authorities are intended to provide for their communities. They are charged with powers to promote the 'well-being' of their area in respect to economic, social and environmental concerns. The modern local authority is therefore seen to have a wider role than providing a range of services largely concerned with social welfare, but is to be the lead agency in the overall economic and social development of their area. However, it is not expected that the local authority is itself to supply the means to achieve local development. To use a phrase popularised in the United States, local government should be 'steering and not rowing' the local boat (Osborne and Gaebler 1992). The modern local authority needs to lead the community by drawing other public and private sector organisations into partrenships which ensure that local organisations co-ordinate their activities and ensure that the most efficient agencies, whether they be public or private, capable of undertaking a necessary service are entrusted with supplying appropriate services. It can, however, be questioned whether this vision is fully formed or even possible. Many of the traditional social service values of local government remain entrenched within the system and remain supported firmly by the rigid legal framework in which local authorities must operate.

There are a range of tasks that are normally assigned to local authorities within liberal democracies across the globe. These include responsibility for refuse collection, pavements and minor roads, street lighting, parks and recreation. There are wider differences concerning more expensive tasks. Education, rented housing provision, social services, hospitals and health care or control of police are not universally local tasks, although many countries assign these tasks to local governments. There are also significant differences in the capacity of local authorities to run utilities with some systems, such as in Germany and the United States, providing gas and electricity, whilst in other countries such as Britain this is generally a matter of private supply and public regulation.

The legal framework

Britain has no single legislative document that determines the role and functions of local authorities. The allocation of responsibility for particular services is assigned by individual Acts of Parliament which collectively comprise a huge body of legislation. A few Acts such as the 2000 Local Government Act or the 1972 Local Government Act are however crucial in defining the powers and organisation of local authorities and will be referred to frequently in this book. The Acts themselves do not exactly define what local governments can do, since they are further refined through the use of statutory instruments. Law relating to local government is further complicated by legal rulings made by judges as to the interpretation of the law which set a precedent that must be followed by the courts.

Any actions of a local authority must, however, be justified by reference to law. A local authority that pursues an activity that has no legislative justification may be instructed by the courts to stop its behaviour through a court order ruling the activity to be *ultra vires*, that is, outside the law. There have been a few, but sometimes spectacular, cases when *ultra vires* orders have been enforced, such as the attempt in 1923 by Labour Party councillors of the London Borough of Poplar to pay their workforce higher wages than was statutorily permissible (Keith-Lucas and Richards 1978: 83).

Some statutes impose a duty on a local authority to undertake a specific activity. For example, the 1944 Education Act requires that a Local Education Authority (LEA) must provide education for any child of school age within its boundaries. If the local authority fails to comply with this Act it may be sued in the courts under a writ of *mandamus*, an order requiring conformity with a statutory duty. In many cases, however, statutes give local authorities discretion as to whether they perform a particular task. There is, for example, no compulsion on any local authority that it should provide parks, swimming baths or promote the arts, since these activities are permissible but not mandatory under the 1972 Local Government Act.

Private acts

Most laws defining local government functions are the product of general Acts of Parliament which apply to all authorities within a specified category. It is, however, possible to frame laws that give a unique power to a particular local authority which may sponsor a private bill through Parliament. In the late nineteenth century many county boroughs gained lucrative trading powers through such means, including the right to generate and supply electricity and gas, and develop tram and bus services. Some of these powers have subsequently been removed from local authorities or consolidated in general legislation. Curious remnants of private legislation still remain. Hull, for example, has until recently run its own telephone service.

Private acts are still promoted by local authorities, but usually for relatively uncontroversial tasks or issues relating to local development. A renewed interest in rapid urban transport has for example prompted some large authorities to seek powers to build tramways in their streets. Some authorities have also gained unique powers to promote industrial development. Many private acts are simply to gain powers to undertake what seem relatively trivial powers. Barnsley Metropolitan District Council (MDC) had to promote legislation to prevent trespassing on the grounds of a school simply to stop teenagers using it as a motorcycle racetrack.

Whilst in the nineteenth century private acts were an important avenue through which local authorities increased their functions, it is now impossible to forward any controversial measure through this means. Demands on parliamentary time ensure that these acts are only subject to formal debate on the floor of the House of Commons, which in practice means that the proposed act is simply announced at each stage of its procedure apart from the committee stage where it may be considered in greater detail by a small group of MPs dealing with such legislation. If any MP objects to the content of a private act, he or she need only indicate their dissent on the floor of the House of Commons to effectively kill the bill since time will then have to be found to debate the issue and this is never allocated. Thus in practice all private acts must have the consent or at least acquiescence of all MPs and also therefore the government.

Statutory instruments

Most acts relating to local government provide only a broad outline of powers or restraints. The acts themselves tend not to provide detailed regulations and, indeed, it would often be impractical to do so. The 1980 Local Government Planning and Land Act, for example, stipulates that any major building contracts required by a local government must be put out to tender, but does not define exactly what size contract must be subject to competition. Given rapidly changing prices it would be unrealistic for a sum to be entrenched into an act that was difficult and time consuming to amend. To solve this problem legislation often delegates to government ministers powers to set and amend more detailed regulations relevant to the principles of an act.

Delegated legislation is promulgated as regulations termed statutory instruments. An act will stipulate whether any related statutory instrument requires the approval of Parliament. In some cases no prior consent is needed. A few acts require Parliament to approve statutory instruments. Parliament must through such an arrangement debate each year changes in the grant settlement to local authorities. Most statutory instruments have however only to be notified to Parliament and, if no objection is made by MPs, they become legally binding. Objections to these orders are not uncommon but usually ineffective. An MP concerned at the paucity of student grants may try to object to a statutory instrument fixing their level but, unless he or she has the support of a considerable number of government backbenchers or the issue is taken up by opposition leaders, little will be made of the complaint. The loyalty of back-benchers to their government ensures that it is extremely rare for a statutory instrument not to be approved. A careful check on delegated legislation is, however, provided by a select committee of the House of Commons which reviews the orders tabled by the government and reports to Parliament on their validity within the framework of existing legislation.

Few powers are given to local authorities without qualification. Legislation usually stipulates many conditions regulating services and these rules may often be varied through the application of statutory instruments. The extent to which controls apply to each particular service will however vary considerably. In some cases, such as local responsibility for distributing housing benefit, councils can do little but administer a task, following a set of rigid rules closely monitored by central government and subject to frequent amendment. Local authorities may, on the other hand, have wide discretion over certain services. For example, there are very few restraints on local promotion of the arts.

Powers of general competence

In the past, powers granted to local authorities tended to be specific to particular services rather than general responsibilities for their communities which would enable them to undertake a wide range of innovatory activities that they felt were beneficial for their communities. Section 137 of the 1972 Local Government Act provided a gesture in this direction allowing local authorities to incur expenditure, strictly limited to a few pence for each rate payer, 'which in their opinion is in the interests of their area or any part of it or all or some of their inhabitants'. The wider powers granted by the 2000 Local Government Act to incur expenditure to promote the improvement of the economic, social and environmental well-being of their communities provide a much more effective basis for local authorities to develop more original strategies for supporting their communities. The powers granted through this legislation cannot, however, override existing legislative restrictions on how local authorities can act and they specifically cannot be used to find new ways of raising revenue for the authority. Specifically, the legislation encourages local authorities to work in partnership with private and voluntary agencies within or outside their area to fulfil the broad objectives set out in the Act. The new powers have made the old section 137 redundant and also sweep away some very restrictive legal rulings on what were the proper duties of local authorities. During the next few years it will be interesting to evaluate how skilfully local authorities use these more general powers and the extent to which the government will avoid the temptation to restrain their use when an authority seeks to act in ways not wholly approved by Whitehall.

In some of the states of the United States and in Scandinavian countries local governments are given powers of general competence that effectively reverse the principle of ultra vires by allowing a local authority to undertake any activity that is not specifically prohibited to it by law. This arrangement may not always be as liberating as it appears, as in the United States there may be an extensive body of prohibitive legislation.

In addition to the more general empowerment of authorities, the Labour Government has expressed an intention to extend this principle by conferring powers of general competence on local authorities that they designate as beacon councils either for a specific service or the authority as a whole. This status will be awarded to local authorities that are regarded by the Government to be particularly efficient and well run. The arrangement will therefore be unlikely to foster particularly radical new departures for local governments but may help to extend what, in the view of central government, may be excellent practice.

In-house provision and contracting out

Following the restructuring of local government in the 1970s, the comparatively large size of British local authorities ensured that they had the resources and the inclination not only to devise policy for those activities for which they were responsible but also that they should implement these tasks. For example, most local authorities not only decided that children should receive school dinners but also expected to employ the kitchen staff and provide the equipment and premises to ensure that this function was carried out.

Until the advent of the Thatcher Governments, central government and its advisors appeared to have shared the assumption that local authority functions were normally to be implemented in-house within a single authority. The Redcliffe-Maud Commission, in particular, promoted the case for larger authorities on the grounds that the bigger the organisation the more efficient. Typical of the Redcliffe-Maud and Government view are their conclusions on the size of social service departments.

In the Home Office's view, for an authority to provide an effective children's service it ought to have a minimum of 250 children in care, 100 of them in residential care, and employ a team of not less than 12 child care officers. Both these considerations in the Home Office's judgement, pointed to a minimum population of 250,000 for a children's authority (vol. I, Para. 140: 39)

Although not stated in the Report, this argument is based on the assumption that, for most functions, each authority would supply all the labour and specialist knowledge required to undertake a service through its own resources.

The ethos that local authorities should provide all their functions in-house is arguably a very limited view that is practised by few local authorities in other nations. Small French communes or American townships regularly co-operate with one another to provide joint services when a larger scale of operation is economically necessary. They will often use private contractors to fulfil many of their functions. Even large cities in Europe will expect private companies to undertake many of their functions. The streets of Barcelona, a city of strong left-wing credentials, are cleaned by private firms working to the orders of the city government.

The Thatcher and Major Governments did much to undermine the view within local government that services should necessarily be provided by the local authority itself, through legislation that compelled local authorities to put many of their services out to tender so that private companies could compete with the local authorities to run the service. Under this system of compulsory competitive tendering (CCT) the local authority drew up a contract which stated what standard of service they required and the organisation offering the cheapest price to run the services was awarded the contract. As a consequence of these values many local authorities lost the capacity to directly implement some services and in the longer term the strategy has inclined increasing numbers of local authorities, including many once radical left-wing councils such as Sheffield, to voluntarily award contracts to private sector companies to manage some of their services as a means of saving costs. The Blair Government has through its policy of Best Value, which is discussed in more detail in Chapter 10, provided a framework in which local authorities do not have to allow private contractors to bid to run their services, but must show if they manage their services 'in-house' that they are providing as effective and cost-efficient service as could be supplied by the private sector. The practice of the 1970s when most local authorities implemented almost all their services is, however, now at an end

The Blair Government has followed the enabling philosophy to further emphasise that local authorities must develop a community strategy as to how they will promote the economic, social and environmental well-being of their communities in consultation with other appropriate local agencies. The emphasis of the Blair Government is upon the idea of partnerships rather than single agencies securing development and service delivery. This strategy links with the Government's idea of 'joined up' government as a means of resolving intractable social problems. High unemployment and rates of crime, poor schools, bad housing and ill health are often characteristic of socially deprived areas where each individual problem feeds off and reinforces the others. The solution to these difficulties cannot lie in tackling only one of a series of inter-linked issues but requires co-ordinating working from a variety of public and private agencies. Local government should be, therefore, a lead agency in promoting task forces and partnerships to bring together all the agencies required to resolve issues of social deprivation.

The status of major services

The preceding chapter showed that from the late nineteenth century, local authorities progressed from being concerned substantially with developing and supplying infrastructure for the local economy to becoming by the mid-twentieth century organisations largely supplying welfare services. In the late twentieth century the pattern of local authority functions started to change again to more of a regulatory and developmental role. Rather than being direct suppliers of local welfare services, local governments are increasingly organisations which regulate the private and voluntary sectors activities in these areas or co-ordinate other public agencies in these fields. However, under the regulatory and partnership framework, the local authority is also becoming more of a lead player in economic as well as social service provision. The change is however one of transition and, as is shown in the following discussion of specific services, characteristics of social service provision and the newer economic and social enabler and regulatory roles can often be found uneasily combined in the tasks currently undertaken by local governments. The following list begins with the more traditional social provision, then regulatory and control functions and finally, the newer developmental functions.

Education

Local authorities took control of education through the 1902 Education Act when school boards, one of the many *ad hoc* agencies that littered the nineteenth century administrative system, were incorporated under the domains of county councils and county boroughs. Local councils which are responsible for education are often referred to as LEAs. The task is much the most costly service operated by local government, although most of the expense is taken up by teachers' wages, which are not subject to local determination.

Education is in many liberal democracies seen as a national rather than a local responsibility. The structure of the French education system and the curriculum is determined by national government although local governments have some responsibility for school buildings. In Germany education is a national and state responsibility. In the United States, school education is normally assigned to single-purpose school boards that are separately elected from city and county governments, whilst states operate publicly funded universities and colleges and even some cities can and still do run their own universities.

Although local authorities retain some control over schools, they lost any responsibility for higher education in 1988 when the Government ended LEA involvement in funding the polytechnics. A more substantial depletion of LEA functions began with a policy of channelling funding for many vocational courses through government agencies rather than the LEAs, principally, after 1990, the Training and Enterprise Councils which were from 2001 restructured into the Learning and Skills Councils. In 1992 the Government removed further education from local authority control with the creation of the national Further Education Funding Council.

The extent of discretion over schools policy is limited. The 1944 Education Act stated that compulsory education should be provided 'by local authorities under his [the Ministers'] control and direction' (Regan 1977: 31) and this position is confirmed in the 1988 Education Reform Act. The exact interpretation of this power is far from clear, but it has sufficient authority to permit the Department for Education and Skills (DfES) to suggest whatever it thinks necessary in educational development and to fund LEAs accordingly. The DfES retains powers to approve or reject local authority plans concerning the types of school they establish for children of particular age groups. The Government approves the national curriculum, the age for compulsory education is determined by statutory order and teachers' salaries are set by national negotiations whose outcome is greatly determined by the Government as paymaster. Standards of teaching are monitored by the DfES through the schools inspectorate, now organised within the Office for Standards in Education (OFSTED).

The 1988 Education Act also changed the role of LEAs from being hands-on managers of schools to being strategic planners of the system. Each local authority is required to devise a formula that must be approved by the government to determine how it will distribute funds to individual schools in its area. The governors of each school, with the executive advice from the head teacher, are responsible for deciding how exactly the money is spent, rather than the LEA. The Thatcher Government further restricted the LEAs' role by allowing schools following a referendum of parents to opt out of local authority control all together and it is probable that had the Conservatives won the 1997 Election they would have removed education as a responsibility of local authorities. The Conservative leader William Hague proposed this idea in July 2000.

David Blunkett, the Secretary of State for Education and Employment in the Blair Government, has however retained LEAs and provided them with a strategic role. Effectively he has brought the state schools that opted out of local control back into the LEA fold and requires local authorities to make plans for catchment areas for schools and arrangements for regulating how schools recruit children from outside their designated area. He has also encouraged LEAs to work in partnership with the private sector by establishing Education Action Zones to improve schools in areas in which examination achievement is poor. However, whilst the LEAs have a role under Labour, they are also faced with further controls over their stewardship of education. The inspection agency OFSTED now also inspects LEAs and those failing to carry out their tasks efficiently, or allowing schools to fail, can be suspended and some or all of their tasks transferred to external managers. The London Borough of Hackney had one of the first LEAs to be subjected to this indignity.

Housing

Local authorities received powers in the nineteenth century to remove what were termed nuisances, disease-ridden insanitary buildings and their attendant middens and cesspools. In 1868 the Artisan and Labourers' Dwelling Act permitted house building. Powers were, therefore, available to clear slums but it was not possible to rehouse slum dwellers on an extensive basis since insufficient funds were given to construct large residential estates. The great breakthrough in housing provision came in 1919 when Lloyd George began building 'homes fit for heroes' for the returning servicemen from the First World War. Local authorities were able not only to build and maintain property but received substantial government grants to enable them to develop this service. Powers to borrow large sums for house building promoted over the next fifty years a dramatic transformation of cities, as appalling slums were removed and new council estates, some to become slums in their turn, transformed the urban geography of Britain.

In the Thatcherite heaven, most property is privately owned by its occupants with a smaller housing stock rented from private owners or housing associations. In order to increase home ownership, the 1980 Housing Act gave council tenants the right to buy their own houses at generous discount prices. The legislation was only partially successful in transferring public housing to private hands. Between 1987 and 1996 the percentage of housing stock controlled by local authorities had declined from 25 per cent to 18 per cent (Office for National Statistics 1999). As a further means of promoting the mandatory sale of houses, the Department of the Environment ended the power of local authorities to subsidise council house rents from the general rate fund. This policy has forced local authorities to dramatically increase rents to council houses making it financially more expedient for all but the poorer tenants to buy their own homes.

In addition to promoting council house sales, the Conservative Governments drastically cut the amount of capital local authorities were permitted to borrow in order to build new properties so that most district councils ceased to build houses and could only raise sufficient resources to undertake repairs or refurbishment of their properties. The Blair Government has not reversed this trend. The responsibility for providing low-cost rented housing has been shifted to housing associations, which are voluntary agencies regulated and funded by the centrally established Housing Corporation. Many housing associations work in partnership with local authorities, often building and owning the houses whilst the local authority provides tenants from their waiting lists.

> Between 1989 and 1998 the stock of dwellings owned by housing associations in England doubled from, 519,000 to 1,048,500 . . . and from 1991 associations overtook local authorities as providers of new homes. (Malpass 2000: 219)

The sale of council houses was clearly not on its own likely to end local authority involvement in the provision and maintenance of housing and steps were taken in the 1988 Housing Act to ease what was left of the rented sector into the hands of either private landlords or housing associations. The measures included provision for the Government to take over a declining estate as a Housing Action Trust. Due to tenant opposition very few were actually created. Even less successful was a scheme, abandoned in 1995, that allowed tenants to vote for a transfer of their estate to a private landlord. These schemes which threatened local authorities with the loss of their housing stock to unacceptable landlords did, however, motivate many local authorities to voluntarily transfer much of their housing to housing associations. By 1999 more than 325,000 dwellings had been transferred to housing associations by 86 local authorities (Malpass 2000: 237).

> Many European local authorities build and maintain housing for renting at low cost to those who would otherwise find it difficult to live in property maintained on the open market. In the United States, whilst some larger cities provide public housing, this has never been developed on the scale of Britain.

The effect of a decade of legislation has been to seriously curtail local authority powers to build houses, retain them or to set rents. As better houses are sold, the remaining council house stock will be the most run down, unpopular and expensive to maintain properties. Local authorities, nevertheless, still have some important functions in the housing field. Whether or not they own houses, they still have a statutory duty to find accommodation for the homeless, although there has been government-inspired speculation about ending this duty. Local authorities are also obliged to administer, in accord with strict guidelines from the government, rent subsidies to poor tenants whether in publicly or privately owned accommodation. In effect, local authority housing powers are becoming an element of a social security system that provides the worst housing available for those unable to house themselves.

Social services

Social service powers have been gradually allocated to local government from a variety of sources, including children's acts that were passed in the first half

of the twentieth century and some of the duties held by the Boards of
Guardians. By the 1960s it was recognised that, whilst local authorities had
major responsibilities in the area of welfare, these were given to them in a haphazard form. Different committees often dealt with care for the elderly, protection of children and general social work practice. To remedy the situation a
government enquiry published in 1968 as the Seebohm Report led to the creation by statute of social services departments in counties and county boroughs
which would be managed by professional social workers and take responsibility for general social work practice and the care of children and the elderly.

Many aspects of the work of these departments have been subject to the
market pressures favoured by the Thatcher Government. A major review of
social care provision by Sir Roy Griffiths in 1988 led to the 'Care in the
Community' approach. Local government is regarded as the lead agency for
securing social welfare, but this must be achieved as far as is possible by ensuring that those in need of assistance such as the elderly, the mentally ill, or drug
addicts and alcoholics are able to remain within the community in 'homely'
surroundings. True to the enabling philosophy, local authorities should not be
the principal providers of care to those in need, but plan and facilitate the necessary arrangements that should be undertaken primarily by private sector or
voluntary agencies. The 1990 National Health Service and Community Care
Act requires local government social service departments to spend 85 per cent
of their community care budget on provision by non-governmental bodies.
Such legislation has led to a mushrooming of private homes for the elderly or
housing association accommodation for the mentally ill, which may be subject
to inspection by the local authority but are not under its direct control (Parrott
1999: 79–83). The Blair Government has, however, established a major
enquiry into social care funding, but this has yet to report.

The new regime for welfare provision has created a number of potentially
serious problems. There is a demarcation struggle between local government
and health trusts and authorities as to the exact distribution of responsibilities
for mental health care or the incapacitated elderly. There is also a problem for
local authorities of ensuring that groups such as the elderly receive a high standard of care that provide them with a comfortable and stimulating environment in their final years. Many private homes for the elderly shelter and feed
their paying guests but do little else to entertain them.

Other aspects of social services seem less exposed to the enabling philosophy.
The routine of social work is not a task that can easily be transferred to the private
sector unless the government artificially created competing social work agencies.
This sector has, nevertheless, been under serious pressure, especially in the area
of child abuse following dramatic publicity in cases where social security departments have been overzealous in taking children into care or allowed abuse to
occur within children's homes. Solutions to such problems are not helped by
underfunding and an increased case load on social workers which prevent adequate time to thoroughly investigate and remedy possible social dangers.

Recreation, libraries and the arts

Local governments' powers over recreation and the arts are less subject to central government regulation than any other of their major tasks. Permission to maintain libraries was firmly established in 1919 when the Public Libraries Act established a county service and abolished restrictions on spending in this field. The 1972 Local Government Act reaffirmed a number of powers conferred on local authorities from parish to county level to maintain parks, sports facilities and sponsor the arts. Larger authorities, especially big city governments, have sufficient resources to operate museums, art galleries, sports stadiums and help sponsor symphony orchestras. At the other extreme, most parish councils only pursue their recreational powers as far as a village hall or a small park, although a few are sufficiently enterprising to maintain recreation facilities including museums, sports centres and swimming baths.

Local authority management of the arts is a testimony to the diversity and richness of provision that can be developed if communities have unfettered powers over a particular service. Large authorities have staged cultural events of international importance and most major cities heavily subsidise their repertory theatres. The Edinburgh Festival, for example, is principally underwritten by Edinburgh District Council whilst the Hallé Orchestra would not survive without the support of Manchester City Council.

Not only are the arts beholden to local government for financial support, they require the innovatory and organisational capacity of local authorities to initiate and sustain these ventures. The arts departments of local authorities often provide the organisational framework from which administrators may seek sponsorship. Such diversity is now extending into the area of sport. Manchester City Council is hosting the Commonwealth Games of 2002 following its unsuccessful bid to house the 2000 Olympic Games. At a less exalted level, many a lowly league football team is beholden to local authority help to sustain its activities and many a sporting hero began training in local authority sports stadia and centres. Calderdale MDC owns a major share of Halifax Town Football Club, whilst Kirklees MDC developed the McAlpine stadium to house Huddersfield's football and rugby league clubs.

Public health

The discovery that filth causes disease promoted a major growth in public services in the nineteenth century. The health boards established in 1848 formed the basis for water supply, sewage services and regular refuse collection and disposal. The task of supplying clean water and sewage facilities was one of the greatest achievements of nineteenth century public enterprise, requiring costly and impressive though now largely unseen feats of engineering.

For most of the last century, the sanitation services have been taken for granted and once important posts in local government such as the medical officer of health and the borough surveyor have declined in importance. Gradually water and sewage services slipped from direct democratic control under the impact of demands for integrated systems of drainage and water catchment. The Water Act of 1945 merged many municipally controlled departments into larger jointly controlled drainage boards and water authorities that were subject to the authority of boards nominated by participating councils. In 1973 a Water Act established nine huge regional water authorities in England and a further authority to cover Wales that would undertake all sewage and water supply services. In 1983 a further Water Act recast the membership of the authorities to remove any automatic local representation on their boards and in 1988 the authorities were privatised, transferring what had been one of the greatest achievements of municipal enterprise out of democratic control. The relative autonomy of Scotland has, however, been asserted at least in the area of water supply. Following recommendations by the Wheatley Commission, water and sewage powers were returned from joint authorities to the control of the newly formed Regions and following their abolition, to three large but still publicly owned water companies.

Local authorities in England and Wales are now left with the residual task of refuse collection and disposal but even in this sector privatisation is taking a severe toll of local responsibility. Refuse collection, a staple routine of district and unitary authorities, is one of the principal areas which were subjected to competitive tendering by the 1988 Local Government Act. It has also proved to be the service most vulnerable to takeover by private firms and, in particular, subsidiaries of large French- and Spanish- owned companies. In both these countries communes do not share the British penchant for undertaking every service in-house and have for many years contracted out refuse collection and street cleaning. Firms dealing with this service have now merged into a few large, highly automated organisations that are able to provide an effective service at a cost to rival that provided by British local authorities. Some new-right local authorities such as Westminster have, as a matter of principle, allocated their cleansing services to the private sector, but an increasing number of authorities are now reluctantly ceding their services to subsidiaries of the continental giants.

Police services

One of the most transparent myths of British political practice is that the police are not a national force but under local control. Maintaining public order was an important function of eighteenth century parish and town government although co-ordination of this function was secured by the Home Office through the work of JPs and the Lords Lieutenant. It is sometimes argued that the first modern police force was established in London in 1829 by Sir Robert Peel. The Metropolitan Police remained under Home Office direction until responsibility transferred to the Greater London Authority in 2000. In the apparently strategically less important provinces, the Municipal Corporations Act of 1835 allowed the new boroughs powers to set up police services, although by 1839 the appointment of a chief constable required Home Office approval. Legislation in 1856 decreed that all counties and boroughs had a duty to establish a police force that would be partly funded by central government and subject to Home Office inspection.

In 1888 it was not thought prudent to hand police powers directly to the newly elected county councils. The influence of magistrates was maintained by the establishment of police committees jointly composed of councillors and JPs. The Police Act of 1919 gave the Home Secretary powers to regulate the control and management of police through statutory instruments. This facility is used to ensure that local police committees have little capacity for interfering in the operations of the police. Not only has there been an increase in central controls over the police, there has also been a steady decrease in the number of authorities with police powers. Before 1945 there were 181 police forces in England and Wales but, in 1946, borough council police were transferred to county council control. More recent amalgamations reduced their number to only 51 police committees and forces in Britain by 1990. Michael Howard, Home Secretary in the Major Government of 1992, unsuccessfully attempted to further decrease the number of police forces but, through the 1994 Police and Magistrates' Courts Act, reduced the proportion of councillors and magistrates on police committees by adding a number of co-opted members from lists approved by the Home Office.

Most police committees now have seventeen members, of which nine are county or unitary authority councillors, three are magistrates and the remainder co-opted members. They administer provision of buildings and equipment for their force and monitor their performance. Attempts to interfere in the use of the police in respect to their operations have met with strong rebuffs from chief constables and the Home Office.

There are wide variations in liberal democracies on local control of police. In some countries such as France, the police are a wholly national force but in others, Spain for example, there may be local police dealing with minor issues such as traffic regulation, provincial police dealing with most crimes and a national force of militarised police dealing with civil unrest and political subversion. In the United States most levels of government employ their own police. Cities, even the smallest, employ their local police force, county law enforcement covering largely rural areas is in the hands of a sheriff and his or her deputies, whilst states provide police services to aid the smaller, less resourced counties and towns. At the national level the Federal Bureau of Investigation (FBI) deals with offences against federal law.

In Britain, although emphasis is still placed on the local accountability of the police, it is difficult to escape the conclusion that the country has an increasingly nationalised force. In 1985, for example, the co-ordination of police forces throughout the country to help break the miners' strike against the views of many members of police authorities further suggests that control of the service lies predominantly with central government.

Transport and highways

Local authorities gained powers to operate tram, and later, bus services largely through their own initiative by sponsoring private acts of Parliament. By 1900 many cities were, in competition with the private sector, running their own public transport companies, usually on a profitable basis and in some cities such as London and Sheffield the municipal authority even constructed their own buses and trams. As with many local tasks, central government has at times promoted and then dashed this activity. Transport acts in the 1930s attempted to remove wasteful competition between bus companies by assigning routes to a specific licensed operator. In many cities the municipal services came to have a monopoly over the transport system which, with the help of government grants, operated on a break-even basis. These established relationships were put into question firstly by South Yorkshire County Council's policy in the 1970s of subsidising bus and rail fares from the rates. This decision, practised widely in Europe, was not welcomed by the Labour Government and then outlawed by the Conservatives who, firstly tried to declare the policy illegal, and when this failed in all areas outside London, passed the 1985 Transport Act which removed route monopolies and decreed that bus services could not be subsidised from the rates. Municipal bus companies now operate as if they were private companies, in competition with the private sector.

> In most European countries, and in particular Germany, public transport receives much greater subsidies from the national government than in Britain and this has led to the development of far more extensive networks of modern tramways and underground rail systems than in Britain.

Road building has, similarly, passed through its phase of growth and then decline as a consequence of centralisation. Responsibility for the maintenance of most roads and highways was transferred, on their creation, to the district authorities from *ad hoc* road boards. The county councils were later given the task of looking after major highways. As road transport increased, the government took the lead in classifying roads and providing funds for the development of major national routes in accord with specifications determined by the Ministry of Transport. In 1936 legislation permitted the Ministry to take direct control of major highways, which were designated as trunk roads. Since the

1960s the major road network has been further enhanced by the creation of the motorways, which are now built and maintained under DTLR direction by a Highways Agency. Local authorities today still maintain minor roads but the most important elements of the network are a central government responsibility, although the Highways Agency may ask local authorities to undertake road repairs for them on an agency basis.

Planning

Local authorities received powers to give planning permission as soon as it dawned on central government that control of building was necessary. The first Planning Act arrived in 1909 and was strengthened in the interwar years. Powers were greatly enhanced through Acts passed in 1947 and 1952 which ensured that any new building had to be approved by the district authority both in terms of its impact on the environment and the safety of its construction. These powers appear to be substantial and, if subject to no other authority than a local council, would permit councillors to determine the future physical environment and economy of their area within the possibilities allowed by market forces. However, these powers are not sovereign and any planning consent is subject to appeal to the government, effectively the Minister for Housing, Planning and Regeneration.

> Planning is a local government responsibility in most liberal democracies, although the extent to which detailed plans can be resisted by local authorities varies widely. In the United States, planning powers are referred to as zoning and allow city or county governments to designate how particular areas of the community should be developed, but generally there is rather less close inspection of designs for specific buildings over and above issues of safety.

The Secretary of State will often support local authority arguments opposing the granting of planning permission and the Department has no wish to use the power to indulge in inspection of every minor building project. However, local authorities are aware that they have little chance of halting schemes such as open-cast mining projects that are favoured by the central government, since developers thwarted at the local level know they will win an appeal to the Secretary of State. As a consequence of the appeals procedure, nationally controversial developments such as nuclear power stations or construction of motorways in scenic parkland, although subject to local authority planning procedures, are analysed, at the government's discretion, in quasi-judicial planning enquiries, chaired by a government appointee from the list of the 'good and the great', which produce a document advising the Secretary of State as to his or her final decision.

Whilst first instance planning powers were given by the 1945 Labour

Government, they also withdrew local authority powers of development in crucial areas. Despite recommendations of a Government committee to allow local authorities to sponsor new town development, the New Town Act of 1946 gave this function to *ad hoc* development corporations which, in effect, gave many local authority powers to a band of doubtlessly worthy but, nevertheless, unelected central government nominees. Local authorities could not be trusted with major developments and are, therefore, in no way responsible for Milton Keynes or any similar planned urban growth. Following the completion of the new towns initiative, the New Town Corporations have been wound up and their powers returned to elected local government.

The Thatcher Governments showed an equal lack of trust in the capacity of local authorities to undertake major new developments. The 1980 Local Government Planning and Land Act made provision for Urban Development Corporations (UDCs) to be formed in areas that the Government considered suitable for major reconstruction. The first UDCs were established to redevelop the redundant docklands of London and Liverpool and a further eight were designated for larger cities. They were controlled by a board of government nominees and an executive director who manages the Corporation. Within their area of jurisdiction UDCs took over the planning functions previously held by the local authority and were primed with substantial funds from central government to offer incentives to incoming business investors. A similar, if lower level, development forged by the Thatcher administrations are the enterprise zones. In these areas, incentives are provided for incoming firms by offering rate and rent rebates and softening of regulations concerning employee training and health and safety.

Economic development

The preceding review of local authority functions suggests that during the last century there has been a continuous movement towards low-level social welfare provision and away from activities that directly affect the local economy. Apart from ritual demands from local businessmen that they should pay less in rates, commerce and local government seemed to pass each other by like ships in the night. Since the 1980s, several local authorities have made a concerted effort to reverse this tendency and become actively involved in their local economies.

Local authority action to secure economic growth is not a wholly novel activity and was a major function of resort towns. In the 1930s, a few towns attempted to relieve the effects of economic depression by using tourist-style publicity to attract new industry to their area. The creation of the new towns and in the 1960s a decline in economic growth led to a revival of attempts to attract industry to a particular area through publicity campaigns and the development of factory estates (Chandler and Lawless 1985). It was not, however, until the late 1970s and the 1980s that more radical economic interventionism became established. A number of Labour-controlled authorities such as Sheffield, and the West Midlands Metropolitan County, followed in 1981 by the GLC, realised that socialism was not simply about social welfare but also about equitably shared economic growth. The economic slump of the early 1980s demonstrated to the satisfaction of these radical authorities that *laissez-faire* capitalism as practised by Thatcher was wholly ineffective and that real growth could be secured by providing enterprising workers with the means to develop co-operatively owned industries aided by local government financial support.

It became apparent after a few years of optimistic enthusiasm from left-wing councils that local authority economic initiatives would only be small scale if managed through direct funding of firms and, whenever they ventured into radical areas, would receive hostile reactions from central government. Authorities such as Sheffield City Council began to retreat from radicalism and adopt more conventional policies to either attract industry or stimulate the local economy by developing schemes in co-operation with local businesses. Sheffield established a rapport with the City's Chamber of Commerce to plan the redevelopment of the Lower Don Valley that had been, until its decimation in the early 1980s, the heart of the City's steel-making and forging industries. This project was forestalled by the Government's formation of a UDC for the area. The Council subsequently engaged in a further major co-operative project by building, with private help, major new sports facilities to host the 1991 World Student Games.

The abolition of the GLC and the metropolitan county councils created a crisis of control for some of the larger agencies and the 1989 Local Government and Housing Act made it much more difficult for local authorities to establish 'arm's length' companies that can avoid being classified as parts of a local authority for the purposes of capital controls. Thus, the enterprise boards have had to be restructured in ways that further loosen their connections with local government. Many have become self-financing agencies independent of local authority control. Generally, they are medium-sized organisations that are not capable of fulfilling the 1980s dreams of local socialists by transforming the economy.

In parallel with these initially left-wing approaches to local economic development, many more centre-left or right-wing authorities were promoting innovatory publicity to attract new businesses which included establishing business parks or reinventing the image of the city. Bradford, for example, gained considerable publicity in the 1980s by promoting the city's industrial heritage as a tourist attraction.

Central government was also concerned to work with local authorities who would channel their efforts into supporting capitalist industrial growth as opposed to those that sought to fund workers' movements and trade union-sponsored activity. The Conservative strategy for reversing urban decline led to schemes such as City Challenge, that required local authorities to devise plans for regenerating areas of industrial and commercial decline by creating redevelopment plans in partnership with local businesses. The public-private partnerships then competed with each other to secure Government support and funding. In 1994 government schemes to further economic regeneration were simplified and brought together within a Single Regeneration Budget (SRB) which is a substantial fund held by the DTLR for development schemes. In 2000, round 6 of SRB awards allocated over £5.5 billion to be spent over 7 years on some 900 schemes (DTLR 2000a). Public, voluntary and even private sector bodies may bid for funds, although they must adhere to criteria established by the DTLR which includes the need to match funding from the government.

> SRB partnerships are expected to involve a diverse range of local authorities in the management of their scheme. In particular, they should harness the talent, resources and experience of local business, the voluntary sector and the local community. (DTLR 2000a)

In general, most larger successful bids are spearheaded by local authorities or are even pushed forward by central government for adoption by a local authority as the lead agency (Chandler 1998). They include, for example, schemes for major redevelopment of city centres or facilitating better training and child care schemes within an area of high unemployment.

> Although a relatively new interest in Britain, economic development has been and remains a central concern of United States city governments, whose populations look to the town hall as a major focus for ensuring the infrastructure to retain existing businesses within a city and attracting new sources of employment. Many cities develop strong links with business interests and so that the formation of public–private partnership to secure redevelopment of run-down areas is regular practice.

Whilst in the 1980s there were several ideological approaches to development, the Conservative Governments realised that such activity was an established and appropriate function for local authorities and began guiding this activity towards a direction that could be controlled by the centre. The 1989 Local Government and Housing Act recognised economic development as a permissible function of local authorities, but also gave the Government wide powers to regulate this function through the use of statutory instruments. The Blair Government has reinforced local leadership of economic development in the 2000 Local Government Act, which gives local authorities the power to promote and improve the economic well-being of their area and also allows the Secretary of State to remove legislative restraints that are thought to detract from local economic initiatives. In effect, therefore, local authorities may apply to the Government to be given greater powers to develop economic initiatives that currently are not open to them.

Other functions

The preceding paragraphs do not provide a comprehensive review of local government services. They have many other functions of importance. Central governments have always found local authorities a useful agent to administer nationally necessary services. Thus, local governments through their education departments handled the administration of the student grant system and currently deal with housing benefit subsidies.

There has been a long tradition of local government protecting the consumer through advice and complaints bureaux and the weights and measures and public health inspectorates. Local government is responsible for protecting the citizen through the fire service and developing emergency planning systems in the event of natural disasters such as floods or major accidents such as a rail crash. County councils have important powers concerning agricultural regulation and inspection and are involved in the prevention and spread of disease in farm animals. A frequently unrealised element of local responsibility is the administration of minor magistrates' courts, which is shared with the JPs under Home Office surveillance. Local authorities are empowered to run markets and are, therefore, in the business of licensing stalls and street traders. They also provide permits through which they can regulate a wide variety of trading practices which range from charitable street collections to licensing taxi firms. The list of minor tasks assigned at some time to local authorities, although exhaustible, is certainly lengthy.

The future for local government services

Local governments in Britain have moved from being highly active in delivering productive and profitable services in the late nineteenth century such as gas, water and electricity supply to being more of an adjunct to the welfare state (Dunleavy 1984). Under the impact of the post-1979 Conservative Governments, many of these welfare functions were moved from direct control by local government to a situation in which local authorities appointed private contractors to supply services or regulate private services providers. There seems to be little evidence that the Blair Government will dramatically reverse this trend, as the Government lays increasing emphasis on local authorities acting as organisations to facilitate the economic and social welfare of their areas in partnership with the private and voluntary sectors under central government regulation. The Best Value framework is specifically aimed at achieving these objectives.

Although in some policy areas such as education British local authorities seem to have greater importance than their equivalent structures in most other liberal democracies, local government in other nations often retain the capacity to operate productive and potentially highly profitable services. In Germany and the United States many city councils supply and distribute gas, electricity and water.

The formal assignment of a function to a particular level of government is, therefore, often misleading. As is indicated elsewhere in this chapter, local control over the police in Britain is largely illusory and the same may be true for education and housing, where there have been strong arguments for removing these services from local control. Although British local authorities, may exercise some powers not always enjoyed by their continental counterparts, they do not have control of some functions that are in other countries assigned to local authorities for the resources to finance their development. The following chapters will consider the important issue of local government finance and then, through consideration of central-local relations, the extent to which British local government has discretion to manage its services.

Further reading

Explanations of functional arrangements and recent theories on local politics are best approached through Dunleavy (1984) and, for a more substantial analysis Stoker (1991) and Hampton (1987). These studies should lead the able student to radical interpretations of local politics in Saunders (1981 and 1984), Duncan and Goodwin (1988) and then Castells (1977), though the neo-Marxist phraseology requires some prior learning, or the much more easily assimilated Cockburn (1977). Public choice texts relate primarily to national rather than local government. King (1987) presents a good introduction. Dunleavy (1991) provides an important analysis of the concept and a critique through his bureau-shaping model.

The concept of an enabling authority as an organisation devoted to providing services requested and needed by citizens is developed in Stewart (1986) and succinctly described in Clarke and Stewart (1990). Walsh (1995) is the best text for analysing how these ideas operate in practice. The popularised new-right version can be found in Ridley (1988) and Beresford (1987) and an 'official' view with tendencies to the right are found in publications of the Audit Commission, especially that of 1988. Stoker (2000) contains the findings of recent Economic and Social Research Council (ESRC) sponsored studies on the functions of local authorities.

4

Finance and its control

Money does not buy happiness, but it certainly helps. Neither does money necessarily buy power, but it is a crucial factor in determining the effectiveness of local government. Large organisations providing a considerable array of services are expensive. Control of finance to fuel these activities is, therefore, an important factor determining the capacity of a local authority to enhance the well-being of its community.

The volume of local finance

Local authority accounts, like those of most large enterprises, cover two separate financial processes. Firstly, a revenue budget catalogues spending on items such as wages and goods and services that are consumed almost as soon they are bought. A second set of accounts deals with capital spending on items such as buildings, computers or refuse trucks that are designed to remain for some years as an asset of the local authority. These two sets of accounts are connected, since capital is acquired largely through borrowing money on which interest must be paid and charged to the revenue account. Table 4.1 outlines the revenue and capital spending by local authorities in Britain in the 1997–98 financial year and Table 4.2 the sources of income for 1997–98.

The local authority budget

Each year a local authority will prepare a budget which is in effect a plan that details how much money is to be spent on each of its activities. The budget will be broken down into statements of the proposed spending within individual departments and on specific services. A local authority is, in theory, able to decide how much money each of its activities will receive but, in practice, there are numerous restraints on the budgeting process, so that the proportion of

Table 4.1 *Revenue and capital spending (1997–98) (in £m)*

	Revenue	Capital
Education	22,856	862
Social services	11,203	159
Housing benefit	11,019	2,349
Police	6,853	234
Fire and civil defence	1,493	51
Transport	3,435	1,136
Local environmental services	5,125	1,135
Libraries and museums	913	59
Sport and recreation	837	206
Courts and probation	924	40
Other services	6,061	158
Total	70,718	6,491

Source: DTLR (1999) *Local Government Financial Statistics* (London, HMSO).

Table 4.2 *Local authority income by source 1997–98*

	£ m	%
Funded by government		
Revenue support grant	18,650	24
National non-domestic rates (business rate)	12,027	16
Grants to specific services	16,374	21
Capital grants to specific services	1,688	3
Local Authority funded		
Council tax	9,265	12
Grants connected to council tax	1,878	2
Revenue from services including rents	13,920	18
Proceeds from sale of assets	2,349	3
Other	783	1
Total	77,209	100

Source: DETR (1999) *Local Government Financial Statistics* (London, HMSO).

spending on particular services usually differs very little from one year to the next. The legal obligations on a county council to operate an effective education service will, for example, require the appointment of a sufficient number of teachers whose salaries are determined by national, rather than local, negotiations. Wide discretion in spending is, therefore, more pronounced in the generally less important services over which local authorities have greater control. In the relatively innovatory area of economic development, some self-satisfied counties and districts choose to spend nothing at all. There may also be wide variations in the resources given to the arts or sports facilities.

> The budgets of British local authorities are comparatively large but this is hardly surprising given the relatively large scale of British local authorities. A small United States city of a few thousand inhabitants or a rural French commune require few resources and will have very simple budgetary procedures.

The budgetary process

The annual budget of a local authority operates for a financial year that begins on 1 April and ends on 31 March in the following year. The budget is finalised usually in February or March, but is determined by detailed consultation among officers and councillors throughout the year. Officers will calculate how much they will need to spend in the forthcoming year in view of expansion or contraction in their services and the effect of price inflation on their spending. These calculations will be made for each service within a department by more junior financial officers and in pre-cabinet-style local authorities the calculations are referred to the councillors on the relevant sub-committee. Backbench councillors in a cabinet-style government under the 2000 Local Government Act will normally only be involved in the budget when asked to approve the final proposals.

Budgeting officers will also estimate the income that the authority could receive from the Government during the following year in grants and commercial rates and also make estimates of how much they may be able to raise in charges and the council tax which they are to some extent able to vary. Expenditure calculations for particular services and the projected local authority income are brought together and presented as a balanced budget to the finance committee. Since the income to be received is determined largely by central government and may be unclear until late in the budgetary planning process, many local authorities develop two or three budget plans during the year which are based on different assumptions concerning revenue. When it becomes clear how much income will be received, a final budget proposal is put before the full council.

Although most of a local authority budget consists of statements on the amount of revenue that will be made available to departments and sections of departments throughout the year, it will also have to determine how much of its funds will be kept in reserve to deal with any unexpected emergencies or to cope with unforeseen overspending by departments. A local authority may build up substantial reserves and can budget to use some of this largesse to maintain spending in the forthcoming financial year. Some councils dip into the reserves in an election year to avoid making high council tax demands. It is however illegal to set a deficit budget in which the authority spends more than it has in reserve.

At the beginning of the financial year, a local government officer is therefore aware of the amount of money he or she is entitled to spend during the year on behalf of the authority. If the officer does not spend everything budgeted to a department, she or he will normally be unable to roll that money into the next financial year but will begin with an entirely new spending allowance so that unspent money, in effect, transfers to its reserves. In theory, a department cannot expect to receive more revenue than the sum assigned in its budget but, in difficult times, it is not infrequent for officers to overspend and, in consequence, deplete the reserve funds of the local authority.

Local authority revenue

Local authorities receive funding from a wide range of sources. At the beginning of the twentieth century taxes on property, the rates and charges for services were the most important components of income. Grants from central government have now become a crucial element of revenue and charges make up a much lower proportion of income. The sources of revenue for local government as a whole in England and Wales is shown in Figure 4.1 and Table 4.2.

Traditionally, through the rates, local governments have had powers to raise as much money as they considered necessary to pay for their revenue services and could, therefore, determine their quantity and quality. The principal restraint on local spending was the extent to which local electors would vote for councillors who increased rate demands. This pattern of funding changed dramatically during the 1980s to a position in which local authority revenue is effectively subject to an upper limit imposed by the Secretary of State for the DTLR. This powerful restraint on local government stems largely from changes to the powers of local authorities to raise taxes and the methods used to distribute government funds.

The current system of determining the revenue for local government stems principally from the Local Government Finance Act of 1992. Central government after consultation with the local authority associations announces in July the Total Standard Spending which is the amount of money the government thinks local authorities should spend for the following financial year. They will also announce how much of this sum they will give to local authorities as grant or through rates that are collected centrally from businesses and how much

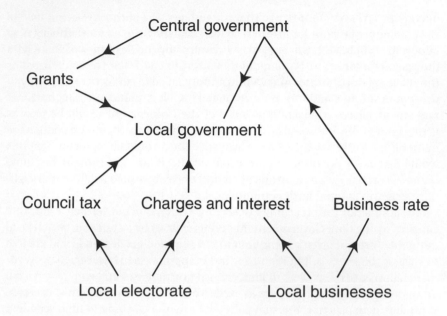

Figure 4.1 *Sources of revenue for local government*

they expect local authorities to raise themselves through the council tax or charges. Following this announcement the government then determines how much each local authority should spend and announces this figure, called the Standard Spending Assessment (SSA), in November. Under the Blair Government SSAs are given for the next three years so that local authorities can more effectively plan ahead their expenditure. The SSA is calculated with reference to seven programme areas, education, social services, police, fire and civil defence, highways maintenance, capital financing and all other services. A local authority can challenge the SSA assigned to it and, after dealing with submissions from several disgruntled councils, a firm announcement on the SSA is made in January.

Once an authority knows what its SSA will be, it can determine its budget for the following year with some clarity and will be able to make a reasonably firm estimate about what it will need to raise in council tax and in charges. Local authorities must set their budget for the financial year that begins each April by 11 March at the latest and send details of its proposals to the DTLR within the following week. If the local authority submits a budget that will spend a higher sum than the SSA, it will need to raise more in taxes than is acceptable to the Secretary of State for the Environment. The Secretary of State has powers to cap the suggested level of council tax if it is in excess of its SSA needs. Under Thatcher and Major, the Government announced before budgets were set the maximum level of council tax they should set. An authority found by the Government to be raising too much council tax was given a month to set a new budget to comply with the level of tax required by the Secretary of State who then put an order before Parliament that determined the level of council tax for the challenged authorities. If a local authority failed to conform to this order, it was not sent funds and ran out of money. In such circumstances, councillors and senior officers supporting defiance of the Government would be seen as acting unlawfully and could be surcharged to repay from their own pockets the money improperly raised. As a consequence they would be bankrupt and this would disqualify a councillor from office. The Blair Government has now removed surcharging as a means of control and substituted a different disciplinary structure of standards committees.

The practice of the preceding Conservative Governments, termed 'crude rate capping' by the Blair Government, has been replaced by a system in which local authorities are not given a clear limit to their council tax demands and are free to suggest the levels of taxation they feel is appropriate. However, the government retains reserve powers to limit council tax increases and will inform local authorities setting what they see as excessive increases that they must decrease expenditure. In practice, this may take the form of a warning to high spending authorities that they will be capped if they continue to spend excessively in the following year (DTLR 2000). Should they continue to defy the government order, the Audit Commission and the newly established regional standards committees will be requested to investigate the conduct of the councillors and can move towards suspending them from office and transferring their responsibilities to another local authority or agency nominated by the DTLR.

Determination of SSA

Setting the annual grant allocation to individual local authorities is like painting the Forth Bridge, a never-ending exercise. In theory, it is the fruit of joint consultation between the local authorities and the Government acting through the Consultative Council on Local Government Finance (CCLGF) which was established in 1975 as a statutory forum for discussions on finance between Government and the local authorities. The full Council is a large body of over seventy delegates, chaired by the Secretary of State of the DTLR, and includes ministers and senior civil servants from the major departments concerned with local authority spending and representatives from the Local Government Association (LGA). The full Council meets three or four times a year, with one statutory meeting in November when the exact terms of the grant settlement are announced. The CCLGF is the apex of a forest of sub-committees which each deal with specific aspects of the fundraising process. These are largely staffed by civil servants and officers of the local authority associations.

The grant allocation cycle is divided into two seasons, with the first half of the year being predominantly devoted to ascertaining the overall sum to be allocated to local authorities. The committees of the CCLGF which are most active in the first half of the year, therefore, deliberate on the needs of each functional area of local authority spending to allow the DTLR to arrive at the Total Standard Spending. The CCLGF is however purely advisory and the final allocation is determined by the Cabinet, on the advice of the Secretary of State for the DTLR and Treasury colleagues. The major decisions concerning funding are made in the bargaining process that takes place between senior spending ministers and the Treasury, which are conducted against the background of the government's public expenditure survey that plans future spending on a three year rolling cycle. Thus, an ambitious Secretary of State for Education who may, for example, wish to lower class sizes by appointing more teachers will seek advice from local authorities through the CCLGF on how much the programme will cost. The Minister will then seek to persuade the Chancellor of the Exchequer and Cabinet colleagues that the project is worthy of resources, usually through meetings and correspondence between ministers or senior civil servants and, on occasion, by courting public opinion through the media.

The second group of committees advising on the distribution of the largesse among each local authority will be particularly active after the Total Spending assessment has been determined, so that an announcement as to how much grant is to be received by each English and Welsh local authority can be revealed in November. It is maintained by ministers and civil servants that the distribution is based on a strict formula concocted within the DTLR with the assistance of CCLGF sub-committees. The distribution is then calculated by DTLR statisticians, who put some ninety or more factors to work in a computer. DTLR civil servants maintain that, given the complexity of the process, it is impossible to manipulate the allocation formula to ensure that one authority receives less than another because of political factors (Chandler 1988: 121). Most local politicians are, however, not convinced that the system is not biased towards favouring those authorities supporting government policy. Computers have, after all, given central government a powerful device for trying a large number of models until the correct desired formula is obtained.

It is difficult to ascertain the extent to which the allocation process is biased against some authorities since very few individuals can understand the whole grant distribution process. Civil servants and their ministers know little of the way in which local authorities arrive at their financial demands but, on the other hand, the mechanics of Whitehall's determination of the rate support grant is a closed book to most city treasurers. The only individuals who see some of both areas at work are the financial secretaries of the local authority associations and senior members of the local authority finance officer's professional association the Chartered Institute for Public Finance and Accountancy (CIPFA), who negotiate with the government. There are also frequent complaints from local authorities that the system is far too complex so that ordinary citizens cannot understand why their particular local authority may have financial problems.

The Blair Government has accepted that changes may need to be made to the system but has not promised any lessening of its complexity (DTLR 2000) and produced in September 2000 a Green Paper, *Modernising Local Government Finance* (DTLR 2000b) to suggest possible methods of making the grant system more transparent and less open to fluctuations in grant without considerable notice to affected local authorities.

The Blair Government has initiated a policy in which, regardless of the SSA formula, there will be a 'floor' level of income which will ensure that no local authority would get an increase in expenditure less than a set amount designated through the SSA process and there is also the possibility of establishing an upper ceiling to the size of any expenditure increase. The Government has also ensured greater financial stability with plans to set grant levels for two years with a more general outline of the income to be received three years ahead.

Local taxes

Local authorities throughout Europe and in the United States do not subsist exclusively on the funds they raise from local taxes but require, in varying degrees, a substantial level of support from national or state governments. In a few countries such as Italy and Ireland, the removal of locally collected property taxes has ensured local governments receive over 90 per cent of their income through grants. In contrast in the United States, most cities raise over half their revenue from local property taxes and municipal trading.

Traditionally, local authorities have raised money from their community primarily through taxes on property known as the rates, in which every property, whether a domestic home, shop, office or factory was assigned a rateable value that was determined largely by the rent that could be charged for the property. A significant exemption is farm land. Local authorities each year decided how much they wished to receive from this tax and then set a rate in the pound to raise the required sum. This custom was temporarily brought to an end by Mrs Thatcher's poll tax, which required every adult in Britain to pay a flat rate charge to their local authority. The hostility to this inequitable means of taxation led to its repeal in 1992 and the return of the rates in the form of the council tax.

Most local government systems in liberal democracies raise at least part of their income through a tax on property similar to the rates. The system is suited to local authorities as it is relatively easy to calculate and collect and, if those individuals owning larger houses pay most money, it is crudely progressive in character in that the rich will tend to pay more than the poor.

The council tax

The council tax is calculated with reference to the market value of each house. The task of valuing property is assigned to a branch of the Inland Revenue who sub-contract the task of valuing each house in the country largely to local estate agents. Each property must be placed in one of eight value bands, ranging from Band A that includes the least expensive properties through to Band H for the most expensive. The assignment of houses to each band differs between England, Scotland and Wales, with the two provinces assigning lower values to each band than in England. As in the case of the rates, only one tax bill is levied for each house, although any person living on their own is entitled to a 25 per cent reduction in their tax bill. The amount paid varies for each tax valuation band, so that those in Band A pay the least whilst owners of Band H palaces pay the most. Councils fix the tax by setting an amount payable for a B and D property and then the payments for other bands are calculated on set ratios. The individual responsible for paying the tax is the legal owner of the dwelling and therefore most tenants do not pay the tax directly but will usually find that the charge is passed on to them by their landlord. Some people are exempt from the tax and, many readers will be pleased to learn, these include students who are living in a property not also occupied by someone who is directly or indirectly liable for payment.

The uniform business rate

The council tax only applies to domestic property. The 1988 Local Government Finance Act which established the 'poll tax' retained a rating system for industrial and commercial property but removed the right of local authorities to set this rate, which is now determined for England and Wales by the Secretary of State for the DTLR and the Secretary of State for Scotland. This arrangement is still in force despite the replacement of the poll tax by the council tax.

The Government determines a rateable value for all shops, offices and factories and each year sets nationally the rate in the pound which will determine the overall payment to local government from a particular business. The sums paid by individual large industries are huge compared with payments made by domestic ratepayers but, in comparison with the overall turnover of a business, as a fixed charge on the business that cannot be easily varied by its directors, its impact on the fortunes of a company will vary depending on whether a firm is financially successful or whether it is in serious difficulties. Although local authorities collect the tax, it is paid into a centrally controlled government account and then redistributed to local authorities in proportion to their population size. This system, in effect, provides a subsidy to rural areas from more industrialised local authorities. The Government is proposing a system to allow local authorities with the agreement of representatives of local businesses to set a higher business rate with the proceeds going straight to the authority, but it

is unlikely that local businesses will agree to such a tax raising substantial sums
for a local authority.

Grants

Since the 1930s, grant aid to local authorities gradually increased as an
element of their income until the Thatcher era, when concerted attempts were
made to reverse this trend, as is shown in Table 4.3.

The most important source of grant income is the revenue support grant
which is distributed throughout the year and may be used by local authorities to
fund their revenue payments as they deem appropriate. Calculation of the grant
is determined through the SSA calculations described earlier in this chapter.

In addition to the revenue support grant, local authorities may be allocated
specific grants directed towards aiding a particular service. Specific grants
accounted for approximately 21 per cent of local government revenue in
1997–98 but by far the largest element of this sum is funding for the police, fire
services, the courts and probation service. A substantial specific grant is also
given to local authorities for administering housing benefit which is, in effect, a
national benefit administered by local authorities. Several smaller grants are
awarded to maintain government programmes covering, for example, inner-city
development, stemming the AIDS epidemic or community support for the mentally ill. In addition to specific grants, local authorities may also receive special
grants which are one-off payments to cover the costs of expensive and unexpected payments such as restoring coastal defences after serious storm damage.

Charges

Local government is widely regarded as a public service which requires direct
or indirect subsidies from taxpayers to maintain its activities whilst private
trading organisations make profits from charging customers for their services.
This is a misleading impression, since it is possible to fund many local authority tasks through trading services at a profit. Local governments were much
more reliant on charges in the late nineteenth and early twentieth centuries,
receiving a substantial portion of their income from trading in energy supplies
and transport services.

In the United States, city governments charge much more extensively for services
such as refuse collection and some will also make considerable income from productive services such as gas and electricity supply or in licensing the right to
supply such services to private companies. As Osborne and Gaebler (1992)
showed, American authorities can be much more entrepreneurial than their
British counterparts.

Table 4.3 *Grants to local government as a percentage of their total revenue (1933–79)*

Year	%
1933–34	31
1943–44	31
1953–54	37
1963–64	36
1973–74	40
1978–79	44
1983–84	40
1988–89	34
1991–92	38
1997–98	46

Source: DETR (1999) *Local Government Financial Statistics* (London, HMSO).

Charges became a relatively minor source of revenue only after the Attlee Government had removed trading services from local authorities and replaced the lost income by grants. Substantial income was still generated through rents from council houses and bus fares, but these charges generally did not meet the full cost of the service. Charges also remained as part payment for a range of minor activities such as the use of sports facilities, cultural events or applications for planning permission.

True to their new-right beliefs, the Thatcher and Major Governments placed greater emphasis on charges rather than adopt the social democratic view that functions such as transport and housing should be provided as a service to the community as a whole. Despite the image of local authorities as being providers of collective services, charges now form a significant element of their income and some major activities, in particular housing and transport, are paid for almost entirely by direct payment from the customer. The 1988 Housing Act, for example, demands that the housing account of a local authority must be maintained separately from the general revenue accounts and cannot receive subsidies from other sources of local government funds. The Act followed a gradual reduction in the considerable subsidy given as part of the block grant to housing, which consequently increased rents for council houses. This policy not only fitted Conservative aims to reduce local taxes, but also with their privatisation policy, since the higher council house rents, the more sensible it becomes for tenants to buy their homes. The principle of balancing accounts through charges has been extended to other areas. The first essay in this direction was enshrined in the 1980 Local Government Planning and Land Act which required Direct Labour Organisations, local authority construction and building departments, to make a surplus each year without the aid of general rate subsidies.

Local authorities still have discretion on whether to subsidise many of their services, to operate on a break-even basis or use the service to make a profit. Decisions as to the pricing of sports facilities, museum admission or home helps fall into this category, even though none of these services, however profitable, can usually generate sufficient income to make a major difference to local authority income. These largely non-essential services are subject to market forces and in many cases higher charges will quickly deter members of the public from using them. Only a few authorities with substantial tourist attractions, such as the City of Bath, are able to make a considerable impact on their finances through profits from entrepreneurial pricing of attractions (Chandler and Turner 1997).

Raising capital

Local authorities have since the nineteenth century been expected to raise capital by borrowing money and paying back interest through the revenue account. Most local authority equipment and property has been acquired through such means, although the amount they can borrow has for over a century been restricted by central government. The annual public spending estimates announced by the government includes a statement on capital spending by local authorities. This statement is followed up by more detailed information to each individual local authority on what they may spend on capital projects for the following financial year. The announcement is not however a promise by the government to directly provide the money, but a statement giving the councils permission to borrow money, up to the limit that is allocated to them. The Green Paper *Modernising Local Government Finance* (DTLR 2000b) has suggested that this current system should be restructured to allow local governments to borrow without direct government approval, provided they adhere to nationally determined formulae relating to indicators, such as the ratio of their overall debt to their expenditure and a limit on the rate at which they could increase their debt.

Local authorities raise capital through a number of channels. They may borrow money on the open market from banks, from the public by issuing interest-bearing bonds at a rate set by the city or county treasurer, or borrow from a government-established body, the Public Works Loan Board. This latter source of funding is usually preferred since it will charge a slightly lower rate of interest than commercial banks. The Treasury, however, sets limits to the amount that may be obtained from the Board as a further means of regulating capital spending.

Capital can also be acquired through the sale or leasing of existing local government assets. The Conservative Governments placed considerable restrictions on the use of the sums that, for example, flow from the sale of council houses and, until recently, the money raised from this source has had to be used to pay back money already borrowed in order to reduce the authority's debts. In practice, local authorities achieve a better return by investing the capital receipts and using the interest to subsidise their borrowing repayments. Pressure on the Government to allow local authorities to release this capital for local development is beginning to force some relaxation in this policy which, as applied to council house sales, has prevented local authorities from ploughing receipts from sales back into improving or increasing their housing stock. A further source of capital funding is through the Private Finance Initiative (PFI) in which public buildings and projects are owned by private sector companies and leased to the public sector organisation. Currently, seventy local authorities are making use of this scheme (DTLR 2000).

Capital may be raised through funds received from the council tax but, given the capping arrangements tied to the projected revenue expenditure of the local authority, this source cannot be used to fund major projects. It is also possible to raise small capital sums for recreational and social welfare purposes through local lotteries. This power, acquired in 1976, led to a flurry of local raffles but it was soon clear that the cost of administrating such schemes was not worth the funds raised.

Auditing the accounts

Local authorities, like any major business organisation, must keep a meticulous record of their finances in accounts kept for departments and sections of departments. Using double-entry bookkeeping, local authorities record the costs and revenue of their services and show the surplus or deficits that they generate. They must keep separate accounts for revenue activities and capital expenditure, ensure that interest on capital is credited to the relevant revenue accounts and also provide an analysis of their assets and liabilities. The accounts for each financial year, along with connected information such as details of staff employed, are published for public scrutiny, although the time taken to compile the final complex report may take a year or more following the close of the year's account.

The work of calculating and reporting the accounts of a local authority was traditionally undertaken by its treasurer's department. Located within this section was a group of internal auditors who monitored the spending and financial procedures of the various services of the authority in order to ensure that their conduct would pass external scrutiny. This task was subject to CCT and is now subject to Best Value so that local authorities must clearly demonstrate that their internal audit can be most efficiently conducted by their own staff rather than external businesses. The accounts compiled and audited within the authority are then subject to external scrutiny. Auditing local government accounts was one of the earliest checks on local government formally imposed by central government and was applied first to the 1834 Poor Law Boards. The independent scrutiny of local government accounts is now the responsibility of the Audit Commission. This organisation was established through the Local Government Finance Act of 1982 to be responsible for monitoring the financial and managerial competence and probity of local government and a number of specified quangos, including the health service. The Commission is divided into districts, with considerable authority delegated to the chief auditor for each of these areas.

The Audit Commission is responsible for the long-established task of inspecting the accounts of local authorities and reporting on their legality and accuracy in order to root out any unlawful or fraudulent practice. The annual accounts of every local authority must be passed by the Audit Commission which can and does comment on areas of irregularity that the council needs to rectify. If the authority is thought to be acting unlawfully, the Commission may start an immediate investigation and if it finds cases of improper action it can initiate legal proceedings against offending officers and councillors.

The power to prosecute local authorities for unlawful action is an important weapon in the armoury of central government controls over local authorities and, although the ultimate sanctions of legal proceedings are used but rarely, cases where action has been successfully pursued through the courts spell out the limits of local government discretion. If, for example, councillors have allowed the authority to spend or raise money unlawfully, the auditor was able to initiate proceedings that made individual councillors liable to repay whatever the auditor calculated had been incorrectly used. Since the sum was likely to be too large for the offending councillors to pay, they were bankrupted and consequently unable to remain as a councillor. The threat of surcharging and disqualification through action by auditors effectively ended the attempts of local socialist authorities in 1985 to raise more money than permitted by rate-capping legislation. Labour councillors in Liverpool and Lambeth were surcharged and disqualified from office. However, the Blair Government through the 2000 Local Government Act has removed the necessity to surcharge and bankrupt councillors and officers who raise and spend local taxpayers money unlawfully, by allowing auditors to refer those thought to be acting improperly to the ethics committees established under the Act which, should accusations be proved, have the power to suspend or disbar the councillor or officers from their posts.

The Audit Commission was given greater powers than solely the duty of checking the legality of accounts. It is also responsible for ascertaining whether local authorities are providing value for money and this has enabled the Commission to comment extensively on the management of local government. Since its creation the Commission has been an enthusiastic supporter of new management values and published frequent reports outlining strategies for competitive enabling authorities. The Commission is not, however, a simple agent of central government and, whilst criticising some local authority practices, has also raised questions about the government's management of local finances.

Financial restraints and local democracy

When the Labour Government was forced to restructure the economy in 1976 through a loan from the International Monetary Fund tied to expenditure cuts, local authorities were included in the cost-cutting package. The Secretary of State for the Environment, Antony Crosland, informed the local authorities that 'the party is over', signalling an end to increases in grant levels. A Green Paper on local government finance published in 1977 maintains, for example, that

> The dilemma which faces local government is to secure and promote an effective local democracy with genuine political choice and at the same time fulfil their responsibilities for the management of the economy and the standards of public services (quoted in Travers 1986: 71).

The Thatcher Government did not, however, see much of a dilemma in these issues and popularised the view that spending by local authorities was out of control and had to be brought into line with the parsimonious regime which was being forced on central government. The post-1979 Conservative Governments began by reducing grant aid to local authorities and then started financially penalising local authorities which raised higher rates to compensate for loss of grant. The Government finally removed in the 1984 Local Government Finance Act the right of local authorities to raise more revenue in taxes than was allowed by the Government and the onslaught on local finance culminated with the disaster of the poll tax which levied a flat rate payment for local government services on every adult. The Act also introduced the uniform business rate.

The Blair Government has, however, done relatively little to remove the constraints on local spending imposed by the Conservatives. There have been no plans to change the council tax and only suggestions that councils may be able to raise higher business taxes with the agreement of local business representatives. Restrictions on capital spending have been slightly alleviated, but still remain under central control. In the first three years of the New Labour administration, Chancellor Gordon Brown imposed severe restrictions on local authority spending and following the massive injection of funding into the economy in the 2000 spending review, local authorities in general received little extra although some of their specific services and especially education were major beneficiaries.

The most controversial restraint on local autonomy that allows the Government to cap the expenditure of the local authority by limiting rate increases remains firmly in force, although it is a less visible restriction since the limit for each authority is not now announced before local authorities forward their budgets. However, in 1999/2000 the Government required twelve local authorities to explain why they had increased their council tax demands and were warned that such behaviour may not be tolerated in the following year.

The Government (DTLR 2000) firmly rejected proposals in a report from the DTLR Select Committee of the House of Commons which called for greater use of locally raised taxes and removal of government capping controls as essential for securing enhanced local democracy and responsibility. The response from the Government argued that it would be unfair to rate payers to suddenly switch the burden of paying for local government onto the rates and if this were done there would need to be complex transitional relief schemes put in place. The Government also thought it necessary to continue with some control over rate demands, since citizens need some form of protection against excessive rises and, because rates are part of the retail price index, excessive rises will give the appearance of higher inflation which will in turn impact on government expenditure.

Accusations of local profligacy are probably as old as local government itself and were certainly a major theme for opponents of active city governments in the nineteenth century (Fraser 1979). There is no evidence that, historically, local government is any more prodigal than Whitehall, as is shown in Table 4.4.

The argument that local authorities, if unchecked by the wisdom of Whitehall, would spend without restraint implicitly assumes that local democracy is of no consequence or effect. This may be the case if most of the extra revenue solicited by a local authority is automatically passed on to them from central funds and, therefore, has no localised impact. Successive governments in Britain have traversed the path of greater centralisation more than the path of autonomy. This trend was been accelerated by the recent Conservative Governments to the extent that few councils seemed to have much discretion as to their revenue. The Blair Government has done little to reverse this development. It is, therefore, now difficult to argue that any financial difficulties faced by a local authority are solely due to their reckless behaviour. If local spending was out of control, then much of the blame must rest with central government.

In countries, such as the United States, where grant levels are much lower, public choice theorists suggest that the levels of local taxation can determine voter preferences and even their choice of residence and local authority (Tiebout 1956). This may only be possible when local authorities are small in size and individuals can choose to live in one authority rather than another without seriously changing their distance from work.

Table 4.4 *Revenue spending by local authorities and central government as a percentage of gross domestic product (1966–95)*

	Local government	Central government
1966–67	8.5	26.7
1970–71	9.6	27.9
1975–76	11.8	35.7
1980–81	11.2	36.7
1985–86	9.9	35.1
1990–91	10.6	29.4
1994–95	10.6	34.4

Source: Office for National Statistics (2000b), *Financial Statistics*, London, HMSO.

Further reading

The problem with any study of local government finance is that it may become factually dated almost as soon as it is written. A succinct official summary is provided in recent editions of the Department of the Environment's *Local Government Statistics* and guides are also published by the Local Government Information Unit and by CIPFA. *Modernising Local Government: A Green Paper* (DTLR 2000b) also has an up-to-date summary of the methods for setting local government expenditure by the Government and like most recent Government publications is available on the web.

There are a number of well-crafted but ageing analytical studies in this area. The standard authority was Hepworth (1984) which received frequent updating in new editions but none has appeared recently. The political issues underlying recent financial change are well considered by Travers (1986) with some updating in Travers (1995). Valuable material on trends in expenditure is also provided by Newton and Karran (1985) and Bailey and Paddison (1988). Local government finance in Scotland was analysed by Midwinter (1984), although this is now becoming rather dated.

Techniques of local government financial management are considered in Jones (1995) and more recently a study of local budgeting sponsored by the Joint Universities Council for Public Administration has produced Elcock, Jordan and Midwinter (1989) and Elcock and Jordan (1987) which provide much valuable empirical information. A more recent financial management study is Rawlinson and Tanner (1990).

There have been a number of studies on the poll tax and its consequences. John (1989) and Hollis *et al.* (1990) are useful studies and in more detail Butler, Adonis and Travers (1995) provide an illuminating analysis of how and why policies fail.

5

Local government
and the State

It is impossible to seriously consider local government as an entity autonomous from the centre. Both central and local governments have evolved a complex network of structures and procedures for dealing with their mutual interests. Despite their labyrinthine qualities, these structures are generally capable of successfully co-ordinating policy towards local authorities and sufficiently flexible to insert central guidance wherever Whitehall considers necessary. This chapter describes the structures and processes through which central government attempts to shape the structure and policies of local governments.

The organisation of central government for local government

The British Constitution ordains that sovereignty is vested in the Queen in Parliament but the realities of cohesive and disciplined parliamentary party politics ensures that effective power lies with the executive. At the apex of the British political system the Prime Minister and Cabinet have the power, subject to ratification by Parliament or judicial review, to make the final authoritative decisions on matters that they feel unable to delegate to subordinate levels of policy making. Thus, any major issues concerning local authorities will be considered in Cabinet. This will include final agreement on proposed legislation affecting local authorities or important policies such as the size of the Total Spending Assessment.

As in all Cabinet discussions, the Prime Minister will be able to exert a powerful influence on an issue, should he or she take an interest in the matter. Richard Crossman, when Minister for Housing and Local Government, observed in his diary that

Certainly it is true that the Cabinet is now part of the 'dignified' element of the constitution, in the sense that the real decisions are rarely taken there, unless the

72

Prime Minister deliberately chooses to give the appearance of letting the Cabinet decide a matter. I was also right to recognise the importance of Cabinet Committees (Crossman 1975: 198).

Cabinet will debate relatively few issues, but may confirm many proposals. Many decisions are, effectively, made in cabinet committees consisting of a number of secretaries of state, non-cabinet ministers and senior civil servants, chosen by the Prime Minister to develop policies relating to a particular issue or policy area. On certain issues, such as foreign policy, Prime Ministers establish standing cabinet committees to co-ordinate policy. The Thatcher Government soon came to see local government as a sector creating sufficient problems to require a cabinet committee which was assigned the issue of local government finance as Mrs Thatcher sought an alternative to the rates. The committee named MISC 79 turned its attention not only to the rates and the poll tax but also the abolition of the metropolitan counties (Chandler 1988: 161). The Governments of John Major established a cabinet committee for local government chaired by Lord Wakeham, the Lord Privy Seal and a further sub-committee to deal with issues relating to London. The Blair Government has continued with a cabinet committee on local government which is chaired by the Deputy Prime Minister and Secretary of State for the DTLR, John Prescott and includes sixteen other ministers including the Chancellor of the Exchequer and Home Secretary. There is also a separate cabinet committee to deal with issues relating to London and a further committee on devolution issues.

The role of government departments

Below the level of the Cabinet and cabinet committees, the DTLR takes the lead in establishing and reviewing policy towards the local government system as a whole and, in particular, issues relating to the structure, general powers and methods of financing the system. In the late nineteenth century it became apparent that control of the network of multi-purpose and *ad hoc* agencies that made up the local government system required a government department that could ensure that these agencies were better co-ordinated. To meet this need the Liberal Government of Gladstone created the Local Government Board in 1871, following the recommendations of a Royal Commission on Sanitation. The Board was merged with other departments into the Ministry of Health in the 1920s. With the creation of the National Health Service (NHS) in 1948, health became less associated with local government and was hived off to a separate ministry whilst local government was allocated to a Ministry of Housing and Local Government (MHLG). In 1970 the MHLG became a central element in a newly created larger body, the Department of the Environment, which also included responsibility for transport and public buildings.

Most European countries assign responsibility for oversight of local government to the Ministry of the Interior, which in Britain is most equivalent to the Home Office, as it also has a lead role on policing. In France the Ministry of the Interior has oversight over all matters relating to local government and, in theory, co-ordinates the demands of other Ministries which oversee services to be implemented by local government. In the United States where the Federal Government has no constitutional powers over local government, the states deal with the structure of local government in their areas and rarely assign this to a lead department.

Although the Local Government Board was allocated oversight of the overall planning of the local government structure, individual ministries still retained, and have continued to retain, their oversight of many functions that are now implemented by local governments. Responsibility for overseeing the policy for individual local authority functions rests therefore with the department most concerned with that issue. Thus, the DfEE deals with all matters relating to local authority schools or the Home Office with the police, even though the final allocation of funds for these functions to particular local authorities rests, in theory, with the DTLR. This complex distribution of tasks, ensures specialist supervision of specialist tasks, but also creates serious problems of co-ordination.

The Department of Transport, Local Government and the Regions (DTLR)

The DTLR was created in its present form by Tony Blair just after the 2001 General Election with, as Secretary of State, Stephen Byers. The Secretary of State for the Department of the Environment as originally established has always been regarded as one of the more senior members of the Cabinet but below the prestige of the Chancellor of the Exchequer, Foreign Secretary or Home Secretary. Since the Department is extensive, the Secretary of State is assisted currently by three Ministers of State and a further three junior Parliamentary Under-Secretaries of State. One of the Ministers of State in 2001, Nick Raynsford, is designated the Minister for Local Government and the Regions and is in charge of the section of the Department concerned with local government as a whole.

Reporting to the Secretary of State is the Permanent Secretary, the senior civil servant in charge of the management of the Department, who advises Ministers about the appropriate action they should take and is the manager for all civil servants in the Department. Much has been written about the relationship of Ministers and Permanent Secretaries both in academic studies, political memoirs and fiction. In certain circumstances a strong civil servant may be able to influence policy more effectively than a weak and hesitant Minister, whilst on other occasions the Secretary of State may be the dominant figure. In practice, due to pressure of work Ministers, will often leave much detailed policy making to their civil servants, but will usually dominate on matters of major importance.

Given the wide range of interests within the DTLR, only a relatively small section is devoted to making policy for the local government system as a whole, but many of the other sections such as housing and construction, the regions or cities and countryside are heavily involved with local functions. Each section immediately below the Permanent Secretary is divided into Groups, which are usually divided into directorates, often led by a Permanent Under-Secretary or Assistant Permanent Under-Secretaries.

In addition to its Whitehall staff, the DTLR has nine regional offices which were established by merging a number of separate provincial departmental offices scattered throughout the country. The offices are delegated decision-making powers concerning housing, planning, economic development and inner-city responsibilities, which can all affect local authorities in their region. They do not have any specific powers concerning local government finance and structures, but they can act as an informal channel through which information and advice on such issues may be channelled between the government and local authorities. Each region is under the direction of an Under-Secretary who reports to the Permanent Secretary of the DTLR. The Regional Directors have a measure of autonomy which may, for example, result in some local authorities getting permission to modernise a council housing estate that would not be granted by another director in a different region.

Local government oversight for Scotland and Wales

Responsibility for the structure of local government in Scotland has since the nineteenth century always been assigned to the Scottish Office and regarded as a matter to be determined by Scottish rather than English interests. In Wales a similar shift of effective responsibility for determining local government structure did not take place until the 1960s with the formation of the Welsh Office. Under the Acts establishing devolved government in Scotland and Wales, responsibility for local government structure and powers is placed even more clearly in the regions. In Scotland, the Parliament has the power to legislate for the structure, funding and functions of local government, provided the function is not an area reserved for the United Kingdom Government. The Scottish Executive thus, can determine subject to Scottish Parliament approval, the structure of local government in the province and has allocated the overall responsibility for the system to the Minister for Communities who is assisted by a Deputy Minister with specific local government responsibilities. The ministerial team are the political heads of a Development Department which, in the Westminster system, supervises the overall structure of the system, although responsibility for many functions such as education or social services that are administered by local authorities is assigned to other departments.

Co-ordination of the system of oversight

The considerable array of central government departments with some responsibility for local authority functions necessitates effective systems for their co-
ordination. Blair has been greatly concerned with this issue and developed the
idea, discussed later in this chapter, of joined-up government to secure integrated policies to multi-dimensional problems. However, the British system of
government has traditionally had a number of devices that help ensure that
government policies are 'joined-up'.

At the highest level of policy making the Cabinet and cabinet committees will
draw together ministers with an interest in a particular issue. A Prime Minister
in an entrenched position as party leader will be able to end quarrels between
subordinate colleagues through pre-emptory decisions in favour of one or other
of the contending factions. Policy co-ordination in Britain is also enhanced by the
hierarchic civil service structure, in which each department of state has one or
two dominant heads, the Permanent Secretaries, and they in turn are expected
to defer to the views of the pre-eminent civil servants, the Cabinet Secretary and
the Permanent Secretaries of the Treasury. Permanent Secretaries regularly
meet in a committee that effectively shadows the Cabinet and serves to co-
ordinate working practices among departments. The Treasury takes a leading
role in this process, since its support can be crucial for any project requiring funds
and it is also the department housing the head of the civil service who has
responsibility for the organisation of the Government's bureaucracy and, most
crucially, recruitment and promotion within the service. The Cabinet Secretary
has influence as the principal official advisor to the Prime Minister and the
Cabinet is consequently able to authoritatively communicate to colleagues what
he or she regards as the views of the most powerful decision makers.

In some European countries, such as France and Italy, the civil service is much
less co-ordinated into a hierarchy and there is no single dominant official as head
of the civil servants in each ministry but rather groups of agency heads each with
equal status.

The civil service has a vast network of inter-departmental committees that
may be established on a standing basis or as *ad hoc* groups to deal with particular issues. The legislation leading to the abolition of the metropolitan county
councils and the GLC involved some 270 civil servants culled from a range of
departments, co-ordinated by a cabinet committee composed of politicians.
Responsible to this group was a civil service, 'officials' steering committee led by
an Under-Secretary in the Department of the Environment temporarily
appointed to take control of the Bill and its implementation (Chandler 1988:
47–8). Apart from these formal structures, civil servants may often be in
contact with colleagues in other departments whose portfolios relate to their

tasks. Any proposal to increase spending in future years will, for example, be immediately referred to the Treasury through the Whitehall grapevine. Richard Crossman observed that the promotion of civil servants rests more with the opinion of the mandarins of the Treasury than himself, as a transient minister, and they will, consequently, leak information to the Treasury before informing the political head of their own department (Crossman 1975: 342).

Linking local and central governments

There is a constant stream of communications between central and local government and the local authority associations. Much of this traffic is in the form of written statements containing orders and advice or requests for information. There are also contacts between the personnel of local and central government through meetings, conferences and telephone discussions. There is, however, relatively little meshing of personnel in both areas to create serious mutual understanding between the two sectors.

Formal commands

The most formal and compelling government communications to local authorities concern legislation. As soon as a relevant Act is promulgated local authorities will receive the document and must respond to its precepts. Its content should not of course come as a surprise to senior policy makers, since they will have monitored its progress from its origins as a ministerial statement. The meaning of an Act is not, however, usually left to the comprehension of councillors, but conveyed in government circulars issued by the relevant departments of state. These provide detailed instructions on how the Act should be implemented as far as the government is concerned. For example, they may suggest dates for completion of Best Value public consultations or clarify membership issues concerning scrutiny committees. Usually these instructions are not binding and can be challenged or ignored, but such a reaction may well result in eventual legal confrontation between a local authority and the government over the meaning of an Act.

Changes to statutory orders must also be communicated to local authorities, accompanied by circulars advising them on the aims and methods of implementing the new directives. Governments can also issue a circular reinterpreting its powers under a long-established Act. The Labour Government in 1976, for example, sought to ensure that all local education authorities adopted comprehensive education by arguing in a circular that it had powers to require this under the 1944 Education Act. Circulars may also be issued to provide a code of practice which informs the local authority of what the government considers to be reasonable behaviour. Whilst not statutorily binding, a local authority may be sued for negligence if it ignores such codes.

Information and advice

Despite their importance, only a fraction of the communications between central and local government involve commands from the government. Much information issued for the benefit of local authorities is primarily advisory in form. These may be reports relating, for example, to public health or information on better road materials or safeguards on waste disposal. There is a mass of routine communication to ensure the day-to-day workings of the system are kept in good working order. This activity involves as much communication from localities to the centre as information flowing from centre to periphery. There is an insatiable demand for statistical material that must be provided on a regular basis. This will include returns of data on issues as varied as levels of local authority spending, the numbers of children in schools, crime statistics, or new housing starts. Such data is published in numerous central government statistical reports. The government may also require information on a more *ad hoc* basis in order to aid policy formation or to satisfy the curiosity of a government minister.

Consultation

Although exchange of routine information is a constant and often onerous duty for both local and central government, these exchanges do not necessarily create greater understanding between the two areas of government. There is, however, more infrequent but crucial communication at times of policy change. Apart from the Thatcher Governments, the process of legislation towards local authorities usually involved comprehensive consultation with the local authority associations and, on occasion, individual local governments. Important enquiries, such as Royal Commissions, solicit detailed evidence from local authorities which is usually published in appendices to the reports. Most White Papers and all Green Papers are issued by the government with a request for local authorities to send in comments by a certain date. Politicians and civil servants may also regularly seek advice from local authority representatives whilst a Bill progresses through Parliament. For example, if an amendment of a highly technical nature is tabled during the committee stage of a Bill, ministers will require their civil servants to advise them on the consequences of the proposal and they, in turn, may seek inspiration from senior officials in the local authority associations.

Serious consultation on major proposals was less apparent under the Thatcher regimes. Apart from the Widdicombe Report, there was little reliance on using major and lengthy independent enquiries as a prelude to possible legislation. White Papers were issued with almost impossible to meet deadlines for receipt of comments and the Government was loath to seek advice from local authorities when piloting Bills through Parliament. The CCLGF became a forum in which Secretaries of State told local authorities what they expected them to do rather than seek their opinions (Rhodes, Hardy and Pudney 1983). The Blair Government appears to have returned more to the preceding pattern of issuing White Papers with sufficient time for comment from local government and of seeking the views of local government organisations on policy.

Local authority associations

Developing policy towards local government requires frequent debate, conflict and discussion between the Government or the provincial governments and the local authorities in their areas. Central government does not usually care to receive a muddled jumble of ideas from the many differing local authorities and local governments themselves prefer to give a stronger unified opinion to central government than a set of conflicting views. Since the nineteenth century, local governments have consequently attempted to co-ordinate their approach to central government through interest groups known as local government associations. Conflict between local authorities of different types until recently led in England and Wales to the development of different local authority associations for counties, metropolitan areas and districts. Since the Redcliffe-Maud Report there had been demands to consolidate the major association into a single group for England but this did not take place until the 1990s restructuring when the local authorities managed to bury their differences to create in 1997 a single interest group, the LGA representing all local authorities in England and Wales above the level of the parish, although within the organisation are sub-groups for particular interests such as the Welsh LGA. In Scotland, the differing tiers of authority decided following the Wheatley proposals in 1973 to develop a single association, the Confederation of Scottish Local Authorities (CoSLA). Parish and town councils are not members of the associations for the larger authorities and many affiliate to a National Association for Local Councils.

European liberal democracies have all developed representative bodies to co-ordinate the mutual interests of their local governments and present these to their Governments. In France, the most influential is the *Association des Maires de France* (AMF). In the United States there are similar organisations representing state governors, city mayors and city managers and county representatives. The impact of such groups is however variable and is much dependent on prevailing cultural attitudes towards interest groups. In France, for example, close links between mayors and national politicians ensures there are additional more direct channels than the AMF to convey local views on the local government system.

Membership of the LGA is not compulsory, but all local authorities regard it as an important and significant organisation for defending their interests. It is also well understood that central government will only discuss general matters affecting all local authorities with the LGA rather than with any individual local government that has decided to opt out of the Association. In the past, a few local authorities have, largely for political reasons, refused to affiliate to their appropriate organisation. During much of the 1980s, Derbyshire County Council, under Labour control, refused to join the then predominantly Conservative Association of County Councils, but soon discovered that civil servants and ministers would not discuss proposed legislation with them.

The LGA is managed and funded by its members. Local authorities will send councillors to represent them on its general council of their appropriate association which will determine the overall policy for the organisation. Since most councils are strongly partisan, the ruling party or parties within the authority will select its own councillors as delegates to the Association. The LGA is, therefore, like its member authorities, organised on party political lines and the party with the majority of representatives on the general council of the Association will control its policy. When the Association was created in 1997, the decline in support for the Conservative Party ensured that the majority on the LGA were from the Labour Party.

Between meetings of the general council of the LGA their affairs are directed by an elected executive which will be dominated by representatives of the party with the majority of seats in the Association. In 2000, the balance of party membership on the LGA Executive reflecting the membership of the Association was five Labour members, three Conservatives, two Liberal Democrats and an Independent. Each association also has sub-committees dealing with areas of functional responsibility, such as education or housing. The chair of the executive, who will also be chairperson of the Association as a whole, is usually seen as the leading political spokesperson for the interest group. The Association employs a permanent staff who advise on policy, conduct research and provide the administrative backing demanded by the association. The permanent officers are led by a chief executive who leads a team of eleven senior officers who in turn head teams of staff dealing with specialist areas of local government, such as education or social services, or tasks such as communication and public relations necessary for the operation of the Association. The staff are usually recruited from the local government service and are often helped by advice from senior local government officers employed by member authorities.

Local authorities and their associations will seek to promote their views in both direct and indirect attempts to influence central government. The local authority associations issue frequent statements that attempt to change national policy. The meetings of the local authority associations are an important means through which the leaders of the local governments can express their opinions. The associations issue reports, parliamentary briefings and press releases in order to forward their case. On occasion, local authorities may initiate major public relations campaigns to court public opinion. The citizens of London could scarcely avoid the skilled campaign launched by Ken Livingstone in defence of the GLC, although the response of the Thatcher Government to an increasing tendency of local authorities to gain popular support in the struggles against her policies was to ban any local authority publicity attacking central government in the 1986 Local Government Act.

Other associations

In addition to the local authority associations, an important network of interests also influencing central-local relations has been developed from professional associations and trade unions representing the interests of local government officers. As will be discussed in Chapters 9 and 11, the influence of the local government professional associations varies substantially but some, such as CIPFA representing chief finance officers, are powerful bodies with a high level of respect within Whitehall. The senior members and officers of such a body may exert considerable expert influence on government thinking. The Government also establishes a number of specialist advisory bodies such as the IDeA, formerly the Local Government Management Board.

Local authorities have also created a number of bodies to co-ordinate their action in particular policy areas. The Centre for Local Economic Strategy develops thinking on economic intervention. Left-wing local authorities along with the trade unions formed a Local Government Information Unit to co-ordinate the strategy of these authorities against Conservative Government pressure. The organisation now has a more informative role. Such action is not however a new departure. LEAs formed an association whose secretary in the 1940s and 1950s, Sir William Alexander, gained such close ties with civil servants that he became a major voice in national education policy.

Joined-up government

The Blair Government has placed considerable emphasis on the need to co-ordinate policy and its implementation across different government organisations and agencies. They are rightly aware that many problems that beset society cannot be resolved by one organisation, but require several separate organisations to work together on the many facets relating to the issue. For example, the problems of a failed school may not simply involve poor teaching or school buildings, but stem form social problems such as unemployment, bad housing or drug taking. Thus, tackling problems of unemployment, law and order or educational deprivation needs joined-up government in which many agencies co-operate to resolve a problem. The idea that agencies must work together is far from new and was a major factor in the idea of corporate management that greatly influenced ideas on local structures in the 1970s. However, following the Thatcher years that emphasised solutions to problems were better facilitated by the private rather than the public sector, the new emphasis on co-ordination has given renewed impetus to resolve issues through public or voluntary sector leadership.

In order to secure joint working, the Government has established a number of task groups to try to resolve difficult problems such as social deprivation or drug dependency. The groups are required to bring multi-disciplinary working to bear on issues that cannot span the interest of one government department or even government as a whole. In addition to the development of task forces, the Government has emphasised the need for organisations such as local government to work more in partnership with private sector, voluntary and other public bodies to secure a co-ordinated approach to resolving problems or providing services. To some degree this approach is the Blair Government's equivalent of the enabling authority, in that local authorities are to be leaders of their community which, rather than resolving issues such as homelessness through the use of their own resources, will be able to bring together the public and private agencies at local and national level to work in partnership on the problem. This idea has influenced not only some of the operations of national government in the form of task forces but in later chapters will be seen to influence Government thinking on how local authorities should be internally structured and how they should manage their responsibilities.

The two worlds of government

Officers and civil servants

Discussions between central and local government are premised on a principle that on general policy, ministers talk only to the leading politicians within the local authority associations, whilst civil servants talk only to its officers. On the occasions when government speaks to individual local authorities a similar minister to member, civil servant to officer arrangement is normally applied. There are, of course, occasional and usually highly informal infractions of this rule, but such occasions are rare and usually conducted outside the more formal channels of communication. For example, a local politician may have a word with a senior civil servant in the entourage of a minister who is visiting the local authority.

On some minor matters, such as local authority pensions, politicians leave the detailed policy making on the issue to liaison between association officials and civil servants. Contacts between the Government and the LGA or between the Scottish Executive and CoSLA are frequent, particularly at officer level where there may be almost daily contact, often by telephone, between, for example, a secretary for local government finance and civil servants involved with this issue. Because of the association officers' knowledge of local authority practice, which is usually a closed book to civil servants, and the officers understanding of civil service practice, the senior association officials may become the most knowledgeable individuals in the country on the working of central–local administration.

There are, however, relatively few links between civil servants and the officers of individual local authorities. Discussions may take place on issues such as planning appeals or requests for inner-city funds, often through regional office civil servants. Senior officers who are used by the local authority associations as spokespersons may meet with government officials in the joint civil service, local authority officer-staffed sub-committees of the CCGLF. These links are however generally formal and unlikely to produce much in the way of close working relationships or mutual empathy.

At a formal level there is, therefore, constant mutual communication between central and local government which keeps the everyday operation of the system in good working order. This element of the relationship is however conducted primarily as an automated impersonal movement of papers involving little personal conduct or mutual discussion. Major areas of possible collaboration are scarcely touched. There is, for example, almost no exchange of personnel between Whitehall and town halls. Exceptionally, the DTLR has seconded a local government officer into its ranks on a temporary basis, but there is no arrangement for regular career movement between local and national civil services. Local government officers inhabit a separate world from civil servants, with dissimilar processes of recruitment, training and promotion let alone any interchange of personnel between the two areas of government.

> There may be greater interconnectedness between the national and local bureaucracies in many other liberal democracies. In Germany, local and central government officers have a common training and may frequently move between levels of government during their career development. In France the system of prefectoral surveillance of local government ensures considerable interchange of ideas between the centrally employed prefectoral staff and local government officers.

National politicians and councillors

Contact between government and local politicians is no more extensive in any formal arena. Discussions at a senior level may take place in established joint committees, especially the CCGLF. At the highest level of its full meeting, senior representatives of local government get a chance to confront Secretaries of State and they, in turn, can use the opportunity to hector or cajole local government leaders. Councillors may also lead delegations on behalf of their localities to petition ministers for aid and support for their area. Politicians from West Yorkshire along with local businessmen have, for example, held discussions with the Department of Trade on the European Union tariffs for woollen goods. In the case of an exceptional crisis, the Secretary of State may personally meet councillors. Patrick Jenkin, when Secretary of State for the Environment, unwisely for him, discussed the issue of Liverpool's refusal to set a legal rate in 1984 with the Militant leadership of the council (Crick 1986: 244–5).

Close contact between councillors and politicians is, however, achieved not so much through government links but through the machinery of the political parties. Details of the party structures of local government are given in Chapter 10, but it should be noted here that all the major parties organise annual conferences for councillors to enable them to listen to the great of their national party and, if fortune smiles on them, forward their own views. Meetings between local and national party leaders may also take place in regional and national party conferences. Perhaps the most important channels of influence are the close contacts that can develop between local councillors and a leading figure in a national party through their mutual work in constituency politics. However, as councillors become MPs and even Ministers, the strength of these links may weaken over time. An MP who had been a highly active local councillor observed that 'I am glad to be out of it' when asked whether they regretted losing their links with local authorities whilst a prominent former councillor, David Blunkett, as Secretary of State for Education has observed that he can only find time to concentrate on issues relating to his Department (Chandler and Kingdom 1999).

Although haphazard links may develop between MPs and councillors, Britain has lost the capacity to closely integrate central and local politicians through dual-office holding. Within the Labour Party, MPs are frequently former councillors, and it this is not unusual within the Conservative Party, however, it is normal practice for councillors, once elected, to drop their local office and concentrate solely on work in Westminster. It is widely held by local and national party politicians that it would be impossible to undertake both the role of a councillor and that of an MP, since the work of an MP and, even more crucially, that of a minister is so time consuming that it would be impossible to adequately fulfil the demands of either duty.

Whilst it is assumed in Britain that national political leaders cannot be local political leaders, this is rather unusual practice in other liberal democracies. Britain is distinguished by the absence of any merging of central and local personnel.

The separation of councillors from MPs is a twentieth century phenomenon. It was observed in Chapter 2 that eighteenth century local government was linked to central government through the representation of the aristocratic Lords Lieutenant and gentleman JPs in the House of Lords or the Commons. These links were still strong in 1900 when many chairman of the newly created county councils were represented in Parliament and prominent local businessmen, such as Joseph Chamberlain, had both local and national government experience. Keith-Lucas and Richards observe that in 1899 there were 101 peers and 87 MPs who were simultaneously county councillors (1978:

Britain is distinctive in its isolation of councillors from national or federal politics. In France most Deputies of the National Assembly, their equivalent of MPs, also remain the leading figure in their local authorities, often retaining the executive post of mayor. Even government ministers will still retain the position of mayor of their local town or city (Machin 1977: 160). For example, as mayor of Marseille, Gaston Deferre was in the early 1980s also Minister of the Interior, responsible for a significant reform of the local government system in that country. The Gaullist Party leader, Jaques Chirac, was elected to the Presidency while holding the office of Mayor of Paris. In British terms this is equivalent to John Major serving as leader of Cambridgeshire County Council during his years as Prime Minister. Through their connections at local and national levels these politicians, termed *local notables*, ensure that national policies can be shaped in their local interest and their local electors will to some extent vote for them through reference to their ability to use their central power to help their locality.

Similar relationships have developed in other countries, although rarely as extensively as in France. In the United States many legislators in state governments are also active in local politics. In some countries such as Italy and Ireland, where such connections have been highly important, recent political reforms have outlawed the capacity to hold local and national representative office. There is concern in these countries, and also in France, that too much power may accrue to a few powerfully entrenched local politicians through the process of multi-office holding, referred to in France as the *cumul des mandats*.

99), whereas in 1994 only 13 MPs were serving as councillors and of these 5 represented Northern Ireland Constituencies, which may reflect the frequency with which southern Irish MPs also serve as local councillors. All of the remaining 8 MPs were elected to Westminster at the 1992 General Election or a subsequent by-election (Dod 1994; Municipal Year Book 1994).

The disappearance of local notables from national politics has had a crucial bearing on the relationship between centre and locality and will be analysed further in the following chapter. Local government personnel generally inhabit a different world from policy makers in central government and hence relations between the two groups are more matters of formal negotiation than accord forged from mutual understanding and common interests. Local government has few friends in the court of Westminster.

Further reading

Whilst there are many studies of central-local relations in Britain which are included in the bibliography for Chapter 6, there are fewer studies of the machinery of central and local government that conducts the relationship. J.A.

Chandler (1988) is particularly concerned with this area and a large and, in its day, the authoritative study by Griffith (1966) is worth consulting. Crossman's Diaries, particularly volume 1 are a valuable source of material on the daily activity of the minister in charge of local government. Rhodes (1986) provides valuable material on the local authority associations.

There are however many studies that discuss how central government generally devises policy and among those to be recommended are Kingdom (1999) and Greenwood and Wilson (1989). A new edition of this latter study on public administration in Britain is currently being prepared. The attitudes and values of the civil service are considered by among others Hennessy (1989) although, significantly, little is said specifically on their views of local government.

6

Stewardship

The preceding chapter shows that central government influences local government through a range of departments and agencies, which may not always have similar aims and interests. Local governments themselves are diverse organisations with differing attitudes to policy or central government or to one another. The relationship between central and local government is, therefore, composed of a network of relationships which, in order to emphasise the complex pattern of connections, is characterised as inter-governmental relations rather than central–local relations.

Although there are many elements in the network of inter-governmental relations it is, nevertheless, possible to discern some broad characteristics of the system. Central government may have many departments and agencies, but has effective means of ensuring co-ordination between departments on matters of principle if not always on detail. The attitude of civil servants and many senior national politicians concerning the role of local government within the state is, as will be argued later, based on some basic and widely ingrained assumptions on the role of the state. It is therefore possible to characterise the nature of inter-governmental relations in Britain, at least as far as central government is concerned.

Models of central–local relations: agency, partnership and bargaining

Attempts to describe the relationship between local and central government have generated widely differing interpretations. Rhodes (1981) suggests that studies tended to depict local government as either a partner or an agent of the centre. Many government reports seek to depict the relationship as a partnership. The 1998 White Paper *Modern Local Government*, for example, concludes with the comment that the Paper's success 'will be assured as councils everywhere join in partnership with the Government to bring about a fundamental shift in power and influence in favour of local people' (Postcript p.1) . However, almost all theorists who use such a metaphor assign local government a subordinate, junior role in the governance of the country. This attitude can be found in the writings of J.S. Mill (1975) and in more modern studies such as the work of J.A.G. Griffith who described local government as having freedom to develop policies within a framework of legislation that lays down minimum standards (Griffith 1966: 17–18). The agency model can more clearly be identified in studies of local government written over the last fifty years. Neither academics nor politicians go as far as observing that local authorities are agents of the centre to the extent that they simply carry out to the letter detailed instructions sent down to them from on high. W.A. Robson (1954), a doyen among academic analysts of local government, pointed out the dangers of an agency relationship and feared that such an arrangement was insidiously inserting itself into the constitution.

Rhodes rejects both the extremes of partnership and agency and characterised the relationship as one of bargaining between two sets of organisations which have differing resources, that is means at their disposal to help them get their own way. The resources identified by Rhodes (1986: 17; 1988: 42) can be categorised as

- their constitutional and legal position,
- political legitimacy, their capacity to mobilise opinion,
- money and finance,
- organisational capacity, command of people, property and services,
- information, knowledge and access to data.

A local authority may prevent central government interference for example, in, their education plans, because they are legally independent from the centre and can challenge the legality of government decisions through the courts. A local authority has resources of expertise, since its officers and councillors may understand local circumstances better than more remote civil servants and may, therefore, be able to convince a government that it is financially or technically impossible to enact a particular policy. Local political support in favour of local ideas can be a valuable resource for councillors, who may convince the government that it would lose political good will and, more seriously votes, were it to press forward with an issue. Finally, local governments are not bereft of financial resources to employ public relations or technical experts, organise publicity campaigns or pay for litigation, in order to pursue their interests.

Although local authorities can sometimes win struggles against the government, the balance of resources and, therefore, power must be seen to rest heavily in favour of the centre. All of the resources held by local authorities are also held by central government, which has its experts on technical, if not local issues, financial resources beyond the wildest dreams of any local authority and the possibility of both local and national political support. Governments also have a further and crucial asset, expressed by Rhodes as the ability to change the rules of the game, through its ability to legislate, change statutory orders and restructure the finance of local government. Thus, local governments may successfully challenge Whitehall on the interpretation of existing law but, unlike the Government, they cannot change the law to suit their own interests.

The power-dependence model has been predominantly applied by British political theorists and has not been adopted in countries such as the United States, where it may seem more appropriate to argue that since the Federal Government is less able to change the rules of the game and so change the resources held by states and local government, that centre and localities are more able to bargain with one another.

Rhodes later (1986; 1988) wove the power-dependence model into the concept of networks and policy communities. A policy network describes the framework of interactions between organisations that are influencing the determination of new policies or the retention of existing practices. A policy community develops when actors in the relationship are aware of each other's influence and form a stable pattern of interaction that often excludes outsider groups. Policy communities, for example, unite separate local authorities into a national community for local government. In general, Rhodes (Rhodes and Marsh 1992: 13–14) sees the wider central-local relationship as more extensive than a policy community and prefers the term 'inter-governmental networks'. Unlike policy communities, which are seen as developing around specific functions, there is a much greater tendency for local government organisations to relate not only to each other and central government but a diverse range of other functional policy communities to create a highly elaborate network of interconnecting groups.

Whilst models, such as the power-dependence theory, and metaphors, such as policy community, capture the complex inter-relationships that takes place between central and local spheres of governance, the images are also used to suggest that both central and local governments can influence each other's actions. This is, however, only true in so far as central government requires the guidance of local governments on how best to secure effective national policies. When serious differences arise between central and local values, it is the national interests that in the long run are the determining factor.

The changing character of central–local relations

The power-dependence model of central–local relations was developed in the years immediately preceding the Thatcher Governments and was therefore modelled on a relationship that was seriously fractured during the 1980s.

What changed was not so much the potential powers of central and local governments, but the attitude of the centre to local authorities specifically and the public sector in general. Following the Poplar confrontation of the 1920s, central–local relations became a quiet area of politics built predominantly on mutual understanding between leaders of the two sides. Local government and its associations bargained with the government behind closed doors in an atmosphere of mutual understanding of each other's role and spheres of interest and thus formed major elements in a policy community. In general, local authorities were happy with their role in playing a significant part in the expansion and delivery of the welfare state and hence there was little ideological difference between local and national politicians and officials.

The common ground that had been forged between central and local government ensured that they could develop a strong policy community in which each element in the relationship listened to each other's ideas in order to mutually reach widely accepted policy goals. The new-right Conservative Governments of Mrs Thatcher shattered this relationship as her Governments sought to roll back the frontiers of the State, which involved not only reducing central government activity but also cutting back the activities of local government and especially their direct role in the delivery of social services.

In the early 1980s a major confrontation developed between the Thatcher Government and several Labour-held urban local governments, primarily over curbs on local spending. In the first weeks of taking office in 1979, the Secretary of State for the Environment Michael Heseltine announced major cuts in grants to local authorities. Local governments responded by raising local taxes which led the Government to forward a complex set of regulations that reduced grants to councils that were judged to be spending too much. The strategy underestimated local government resolve, as the more radical authorities continued to raise local taxes with the support of their electorate despite serious loss of funding from central government.

After several unsuccessful attempts to curb local spending, the Government arrived at a formula, the 1984 Rates Act, which ended the capacity of local government to raise as much money through the rates as they thought necessary and electorally feasible. The reaction of some radical urban authorities was to defy the Government and refuse to set a legal budget based on the lower level of spending demanded by the Government. The attempt at illegal defiance was however a disaster that underlined the principle that central government in Britain constitutionally has the right to enforce its ideas through legislation on any public or private organisation. The authorities that opposed Mrs Thatcher's rate-capping legislation were warned that if they persisted in setting illegal budgets, councillors supporting the action would be surcharged for illegal spending, made bankrupt and be obliged to resign as councillors. Consequently all the rebellious councils withdrew their defiance and were forced to accept the Government's policy and the Labour councillors on the two Authorities which stood longest against the Government, Liverpool and Lambeth were subject to surcharge and thrown off the Councils.

Following the rate-capping confrontation, the Conservative, Government moved to neutralise criticism from left-wing local authorities and demolished many of the policies that they had devised during their period to extend their left-wing credentials. These included high levels of subsidy to local transport services or support for small businesses. The Conservative Party, emboldened by its success and also irritated by local defiance of its ideas, subsequently set about remoulding many features of local governance. The Labour-controlled GLC and the metropolitan county councils were abolished in 1985 and the following year to prevent a further irritation consequent on the abolition campaign, passed legislation to stop local authorities politically criticising the Government. In 1986 many local services were subject to compulsory competitive tendering and could therefore be provided by the private sector. Bus services and further education were removed from local government control, schools were allowed to opt out of local control and public housing was increasingly transferred to housing associations.

Attempts to find loopholes in legislation were initially an effective method of thwarting Conservative policy. Such action not only directly prevents the implementation of a government's intentions but may also necessitate further legislation to stop up the loopholes, which consumes the time of Parliament and the resources of civil servants and also delays the development of new legislative changes that are proposed by government. The strategy of prevarication and delay was particularly successful in the early 1980s, since the Government was incapable of understanding the intricacies of local government administration and also miscalculated the extent to which the electorate were willing to pay higher taxes to their town hall.

Although battles were won by local authorities, individual victories do not necessarily win a war of independence. Despite delays in legislative time, the Thatcher Governments persevered in restricting the powers of local authorities. As the Government became more experienced in the methods used by local authorities to find legislative loopholes, Whitehall draughtsmen wrote bills that gave Secretaries of State greater discretion over the use of statutory instruments and were increasingly difficult to evade. The Thatcher Governments used its powers to change the rules of the game in order to blunt many of the more potent local authority weapons that had been used against it. Inter-governmental relations in the early 1980s were characterised by a Tom and Jerry syndrome, in which the central authority cat believed it had caught the local authority mouse through new legislation, only to find that the creature had again escaped from its clutches, resulting in further central pursuit of the hapless mouse, which was eventually caught and was unable to escape.

Has Blair continued the relationship of control?

The Government of Tony Blair promised in its 1997 Manifesto that 'Local decision making should be less constrained by central government' (p. 54) and has
in style if not substance ushered in a rather different framework for central-
local relations. As described earlier, the Labour Government has been more
willing to consult local authorities on changes to policy and lifted some of the
restraints imposed by the Conservative Governments on revenue and capital
spending and is proposing to remove restraints on local authorities' capacity to
benefit their communities.

However, despite this more relaxed attitude to local authorities, many of the
underlying controls established by Mrs Thatcher remain as reserved powers.
Although the Government does not set rigid targets on local expenditure, it still
retains powers to order local authorities to reduce spending that they feel is
excessive. CCT has given way to Best Value, which restores to local authorities
some discretion as to whether they operate services themselves or allocate them
to the private sector. However, the legislation also establishes further bench-
marking for service standards, increased inspection to ascertain whether
minimum standards are fulfilled and provides further means through which
the centre can take over failing services. The 2000 Local Government Act is
bringing in tighter regulations on the ethical conduct of councillors and impos-
ing reforms to the internal structure of local authorities, obliging them to
accept executive government and possibly local mayors, even though there is
no great enthusiasm among local authorities for the idea. Some of the more
draconian restraints imposed by Mrs Thatcher also remain on the statute book,
such as the 1986 Local Government Act that prevents elected local authorities
from criticising central government.

Local government as a steward

The capacity of the Thatcher Government to force new-right policies on a
largely reluctant community of local authorities illustrates that whilst local
and central government may bargain with one another in closed policy communities as partners on a broadly equal footing, in reality if central government
has ideological values that differ from most local governments, the centre has
the capacity to restructure local government's role within a relatively short
period of time.

Although the Governments of Thatcher and Major may have sharply
increased legislation controlling local government, the Blair Government,
despite a more relaxed consultative relationship, has not reversed the extent of
central control. This trend has origins long before the 1980s. In the 1920s local
government suffered a major, if not at the time too obvious, defeat when
Parliament refused to accept any but the most innocuous private bills. During

this decade a process of cat and mouse conflict arose between the Conservative Governments and the London Borough of Poplar with its associated Board of Guardians which was not dissimilar to the local socialism battles of the 1980s. Both the Labour Party councillors and guardians of Poplar on several occasions refused to accept Government regulations on wages and rates of poor relief and at one point were imprisoned for contempt of court, only to be released because of popular support (Branson 1979). In the longer term, their intransigence led the Government through legislation to change the rules that ensured that councillors who were surcharged for supporting unlawful local expenditure were not sent to prison for contempt of court if they refused payment but, as a consequence of their being made bankrupt were disbarred from holding locally elected office. This procedure was successfully used by the Thatcher Government to rid themselves of troublesome councillors in Liverpool and Lambeth.

The power of the centre to determine the policies of local government is clearly evident in the restructuring of the system from the inception of the Redcliffe-Maud Commission to the Local Government Act of 1972, which was dictated by central rather than local interests and pushed through despite the strong objections of the associations for the urban and rural districts.

> Wholesale redrawing of local government boundaries has never been acceptable in France or United States politics where the boundaries of local authorities have changed relatively little during the last 100 years.

Despite some victories by local governments during the last century, they are losing the battle for autonomy and have failed, in the long run, to successfully maintain their independence and integrity from central government. There have, of course, been many periods of co-operative working between central and local government when there appeared to be no conflict between the two sectors. There are also many examples of central government taking on board ideas that were generated locally, such as the development of local initiatives to publicise the attractions of an area for footloose industry. However, this deference to local interest is a consequence of *noblesse oblige* on the part of central government. Ministers and civil servants are happy to tolerate, or even encourage, local initiatives that are consonant with central policy interests and their interpretation of the proper role of local government. Where localities move into areas that seriously oppose the objectives of the centre the government, throughout all but the first decades of the twentieth century, has intervened to suppress the practice.

The essence of central-local relationships in Britain cannot be analysed simply in terms of structures and sources of power. Underlying the system are values and traditions that have been shaping the system over the last two centuries and inform the behaviour of central politicians to the periphery. This entrenched attitude may be characterised as one of stewardship. The policy makers in central government, whether party politicians or bureaucrats, use local authorities as their steward in much the same way as the aristocratic owner of a large eighteenth century estate would have employed a steward to manage his country estates. The steward was given a measure of discretion to manage his lord's estate as efficiently as possible, but this discretion was always constrained by rules determined at the whim of the aristocrat. Free from detailed managerial duties, many landed gentleman could absent themselves from their estates in order to indulge in the pleasures of luxury, politics, war or religion. Many landowners granted their stewards a very free hand but, should they learn that the steward was acting contrary to their principles or against their instructions, they had the means to admonish the false steward or remove him from office. Some landed gentry, however, chose to interest themselves in the day-to-day management of their estates and constantly plagued their stewards with rules, regulations, advice and caprice.

Similarly, within central government, there is a pervasive ethos that perceives local government to be a generally useful but subordinate arm of a national political system controlled by Whitehall and Westminster. Local authorities are of value because they take from the centre the tedious and detailed task of applying general policies to fit local circumstances. Politicians and senior civil servants can concentrate on major affairs of state and leave matters of detail to their subordinate stewards. On occasion, the government will consult with local authorities and even defer to their opinions since they may also be of help in advising the government on problems of implementing policy. Good employers will always consult with their stewards to understand whether their general policies will work in practice and also to ensure that they have the resources to fulfil their assigned tasks. However, the centre may often refuse to take local advice and will certainly discipline or *in extremis* remove local units that oppose central interests.

The pervasive assumption that local authorities are always subordinate to the demands of the centre can be perceived in most official studies of the role of local authorities. The Widdicombe Report was praised as upholding local government since, to the relief of many supporters of the system, it argued for the continuation of local authorities. However, the enquiry discerned only a limited role for localities and firmly underlined the convention that, whilst local government may be a useful administrative device, the system should be subordinate to the interests of the centre.

> It would be . . . wrong to assume that . . . conventional convention amounts to or derives from any natural right for local government to exist. It is a convention based on, and subject to, the contribution local government can bring to good government. It follows from this that there is no validity in the assertion that local authorities have a 'local mandate' by which they derive their authority from their electorate placing them above the law. (Widdicombe 1986: 48)

This view of local involvement in national policy making has echoes in early Fabian ideas of municipal socialism, as advocated by the Webbs (1920) and Bernard Shaw (1908). It is, however, wishful thinking and, at best, can be seen in episodes of glorious failure as radical local governments have clashed with the centre as in Poplar in the 1920s and Liverpool and Sheffield in the 1980s. In all these instances of central-local conflict, in the long run, the central ethos of stewardship has prevailed to place the aspirant local authorities firmly in a position subordinate to central interest. Whilst a few local politicians, including at one time David Blunkett (1987), have suggested a different balance of central-local relations, for the most part local activists have absorbed the utilitarian stewardship ethos. Apart from the dramatic events of the 1980s central-local relations have been relatively placid and local politics viewed as an unproblematic area of politics. This is as much a reflection of the extent to which local councillors have accepted the role of steward assigned to them by the centre.

Explaining stewardship

The stewardship model is a metaphor that describes the relationship between central and local government but does not in itself explain why this relationship evolved and how it is sustained. Marxist theory presents a number of explanations for the arrangement. At its simplest level, local government is viewed as part of the State and, therefore, a mechanism through which wealthy capitalists sustain a political system that exploits the workers in society. Such an argument may have seemed reasonable in the nineteenth century, but cannot explain the current role of central and local government in providing support and welfare for the least able in society.

A more sophisticated neo-Marxist explanation of the role of urban government put forward by Castells (1977) formed the basis for an explanation of inter-governmental relations that was particularly fashionable in the early 1980s. Urban society was essential to facilitate what Marxists term the 'reproduction of labour', a need to provide education, housing, health care and recreation facilities for workers, so that capitalists can rely on a continuous supply of effective workers, with sufficient understanding to adapt to changes in technology in order to keep the wheels of industry and commerce turning. Urban society and urban government emerge as the most efficient device for providing the necessities to ensure the reproduction of labour through, for example, schools and cheap housing. Under this model it may be argued that in the late nineteenth century, when industrial capitalists controlled large city governments, the municipality was far more concerned with providing services necessary for direct production such as gas, electricity and transport. The growth of industry into large multi-national businesses rather than smaller firms owned by a family rooted in one area of the country and the emergence of democracy and the Labour Party as a governing party in large towns, led central governments in Britain to take into their direct control activities that affect capital production, but found that local government led by local people would remain interested and capable of running those services dealing with the reproduction of labour that had a direct effect on individual welfare and a more indirect effect on production. However, even in the provision of welfare services, central government did not trust some local authorities to use their powers of taxation to provide what was seen as essential for welfare and not use their powers to reallocate the riches of wealthy individuals and businesses to the poor.

Such explanation may provide some answers to the explanation of steward-ship in Britain, but cannot be the sole solution. Not all welfare services are pro-vided locally and productive services are not exclusively reserved by the centre. The Health Service remains firmly outside the orbit of local authority control, whilst planning policies and economic development tasks that affect business are still important local responsibilities. Whilst the relationship between labour and capital is a crucial element forging political systems, it is doubtful that is the only factor that should be considered. There are specifically British factors that have helped shaped the current relationship.

The central government ethos that subordinates local authorities to the role of a steward evolved with the growth of utilitarian liberal values in central government thought during the nineteenth century. The values expressed by Redcliffe-Maud or Widdicombe are echoes of the writings of the most impor-tant proponents of liberal values in England. Bentham, the fount of much English political liberalism, assigned a highly subordinate role to local govern-ment in his ideal constitution. Indeed, there could not be local government, but rather local administration. Political decisions had to be made so as to provide the greatest happiness for the greatest number in the Nation as a whole and this could only be achieved through the deliberations of a nationally elected repre-sentative Parliament. Thus, it was not possible to allow a smaller body in the Nation to put forward ideas contrary to those of Parliament since the group, if it disagreed with the majority view, could only be seeking favours for that par-ticular group and not the Nation as a whole.

This view was largely accepted by J.S. Mill, whose writings present the most influential philosophical justifications of the British political system as it evolved in the nineteenth century into a liberal democracy. In his *Essay Concerning Representative Government*, Mill argued that the national Parliament will have greater wisdom on the correct principles by which the Nation should be governed than any smaller locally elected body.

> ... local representative bodies and their officers are almost certain to be of a much lower grade of intelligence and knowledge, than Parliament and the national executive (J.S. Mill 1975: 375).

The national assembly and government were, however, not necessarily as conversant as parochial opinion on the detailed needs of a locality and hence local government had considerable value as a means of ensuring that the principles of political and moral action determined by the sovereign Parliament were fitted efficiently and effectively to local circumstance. J.S. Mill therefore advocated a central–local relationship based on the principle that

> The authority which is most conversant with principles should be supreme over principles, whilst that which is most competent in details should have details left to it. The principal business of central authority should be to give instruction, of the local authority to apply it (1975: 377).

This view informs much of the policy making by central government towards local authorities. The role of local government is chiefly to implement policies whose principles are drawn up by centre so as to adapt the general principles to local circumstances.

J.S. Mill also suggested a further subordinate function of local authorities as training grounds for national politicians and also as instruments to help educate the public to understand the practice of civilised politics. Thus, for J.S. Mill, local politicians could make the errors of apprenticeship at local level so as to become skilled politicians if translated to the heights of national politics. Although liberal utilitarian theory has been consonant with current attitudes within central government, it would be incorrect to assume that these values were the direct result of Bentham and Mill's weighty arguments. Political theory does not so much persuade individuals to accept other values but clarifies and justifies existing interests.

In contrast to British liberals such as Bentham and J.S. Mill who concluded that local government should be subordinate to the nationally expressed will of the majority, in the United States and France liberal theory supports the independence of local government as a means of securing greater individual liberty. The French political philosopher Jean-Jaques Rousseau considered that democracy was only viable in small communities where individuals could all participate personally in decision making. Most influential in the United States are the views of de Tocqueville, who argued that the townships of New England in which all citizens of the community participated in town meetings was the best guarantee of individual liberty. He developed the idea, similar to that now accepted by the European Union as subsidiarity, by advocating that decisions that affect principally people in a small community should be made at this level, allowing individuals in that community the greatest freedom to determine the decisions that affect them.

   Bentham and J.S. Mill represented the manufacturing and commercial interests which were transforming British during the industrial revolution from a
State based on landed estates held through the traditions of inheritance and
custom to a capitalist regime founded on rational thought and meritocratic
achievement. The old system of local government based on parish and county
was dominated by traditional landowners and was hence becoming an anach-
ronism. Good government should be controlled by the most innovative, hard-
working and successful members of the community. Practical utilitarians such
as Chadwick had no time for government controlled by the minor worthies of
the parish or the Tory squire and advocated central surveillance of these individuals. As liberal values gained strength, so also did the view that Parliament
and Whitehall needed to retain powers to supervise the local system of government, at least in rural areas. These values were retained into the twentieth
century when the rise of the Labour Party in the large cities ensured that civil
servants and liberal politicians who had established controls to modernise
Tory-held rural authorities now developed those controls and the values that
underlay them to restrain local socialist radicalism. Once in power, Labour
Party moderates inherited this culture and used central stewardship to dampen
down their more radical supporters as well as ensure Conservative local governments were obliged to provide standards of service required by their
Governments.

> The pattern of centralisation in Britain is not replicated in the United States,
> where politicians did not have to struggle against a non-liberal elite dominating
> rural society, as was the case in eighteenth century Britain. Once the British were
> chased out of the country, the United States liberal politicians were concerned to
> limit the power of central government to avoid the imposition of a King or pow-
> erful aristocracy. Independent local government was one of several means to
> ensure an effective separation of powers to help secure this aim.

Further reading

The study of intergovernmental relations in Britain received a major impetus in
the late 1980s through the development of a research council-sponsored
survey of the subject. Rhodes (1981, 1986 and 1986a, 1988 and 2000) developed the theoretical framework underlying a series of studies on this theme,
which has included Gyford and James (1983) on the role of political parties and
Laffin (1986) on professional associations and Rhodes (1986) on the local
authority associations. A summary of more recent work on this area is provided in an article by Stoker (1995)
   Chandler (1988) considers the mechanics of central local relations from the
perspective of the organisation of central government and also develops a

differing interpretation of inter-governmental relations in this study, and in a comparative context in a later article (1992).

A more historical approach is developed by Bulpitt (1983) and for a nineteenth century insight Redlich and Hirst (1958) is still of importance. To get an insight into nineteenth century liberal values Mill (1975) is very readable and also a seminal study.

7

Policy making
and democracy

Local government claims to be a democratic institution. In theory, local authority policy is determined by its elected representatives, the councillors or, following recent legislation, a popularly elected mayor. The electoral basis of local
authorities gives them a unique and authoritative role among the plethora of
sub-governmental institutions. The decisions of a local authority cannot be
passed off as solely the views of an appointed elite, but derive from a body representative of the local population as a whole. Despite this seal of democratic
authority, local government has for many years been accused of being representative not of the majority of electors but small self-interested elites and, consequently, the status and support given to the institution has been seriously
undermined. Criticism of local democracy is not however universal and the
value of locally representative community government also has its powerful
defenders. In the second half of this book, after describing the institutions of
local democracy, the role of councillors, officers and interest groups in local
government, Chapter 12 will return to the central issue of local democracy.

The local electoral system

With the exception of the Greater London Authority, local councillors in Britain
are normally elected for a four-year term of office to represent an electoral ward
which in local terms is the equivalent to the constituency which returns an MP
to the national Parliament. Exactly when a councillor's term of office expires is
dependant upon the type of authority she or he represents, since local authorities do not all go to the polls in the same year, nor do all members of a council,
necessarily, stand for election at the same time.

County councils, London Boroughs, the Greater London Authority and
some district and unitary authorities hold elections for the full council once
every four years. In metropolitan districts which have three councillors representing each electoral ward, only one councillors stands for election in any year.

Table 7.1 *The timing of elections*

	2000	2001	2002	2003	2004
County councils		*			
London Boroughs			*		
The Greater London Authority	*				*
Metropolitan districts	⅓		⅓	⅓	⅓
Some non-metropolitan districts	⅓		⅓	⅓	⅓
Some non-metropolitan districts				*	
Some English unitary authorities				*	
Some English unitary authorities	⅓		⅓	⅓	⅓
Scottish districts				*	
Welsh districts				*	

* = elections are held for the whole authority.

Thus, there are elections, in which one-third of the council is to be elected, in three out of every four years in metropolitan districts. The fourth year, when there is now no contest in these areas, was the year for elections to the now defunct metropolitan county councils, although the Government proposes that this year will be used in future for the election of an executive mayor. Some non-metropolitan districts and unitary authorities also operate an electoral system similar to that of the metropolitan districts. The Blair Government has proposed, but so far not legislated into practice, that all local authorities should have elections for councillors each year. Thus, in areas where there is a single-tier authority, elections would follow the current practice for metropolitan authorities, but if there are two-tier arrangements the county council and the district council will elect half their members each alternate year. Given the complexity of these arrangements, some local elections are taking place each year. Table 7.1 indicates the present pattern in a four-year cycle. In Scotland and Wales local elections are held for all members of each council on a four-year cycle. A report to the Scottish Parliament, the McIntosh Report, has suggested that the elections for local authorities in Scotland should take place two years after the four-yearly elections for the Scottish Parliament.

A significant difference between the national and local electoral system is that local elections are statutorily held on a specific date and not at the convenience of the leading councillors. The date is normally the first Thursday in May. Should a councillor resign or die between elections, according to the 1972 Local Government Act, then a by-election to replace the departed politician must normally be held within forty-two working days of the notification of the vacancy. An important consequence of the fixed date for elections is that political parties in control of a council are not able to aid their chances of re-election by choosing to resign, as does the national government, at a time most favourable to them. Only individual councillors can resign and there is no way in which the leader of a local party can force his opposition rivals to vacate their seats by dissolving the whole council. On occasion, party groups of councillors have threatened to resign *en masse* to force new local elections in order to stress their popularity over an issue on which they are challenging the government. In very few cases has this threat ever been practised.

The restrictions on eligibility to stand for election that are applied nationally also apply locally. Candidates must be at least twenty-one years of age, be registered voters and have no undischarged criminal sentence or be certified as insane. Council candidates must also demonstrate to the returning officer that they are either resident in that local authority, own property or have their main place of work within its borders. In contrast to national elections, local political parties cannot simply invite a famous or able candidate who does not have the links with that community that qualify him or her to be a candidate to stand for their local council or as an elected mayor. There are, of course, strong arguments in favour of ensuring that local councillors are part of the community that they represent, but this is one of many instances where good practice is imposed on local government but not extended by the government to its own proceedings.

Candidates cannot be employed by the local authority for which they wish to stand. Legislation in 1989 restricted the capacity for senior local government officers to become councillors in order to curtail a mutual self-help mechanism being evolved by some neighbouring authorities in which they agreed to employ, in not particularly arduous jobs, senior councillors from the adjoining authority so as to provide them with a reasonable salary and time to pursue their political work. These restrictions can be unfair. A local dustman or a school teacher, whose salaries and conditions of service will be effectively fixed by national negotiations will, in practice, have less to gain personally by being a councillor than, for example, a local estate agent interested in property development in that community.

The method of balloting for local elections has always been similar to the procedures for national elections, but concern within the Blair Government about low turnout in local elections, has led to ideas for using local ballots as a means of experimenting with new voting procedures. In 2000, legislation was passed that allows local authorities with the agreement of the Secretary of State to experiment with the place and timing of voting so that, for example, balloting can be held in supermarkets or greater use can be made of postal ballots. In Scotland, studies are being made following the McIntosh Report on similar schemes to make it less troublesome for the less than interested potential local authority voter to cast their less than informed and interested vote.

The implementation of the electoral rules are in the hands of a returning officer, usually the mayor or the chief executive of a district council. He or she is responsible to the courts for the correct conduct of the election and could be sued or prosecuted for bad practice. The returning officer is, however, usually a figurehead and the real work of electoral organisation is undertaken by a deputy who will normally be a full-time local authority officer charged with running a small office concerned with the management of elections both for the local authority and for Parliament. This officer's principal task is to compile each year the register of electors, draw up the timetable for an election, receive and check the validity of nominations for candidates, arrange for votes to be cast and counted and receive and act on complaints about the conduct of the elections. The returning officer rather than the deputy nevertheless usually steals the glory of announcing the winner of a parliamentary, if not local, election.

The electoral system and adversary politics

Most elections follow the first-past-the-post, simple plurality voting system that is used in Westminster elections. The candidate with the highest number of votes wins the contest. This system has attracted strong criticism since, as in general elections, smaller parties may win a considerable proportion of the vote city-wide, but gain no seats. Thus, the system benefits the larger local parties, which receive a much greater proportion of seats than their share of the popular vote would merit. If a system of proportional representation were adopted for British local authorities, in which the seats won on the council reflected the votes cast for each party across the local authority, then far more councils would be 'hung' councils in which no one party had majority control.

Smaller parties, such as the Liberal Democrats, complain that they have far fewer councillors than they feel they ought to be entitled to on the basis of their national vote. However, whilst they are sometimes under-represented on a national scale, smaller parties can reap the benefits of undisputed control of a local authority in those areas where they are a dominant political force. The system did not prevent the Liberal Democrats from securing overall control of a large cities such as Liverpool or Sheffield. Independents may also benefit from the system, since it is possible for active individuals to win local elections if they are well known in a ward but not recognised throughout the local area as a whole.

Most European local government systems utilise some from proportional representation to select their councillors and multi-ballot systems to select the mayors when they are directly elected. The United States like Britain, however, remains firmly wedded to the first-past-the-post system although many 'reformed' local governments elect councillors or commissioners to represent the city or county as a whole rather than for wards.

In response to pressure for electoral change, the Blair Government has established a system of proportional representation for elections to the Scottish Parliament and Welsh and Greater London Assemblies through a system similar to that adopted in Germany for national elections in which, in addition to representatives elected on a first-past-the-post basis from single member constituencies, further members are selected from lists drawn up by the parties, so that the final assembly has representation from all the major parties in proportion to votes cast within the province as a whole. For the Mayor of London and for proposed mayoral elections outside London, the Government has adopted a half-way house arrangement between full proportionality and the first-past-the-post system. The arrangement, which is termed the supplementary vote, allows voters to mark a first and second choice on the ballot paper if more than two candidates are standing. If no candidate gets over 50 per cent of the first choice votes cast, the candidate with the lowest number of first choice votes is eliminated and his or her second choice votes are then assigned to the remaining candidates. The candidate who then has the largest number of votes is selected. The system, whilst favouring well-supported third-ranking parties, generally in England the Liberal Democrats, still falls far short of the principle of full proportionality and is unlikely to favour smaller parties such as the Greens. In Scotland the McIntosh Report has suggested that their local authorities should secure proportionality by adopting the German-style added members system and this idea was in 2000 subject to further study by a working party of the Scottish Parliament.

The council and its committees

The policy and management structures of local authorities are currently undergoing their most radical reform since they became elected organisations in the nineteenth century. Between 2000 and 2005, there will be a process of change as all but the smallest district authorities, which have populations below 85,000, must restructure their decision-making structures to adopt new styles of executive cabinet government established in the Local Government Act of 2000. As some smaller districts may continue with the old system and, during the currency of this edition of the book, more laggard larger authorities may be slow to change their structures, both the older traditional system and the new structures are described.

> Most but not all liberal democracies establish local government on similar democratic basis. There are a few exceptions, such as Malaysia. In the European Union and the United States the structure of local democracy is based on either an elected council which chooses an executive or a directly elected mayor and an elected council that either approves or scrutinises the activities of the mayor.

The traditional system

Until the 2000 Local Government Act, all decisions made by a local authority were the responsibility of the full council, which is the meeting of all elected councillors for the local authority. The size of the full council varies depending upon the population of the local authority, although there is no exact proportion of seats to population. The smaller districts will have between 24 and 60 councillors, whilst large cities or counties have between 50 and 100 members. Birmingham City Council has the largest membership with 126 councillors, although its population was not, prior to 1996, as great as some counties, such as Essex which has 97 councillors. Scotland seems to be less enthusiastic about councillors, having proportionately fewer members than in England. The smallest districts have but 10 councillors whilst Glasgow, with a population of over a million, has only 72 elected members.

The full council of a local authority determined the frequency of its meetings, although statutorily they must meet at least once a year. Many metropolitan district councils deliberated once a month, but in non-metropolitan districts there was usually a meeting every six or eight weeks. Many county councils gathered even less frequently. Some authorities, such as Oxfordshire or Buckinghamshire County Councils, met only four times a year. The frequency of council meetings had considerable importance in setting the pace of local authority work. Since all decisions needed to be ratified by the full council, the many sub-committees of a local authority had to gear the frequency of their meetings to that of a cycle set by the timing of the full council meetings. Thus, an authority with relatively few council meetings also had fewer sub-committee meetings and there could be longer delays between the time an issue was put before the local authority, for example a request for planning permission, and the time when a final decision was made. The timing of council meetings also had implications for the relationship between councillors and officers. A longer cycle usually implied that councillors were less involved in detailed business and met largely to discuss policy, leaving much more to the day-to-day activities of the appointed staff.

The meetings of the council are presided over by a 'chairman'. The Equal Opportunities Commission might wish to note that the 2000 Local Government Act uses the male-orientated designation. The person occupying the chair is elected on an annual basis by and from the members of that council. Historically, the chairman in chartered boroughs and, after 1835, municipal boroughs was accorded the title of mayor. This title is conferred on all chairs of metropolitan districts, London boroughs and many district councils which have pretensions to being urban areas. Any of the authorities created in 1972 are able to petition the Queen to confer upon them a charter giving them the status of a borough and the right to elect a mayor. Parish councils, especially those covering old urban communities, that formerly were boroughs or districts in their own right have petitioned for the right to become town councils and dignify their chairperson with the mayoral accolade. Larger local authorities which have been granted by Royal Charter the status of a city appoint a Lord Mayor. Counties have always remained content with a mere chairman. In Scotland, the chair of the district council is often referred to as the Provost or, in the large cities, the Lord Provost. The chair is, in most cases, an active and distinguished member of a political party but is expected to maintain, like the Speaker of the House of Commons, strict neutrality in her or his dealings with the council. Very occasionally neutrality may go out of the window, since the chair has a casting vote in the case of a tied vote in council and, should party groups in council be evenly balanced, the political preferences of the mayor may be crucial in determining which party controls the local authority.

Since the position of mayor is awarded through a vote of the council, it is possible for a majority party to ensure that their friends always retain the chairmanship or mayoralty within the party. Most local authorities will, however, ensure that opposition groups have a share of the honours and it is frequently the case that each party gets a turn at nominating one of its members to be the mayor, in conformity with the size of party groups within the council, under a well-established principle of equity and 'Buggins' turn'. It is, therefore, not infrequent for a Labour-controlled authority to have, from time to time, a Conservative Party mayor and visa versa.

Council meetings

Under the old system the full council, although the sovereign body of the local authority, in practice makes few serious decisions, even though almost all matters affecting the local authority must pass through the council for approval. Most of the detailed work is undertaken in sub-committees of the council, which forward to each full council meeting a huge agenda of items for ratification. Most of the issues are so uncontroversial that they do not raise the slightest hint of debate, whilst others may be settled by argument in a lower committee. The full council, therefore, debates only a few issues of major importance to the political parties at each meeting whilst the rest of the agenda is passed without discussion, 'on the nod', by simply approving the entire raft of items on the council agenda submitted by a sub-committee. If, for example, a small district council decides to repair a council-house the decision to undertake this task will be made by a sub-committee of the housing committee and then included on the agenda of the full council under the housing sub-committee section. If there is no controversy about this item at the full council, the chairman of the housing sub-committee moves that the proposed items on the agenda be accepted and the motion is seconded and agreed unanimously. Under this system, the agenda for the meetings of large local authorities was, therefore not surprisingly a book length document listing numerous minor items such as repairs, material requisitions, or the creation of new posts.

The committee structure

Membership of committees is determined by the party leaders in the local authority, who normally proportion the party balance of major committees in conformity with their representation on the full council. A local authority which has a majority ruling party consequently secures a majority on all committees and also ensures that its members are elected to committee chairs. The chair of a major sub-committee is a key political figure who is expected to initiate and monitor the policy and operations of that committee. The chair of an education committee will, for example, be regarded as the most important political spokespersons for this service in the authority and have a role over policy making in this area not dissimilar to that of the Secretary of State for Education and Skills at the national level. Such responsibility ensures that the chairs of major committees are part of the inner oligarchy of council leaders.

Within a large authority, the number of committees were Byzantine in their complexity. The local authority was divided into major sub-committees dealing with the most important functions of the council. The major committees were usually divided into further smaller sub-committees to deal with more specialised issues and these too can be further sub-divided. Thus, in a county council, the education committee will have had reporting to it separate smaller subordinate sub-committees on, for example, secondary education or maintenance of school premises. Issues discussed at this lower level were accepted, often without debate, in the major committee before being presented to the full council. This pattern can be further complicated by the creation of joint committees reporting to more than one committee established to deal with some major event or an issue that touches the interest of more than one department. Many authorities also formed advisory committees to include non-councillors, for example, as a means to regularly consult with local business interests.

Corporate management

The committee structure of local authorities had for many years been subject to serious criticism but only piecemeal reform. A central objection to the management structure of local authorities was that they effectively consisted of a number of semi-independent committees whose chairs and chief officers built moats and ramparts around their fiefdoms and defied other functional interests within the local authority to invade their territory. In 1964, an enquiry chaired by Sir John Maud was established by the Government to review local government management. The subsequent Maud Report not unexpectedly echoed the prevailing criticisms of departmentalism and suggested the establishment of a smaller policy-making group within local authorities which would be paralleled by a more hierarchic officer structure. This view anticipated some of the ideas now established in the 2000 Local Government Act.

The Maud Report was not, however, widely welcomed and its ideas were eclipsed when the self same Sir John was appointed to chair the Commission to restructure the whole of the local government system. As the new structures began to emerge in the 1972 a working party chaired by the Chief Clerk of Kent County Council, Sir John Bains, was appointed to report on the ideal managerial structures for the new authorities. The membership of the working group was designed to take a managerial perspective and eschew political division, since it contained a businessman and local government officers but no councillors. A parallel working party was created to deal with reforms in Scotland.

The Bains Report, published in 1972, had a considerable influence on local authority structures. The committee accepted what was by this stage an orthodox view that there should be greater integration within local authorities, but rejected the Maud prescription of a drastic reduction in the number of committees or the creation of a board of councillors standing between the full council and the major committees. The Report suggested a reduction in the number of major committees reporting to the full council and the creation of a lead committee to co-ordinate the general policy for the authority which would include committee chairs and, unlike the British cabinet at national level, also leading members of opposition parties on the council. Strategically important service committees concerned with, for example, finance would also report to this policy committee. The Bains Report also recommended the appointment of a chief executive who would be the head of the local government service within an authority and a management committee of senior officers to co-ordinate their activities. There should also be a corporate policy unit attached to the chief executives' department, whose officers would advise on the overall strategy of the local authority.

Leader and chairs

The leader of the council under the old system is the chair of the policy committee and is, in many respects, equivalent in authority to the position of Prime Minister in central government. In most local authorities, where party politics is dominant, the leader is chosen by the councillors of the majority party group. The councillors representing smaller parties which do not have the majority of council seats also select a leader from their numbers who is recognised as a minority party leader and the principal policy maker and spokesperson of that group. The leader usually has no departmental responsibility but is expected to have oversight of the overall policy of the council. The leader is usually responsible for selection of the committee chairs and can also dismiss them from office. He or she will also be called upon to resolve differences of opinion between rival committee chairs. The press, radio and television will usually require comments from the leader of the council on any major issue affecting the local authority and hence he or she is often the most well-known council politician within the locality. The leader's authority, like that of the Prime Minister, is, however, a reflection of their standing within their political party.

The other members of the policy committee will normally be either committee chairs or shadow chairs of committees from the parties in a minority position on the council. These senior committee chairs gain their exalted status as prominent and respected party politicians selected by their party group of councillors, usually on the recommendation of the group's leader. The policy committee can therefore expect that its decisions are effective, since its members will normally have the authority to ensure that more junior councillors and party colleagues will accept their decision. In practice however, the committee may become little more than a device whereby established committee chairs seek to ensure that the trenches dividing them from rival chairs are as wide as ever. The key to political relationships at this level of policy making is, like the power of the leader, often inextricably linked with relationships within the majority party group of councillors.

The new structures for local policy making

The Bains proposals never completely ended debate on the need to streamlining local authority decision making and pressures for change were sharpened by the new public management movement that emerged during the Thatcher years. Public bodies such as local authorities would, it was argued, be far more efficient if they operated rather like private businesses, which were controlled by a small executive and a clearly identified leader who would be seen as responsible for the successes and failures of the service. This view was taken up by Michael Heseltine when he returned as Secretary of State for the Environment in the first Government of John Major. In addition to restructuring local boundaries, Heseltine advocated that all local authorities should be governed by elected mayors. The idea was not warmly received by many of his Cabinet colleagues, who feared this idea may create a further host of Ken Livingstones to harry the Government from positions of local power. The idea was, however carried forward by an interest group seeking to revive the fortunes of local government, the Campaign for Local Democracy, which has been highly influential among some of the leaders of New Labour. The Blair Government came to power promising an overhaul of the decision-making structure of local government and announced their plans in the 1998 White Paper *Modern Local Government: In Touch with the People*. The proposals formed a central element of 2000 Local Government Act which is determining a major restructuring of the policy structure of local authorities.

The new structures for local government concentrate decision making and responsibility for policy implementation in the hands of small executive cabinets of local politicians led, either by an elected mayor or a more old-style leader of the council. Local authorities must adopt one of four models for executive governance.

1 The councillors elects a leader, who chairs a cabinet formed from among the councillors selected either by the leader or the full council. The cabinet is responsible for developing and implementing local authority policy. The leader will depend for his continued role in office on the support of the council and can be replaced by the council.

   The leader council structure is the least radical and probably least preferred by the Blair Government of the systems open to local authorities. The adoption of a cabinet system is, nevertheless, a radical change in approach to undertaking council business. In the former system, council leaders were not legally recognised but was a position that had evolved by custom and practice and it was possible to have local authorities without a designated leader. Under the old system the co-ordinating policy committee also had to be composed of representatives of all the parties elected onto the council. Under the new system the cabinet can consist of entirely members of one party.

   A further and crucial difference between the new and old systems is that the cabinet is responsible for policy making and ensuring its implementation rather than all members of the council. Unlike a prime minister, the mayor can appoint no more than ten members to the cabinet which is expected, therefore, to be a relatively compact group with considerable authority, concentrated in the portfolio of each member. The backbenchers as discussed below will be assigned a role in scrutinising the work of the cabinet.

2 A mayor elected by all voters in the local authority selects a cabinet from the councillors to form the cabinet for the authority. It will normally be expected that each member of the cabinet will be responsible for one of the major departments and group of services for the authority.

   The Blair Government expects that, in local authorities which adopt this system, the mayor will become a far more prominent public figure than a leader and a more dominant focus of the strategy and policy of the authority. This system has some similarities to the structure adopted for the Greater London Authority in which the mayor is regarded as dominant strategist and figurehead for the city. However, unlike the Greater London Authority, the mayor must select the rest of the cabinet from the elected councillors and will not have a totally free hand to choose any person he or she thinks will be most beneficial to the community. Thus, the system effectively closely resembles the procedures of the national government, where the Prime Minister selects his or her cabinet from prominent MPs within his or her party.

   It remains to be seen how the system will work in practice in Britain, since there is a potential for serious conflict if the elected mayor chooses to pursue different policies from those preferred by the majority of councillors. It would, for example, be possible for a mayor to be selected representing a party with a minority of councillors, but who could still choose a cabinet from his or her own party and have to face the hostility of backbench members.

In France the council elects a mayor, and in Germany councils elect a similar political executives the *burgermeister* who is regarded as the political leader of the community. Italy has started to adopt a system of separately elected mayors and councils. In the United States, there are a variety of local governance systems. Many cities, such as New York, have a strong mayor system in which the mayor is separately elected from the council and serves as the head of an executive-style government and appoints its members but in others, termed a weak mayor system, the council chooses the mayor or he/she may be separately elected, but in either case the councillors have the power to appoint other leading executive politicians. Weak mayors can nevertheless be effective leaders of the council, as in Chicago, if the city has a disciplined dominant party of which the mayor is leader. In some mid-sized cities, a smaller number of commissioners are elected to jointly run the authority. In many, although by no means all, of the United States cities, the mayor, councillors or the commissioners will appoint a city manager to run the city in accord with the strategic lead established by the mayor or commissioners.

3 An elected mayor and an officer appointed by the council who is called the manager for the authority and runs all the local services with aid of subordinate departmental officers. The mayor operates like a non-executive chair of a company, in that he or she guides the policy framework of the authority whilst implementation is left to the manager.

   The mayor and manager system resembles the United States mayor-city manager structure and is a highly radical departure from preceding democratic systems in Britain that base the authority of an executive on their support from elected legislators. Under such a system, the policy-making role may be in the hands of the appointed city manager rather than the elected mayor. The mayor would be expected to take a longer term strategic vision of the progress of the authority and the manager would be expected to put the vision into practice. As the council and not the mayor appoints the manager, the structure may result in a situation where the mayor and manager are not in agreement although, in practice, it is probable that the mayor as the likely leader of the dominant political party in the authority will also be able to influence his or her party members on the council to choose a manager who will accept the mayoral vision and strategy for the authority. It remains to be seen, if such a system were adopted, who would be recruited as a city manager and how much the elected mayor or the appointed manager would determine the policies for the community. Existing local authority chief executives may be the most likely candidates to obtain the positions of city or county manager, but it will also be possible for a council, perhaps under the mayor's influence, to import someone from a business background or even a fellow travelling politician.

4 A further design-your-own-system possibility is open to local authorities,
   who may propose to the Secretary of State that they are allowed to adopt a
   different structure for their cabinet government based on variations on the
   three patterns outlined in the 2000 Local Government Act. They could, for
   example, develop a system in which all cabinet members in addition to the
   mayor are directly elected or that some specific cabinet posts, such as the
   head of education or social services, are directly elected.

Implementing the new structures

Local authorities are given the responsibility for initially deciding which policy-
making structures they will adopt, but if they decide to have a system involving
a directly elected mayor they are required to put the idea to the electorate in a
local referendum. It is also possible for members of the public to petition the
council to hold a referendum to establish a system with an elected mayor and it
is mandatory for the council to hold a referendum if they receive a petition for
such action from at least 5 per cent of the electorate of the local authority.

It remains to be seen how local authorities and public will react to the proposed new structures, but current evidence suggests that most local authorities
prefer the leader/cabinet system rather than structures involving an elected
mayor. A considerable number of local governments, for example the cities of
Barnsley and York and Kent County Council, anticipated the thinking behind
the new legislation and adopted a cabinet/leader style of government in
advance of the 2000 Local Government Act. However in some large cities, such
as Liverpool and Birmingham, there are strong political and popular pressures
to seek the adoption of a system involving an elected mayor and there is current
press speculation that prominent local politicians currently serving as MPs
may be interested in such a position. It is possible that for large cities the elected

In the United States where many, but not all, mayors are directly elected, there is
less likely to be a total breakdown in the relationship between the mayor and
councillors, even if the majority of councillors are from a different party than the
mayor, since party loyalties are generally far weaker and politicians are rarely disciplined if they vote against the party line. This relationship is most clearly seen
in the Federal Government where the President, as under the later years of
Clinton's term of office, does not have the support of a majority of his own party
members in Congress. As a consequence of much weaker party loyalties, the
President can however still get policies through Congress and is not constantly
facing votes to remove him from office. In France, as the mayor is elected by the
councillors, he or she will generally be supported by a majority of councillors and
can remain effective, despite a more partisan political system than in the United
States.

mayor may become a resting place for ambitious politicians who have not quite made national leadership status. The selection of such figures will also however be dependent on what selection strategies for their mayoral candidates are adopted by the major political parties who will, apart from the Liberal Democrats, be mindful of the disasters that accompanied their selection procedures for the London mayor candidates.

The council

Under the new structures the role of the backbench councillors and of the full council is dramatically altered. Councillors who are outside the cabinet are not directly involved in making policy or directing the activities of officers. A major function of councillors is to scrutinise and check the work of the executive and where necessary call the cabinet or its members to publicly account for their actions. Councils appoint one or more scrutiny committees, which can demand that cabinet members or officers appear before them to explain their policies and the scrutiny committees can request the cabinet to reconsider policies or actions that are thought to be unacceptable.

The system appears to parallel the arrangement of select committees in the House of Commons, which can, on occasion, be influential in raising difficult and embarrassing issues for the government that can be taken up by the press and become matters of public interest which help determine voters attitudes to the government. Many of the accusations of sleaze and cash for questions in the Major Government were made more transparent through the operation of select committees. However, it remains to be seen whether the similar scrutiny committees of local authorities are likely to raise issues that will so excite national or even local media attention that they will have any impact on local elections. In addition to their critical role, most Parliamentary committees work quietly and without much publicity on valuable investigatory work that often provides useful research and ideas that can be used by the government. It is more probable the local scrutiny committees will largely be a source of possible ideas to resolve local problems that will be on occasion used by the local authority executive or probably more often ignored.

A further and potentially important function of the full council will be its capacity each year to comment on the policy proposals put forward by the cabinet for the following year and its power to approve or reject the budget proposed by the cabinet. It is only possible to speculate at the time of writing how councils and executives will use these powers. In the Westminster Parliament, should the government lose the vote on the annual Queen's Speech which sets out the government's policy proposals for the forthcoming year or the vote on the budget, convention dictates that the Prime Minister and Cabinet should resign and new elections should be held. Under the 2000 Local Government Act, there is no requirement that the cabinet or leader, mayor or city manager of a local authority should resign if their budget or policy proposals are rejected and the possibility is raised of a local authority cabinet remaining in office even though it has no approved budget. However, since it is illegal for a local authority not to set a budget, some resolution of a conflict on the budget will have to be reached between an executive and its council. Whilst the executive or mayor of a local authority may in practice be forced to compromise with the council on the budget and the policy programme, the council will have few powers to ensure on day-to-day local authority business that the executive pays serious attention to its demands.

> A system that effectively separates the powers of the elected mayor and the council operates in practice in many local authorities in the United States, as it does in the Federal Government, but it remains to seen how it will work under British conditions where party loyalties are much stronger.

Modern Local Government: In Touch with the People (1998) clearly suggested that in the Blair Government's view, councillors would not be involved in the details of policy making but have a far more limited role than has traditionally been the case, at least for a councillor of the majority party on the local authority. The White Paper suggested that a major advantage of the new system would be to ensure that local councillors could devote far more of their time to work in the community. It is anticipated by the Government that backbenchers will not as they seem to see it, waste their time sitting in endless committee meetings in the town hall, but be out on the streets and footpaths of their wards talking with and working for their local electors and reporting back to the executive their needs and demands. As a result of this changed role councillors will, so the Government hopes, become far more involved in the work of their community.

It is difficult, however, to see how the hope can be fulfilled that under the new arrangements backbench councillors will be henceforth more active in the community and as a result create greater enthusiasm for local government and facilitate greater local democracy. Much of their work may still have to be within the town halls, engaging in even more futile posturing on scrutiny committees or trying to gain the attention of remote cabinet members to draw their attention to issues relating to their ward. The effectiveness of the new arrangements will be considered again in Chapter 13 against the wider background of local democracy and party politics.

Further reading

The basic internal structure of local authorities are covered in most textbooks, but more detail on the ideas behind new management can be obtained from Leach, Stewart and Walsh (1994). Walsh (1995) provides a wider theoretical

view of new management thinking. The earlier ideas on corporate management produced an extensive literature and are best approached through of one
of its principal advocates Stewart (1971 and 1974). Also of value is Greenwood
and Stewart (1974) and Greenwood *et al.* (1980). The Bains Report (1972) is
also worth reading to gain an impression of this management style. Policies
concerning decentralisation are best covered by Hoggett and Hambleton
(1988) and by Burns, Hambleton and Hoggett (1994) and Chandler *et al.*
(1995). The theory of post-Fordism as applied to local government is considered by Stoker (1991).

8

Leaders, councillors and the party system

Throughout the nineteenth century, it was legally considered that the decisions of a local authority reflected the majority view of elected councillors who were supposedly representative of the citizens who voted for them. Democracy seldom operates like this in practice. Even before the 2000 Local Government Act established small policy-making executives, decisions within all but a few of the principal local authorities in Britain were made, not in formal committees of the local authority, but in the informal conclaves of political parties. Representation of the electorate is also not a simple relationship between councillors and constituents, but is mediated through the campaigns and programmes of local and national parties.

In the late nineteenth and first half of the twentieth century, many commentators on local government regretted the rise of partisanship and the decline of the independent councillor. Recent government studies such as the Widdicombe enquiry recognise that

> In common with the great majority of those who commented in the evidence, we regard the continued presence of political organisation in local government as inevitable for the foreseeable future. Indeed we would expect to see a continuing trend towards political organisation in those authorities which at present are relatively apolitical. We do not regard this in itself either as desirable or undesirable. (Widdicombe 1986: 61, Para. 4.16)

Not only are local authorities organised along party political lines, it is now generally the case that the party groups within a local authority, that is the collection of councillors affiliated to a particular party, form the conclave in which most of the crucial policy decisions are made, especially where a party group is in the majority.

By no means all party groups, which are sometimes referred to as the party caucus, are well-disciplined and expect each member to vote in unison with their colleagues. In some local authorities, party membership may only be

Within most European Union countries party politics is a major feature of the political life of all larger authorities, but in smaller local governments, such as rural French communes, it may have little relevance and councillors are effectively independent of party ties. In the United States the movement to reform city government in the late nineteenth century led several cities to forbid political party affiliations being part of local elections and in such cities councillors stand as independents. The consequence of this arrangement is to advantage middle-class candidates, often with business affiliations, who can afford the personal cost of standing for election.

valued as a means of securing electoral success and that once members convene in the council chamber, party affiliation is virtually forgotten. A.H. Birch in his study of the Lancashire town of Glossop observed that

> The influence of party affiliations in the subsequent work of the Council is not easy to trace. The Liberals do not believe that their Council members should be tied to any particular policy and they do not hold caucus meetings; the Conservatives generally regard party agreement as desirable but they have abandoned the practice of holding caucus meetings and frequently disagree in debate; the Labour members still hold caucus meetings but no binding decisions are taken there and it is quite common for Labour councillors to be on opposite sides in Council debates (1959: 119).

Such independence was normal practice in many of the smaller pre-1974 reconstruction authorities and was also not unusual in county councils. By the 1930s, most cities had established more rigid discipline among the party rank and file and the decisions of the party group were expected to be binding on members. It is now generally assumed that since 1974 local politics has become more partisan and that this includes a much greater tendency for party groups to vote cohesively (Widdicombe 1986: 60).

The organisation of the party group

Most party groups in large authorities will convene before any full meeting of the council in order to co-ordinate their strategy towards items on the agenda and will often meet at other times to discuss ideas and problems. Council groups in the Labour, Liberal Democrat and most Conservative Parties will usually make decisions on a majority basis, although this should not be taken to mean that each member has equal power. Each group of any size will have an elected inner executive committee composed of the most respected and authoritative party members, which will recommend what action should be taken on important issues and initiate many of the policies to be adopted by the group. Most members of the executive will be either committee chairs or shadow committee chairs. A chair, who is often an elder worthy of the party, is elected to control the group's meetings. A secretary arranges the meetings, circulates their agendas and takes the minutes. A group whip has the task, like the House of Commons equivalent, of informing members of their strategy in any debate, monitoring how colleagues vote and, in consultation with other senior party members, instituting disciplinary procedures should a member fail to follow the party line.

The effectiveness of the group in delivering a common stance is primarily a function of its ability to discipline its membership. The cohesion of party groups is a seriously under-researched area but the problems of disciplinary procedures that apply in national politics are also applicable at the local level. It is clearly less of a problem for the group to deal with a rebellion among one or two of its members if it enjoys a substantial majority in the council than it is to deal with a rebellion by a numerous entrenched faction when it has but a slim majority. Party groups are insulated from the fear that motivates party cohesion in Parliament, that a rebellion that results in defeat for the party on an issue of importance will lead to new elections and loss of power. Discipline is, therefore, in part, secured by the fear of loss of status, promotion prospects and positions of responsibility in the party and local authority. The greatest constraint is, however, expulsion from the party group since, should the district or county party accept this decision, the errant councillors will not be reselected as the party's candidates in the next election and have to take their chances as independents. Expulsion from the party is not uncommon and it is even more frequent for councillors to resign from the party ahead of the threat of expulsion.

The party leader

The most important elected member of a party's group of councillors is the party leader, although it remains to be seen if directly elected mayors will change this pattern. The party group leader will generally also be leader of the council if his or her party enjoys a majority of seats on the council. The leader will expect to initiate the major policies of the council group, set the tone and style of its strategy, co-ordinate its activities and mediate between its members and determine which colleagues will serve in the cabinet for the authority or, if the party does not enjoy a majority, be its chief spokesperson on important policy areas.

The power and authority of a party leader will, however, vary depending on personality and political circumstances. The position is achieved through election by the party group in what may be a strenuous and sometimes bitter contest between rival political leaders. The outcome of the vote may radically change party policy. For example, the election of Ken Livingstone as leader of the GLC in 1982 was a triumph for more radical forces with the Labour group of councillors and signalled the beginning of confrontation with the Thatcher Government.

Few party leaders will, however, be so popular with their fellow councillors that they can alone determine policy and assume that their more junior colleagues will accept their opinions. In order to get their ideas accepted by the party group, a leader or an elected mayor will need the support of most of their more authoritative colleagues on the party executive and, in turn, at least in the pre-cabinet systems, they will have to be in tune with backbench councillors. There are many instances where party leaders do not always get their policy accepted. Despite his national prestige and work in initiating the challenge against rate capping in 1985, David Blunkett, then leader of Sheffield City Council, was unable to immediately persuade his fellow councillors to back down from confrontation after it was clear most other rate-capped local authorities had given up the fight. In extreme cases, a powerful majority section in a party group may keep in power a figurehead leader who will be obliged to largely follow the majority view. This eventually occurred in Liverpool after 1983 when the dominant Militant Group chose to retain the milder mannered John Hamilton as Council leader, although real power lay with the deputy leader Derek Hatton (Crick: 1986).

Although party leaders, like many Prime Ministers, are not necessarily all-powerful, some can, over time, reach a position of dominance over the local authority to the extent that no policies are enacted without her or his acquiescence if not approval. Dominant party leaders achieve their status partly by careful and judicious appointment of friends or, potential, but subornable, rivals to senior positions in their entourage. The executive of the party group will often be composed of individuals who are indebted to the leader for their political status and fully in accord with his or her policies. Some local politicians such as Sir Jack Smart, leader of Wakefield District Council throughout much of the 1980s and for a time Chairman of the Association of Metropolitan Authorities, occupy not only the position of leader but several other strategically important party posts such as chair of the district party or of a locally

---

The image of a city 'boss', a dominant politician who controls the governance of a community, is most firmly identified with the United States, where some mayors have been in a position through dominance in the local Democrat or Republican Party machine to dictate, not only who held office in local government, but also who represented the area in state and federal elections. Generally, it is thought city bosses are more a pre-1945 phenomenon. Mayor Richard Daley of Chicago was in the 1960s viewed as such a leader, although he had limited powers in the State of Illinois. Powerful political leaders, the *local notables*, are perhaps more strongly entrenched in France which has a more disciplined party system. A politician such as Gaston Deferre, who in the 1980s reformed French local government structures as Minister of the Interior, was simultaneously Mayor of Marseille, where he dominated both local and departmental government and representation from the City in the National Assembly.

dominant trade union branch. It is possible in such a position for leaders to influence the attitudes of party members and, without recourse to overt discrimination, ensure that dangerous opponents to their policies are not often nominated as council candidates.

The party system under cabinet government

It remains to be seen how the development of cabinet government and the introduction of directly elected mayors may influence the role of the party group. In local authorities that have established cabinet systems, especially those with a dominant party, the changes have done little to alter the role of the party group in determining policy. In effect, the leader of the council is the chosen candidate of the dominant party group and the cabinet are the senior group members who would form the majority on the party executive. However, as the cabinet does not have to share power with opposition parties, it is possible for this group to discuss matters that they may in the past have referred to the more secretive group executive. It remains to be seen, how the power of party groups will be modified within systems with an elected mayor, and there may be a major loosening of the influence of the party as directly elected mayors seek to gain, like Ken Livingstone, local electoral support that transcends party loyalties. In such circumstances a popular mayor may be able to largely ignore the local party group by threatening to stand as independent.

Local party structures and the selection of candidates: the Labour Party

Political parties do not regard their groups of councillors as isolated organisations that are unaccountable to the party at large. There are important connections between local political parties and their councillors, especially in relation

It is possible but rather dangerous to speculate on the basis of comparative studies how party systems in Britain will adapt to the restructuring of local authority management. For example, in the United States which has, compared with Britain, a generally weak and less disciplined party system, it is far easier for directly elected mayors to appeal to the electorate on the basis of their personality rather than party loyalty and thus be more able to circumvent whatever controls the local party may impose on them. Similarly in Italy, elected mayors are popular in part because of the widespread dissatisfaction over the corruption within the major parties and the delays and in-fighting caused by coalition government. In Britain, where party affiliation has at least until now been the principal criterion for determining who wins in a local election, these examples drawn from weaker party systems may not be applicable.

to the procedures for electoral campaigns and the selection of candidates. In theory, the Labour Party is a democracy in which policy is determined by its rank and file membership, unlike the Conservative Party which has never pretended to organise itself internally under democratic principles. It was argued by Robert McKenzie (1963) that both organisations are, nevertheless, at least as regards national policy-making oligarchies.

When the Labour Party was formed in 1900, it was composed of trade unions and socialist societies which affiliated to the organisation. A new constitution, written in 1918 in a flush of post-war radicalism, grafted individual membership to the structure, so that the party established members branches at local government ward level as the basis of an organisational hierarchy. Ward parties nominate delegates to the constituency party which covers the area returning an MP to Parliament. This body also includes delegates representing members affiliated to the party as a consequence of membership of trade unions or socialist societies that are corporate members of the national party.

Each local authority is shadowed by a committee which is called, as appropriate, the county or district Labour Party. These organisations are relatively large and may have a membership of up to 300 members. Most of the active delegates to these bodies are chosen from constituency parties, although in practice it is common for many constituency parties to select at least one delegate from each ward in their area. Affiliated party members are also represented on the county and district parties and in many areas trade unions, could potentially compose the majority of the district party membership, but, normally, few trade union branches bother to send a delegate, either through indifference or because the nominee must also be an individual party member. Each year the district or county party will choose a small executive which may have considerable authority in steering debate within the party and undertaking its day-to-day functions. In wealthy or electorally marginal areas, the secretary of the district party may be a professional party agent.

The function of the district or county party is to consider issues pertinent to the local authority area, and to organise and fight the local elections. This role includes powers to supervise the selection of candidates for elections to the local authority and to approve or reject nominees. Through its executive, the local party has joint responsibility with the councillors group for drawing up the manifesto for local elections. The party is also entitled to send a few delegates who are not councillors to the Labour group.

Most of local parties take their powers seriously. In a large city with strong Labour Party representation, the district party will generally meet once a month and debate resolutions concerning the policies of their councillors and may expect reports from the leader of the council and his senior committee chairpersons. District parties may also convene extraordinary meetings to debate a single vital issue such as their defiance in 1985 of the Government's poll tax legislation. Some district Labour Parties establish standing working

parties composed of district party delegates and councillors to monitor the decisions of council committees and devise policy to be presented to the joint executives of the Labour group and district party that draw up the election
manifesto.

Potentially, a district or county Labour Party will have considerable powers
to influence the activities of its local councillors although in practice they may
often have little impact. In areas of the country where the Party elected few, if
any, councillors the district or county party may meet infrequently and its
debates have but an academic quality. In many cities, the executive of the district party is dominated by councillors who are able to control its proceedings
as a consequence of their cohesion in the face of external criticism and their
authority as prominent local politicians (Hall and Leach 2000: 162). Complete
domination is, however, not always the case, and there can be bitter conflict
between the district party and councillors. During the Banham Commission's
restructuring of local government, the District Labour Party of Chesterfield
supported by the County Labour Party successfully undermined Chesterfield
District Council Labour Group's policy on advocating a unitary authority status
for the area by threatening to deselect councillors favouring such a policy (Hall
and Leach 2000).

Candidate selection

Potentially the most effective power held by a district or county party is its
control over the selection of electoral candidates. The executive of the district
party must draw up a panel of party members who are fit and proper persons
to be chosen as party candidates for future elections. Ward parties can only
select as their candidate a member who has been placed on the panel. A Labour
Party councillor will, therefore, only become a candidate if acceptable to the
district or county party. Members are included on the panel if they are nominated by a ward party or affiliated trade union branch, approved by their constituency party and then by the district or county party. In many local
government areas, inclusion on the panel is almost automatic following nomination by a ward and constituency party. Some large city parties will, however,
interview prospective candidates and not endorse anyone they feel lacks knowledge and understanding of the role of a Labour Party councillor. Such action
may even involve the removal from the candidates list of a sitting councillor
who is thought to be too ill-disciplined or incompetent to continue to represent
the party. An aggrieved candidate has a right of appeal to the regional and
National Executives of the party.

Once established on the panel of candidates, the prospective councillors may
be shortlisted by a ward party and invited to attend a selection meeting. Along
with other candidates he or she will address the branch delegates and then be
asked questions. The final selection is undertaken by an exhaustive ballot, so
that if no candidate gets a majority of votes on the first round of voting a new

ballot, is held in which the candidate with the lowest vote drops out of the contest. This process is continued until a candidate emerges with the majority of votes. The selection is supervised by a representative from the executive of the district or county party, who will ensure that the selection process was conducted according to the rules. The candidate is not officially adopted until the county or district party approves the selection.

If all is well for a local party, the selection of a new candidate will be made from a number of very capable shortlisted party members. In reality, in areas of the country less favourable to the party, there will be serious difficulty in finding anyone willing to stand and hence circumstances will effectively make much of the selection procedure only a formality. It is not unusual even in city parties for the shortlist to contain fewer potential candidates than there are vacancies so that once the safe seats have been allocated the unattractive no-hope candidatures are foisted on any party member who can be cajoled to put his name forward to fill an otherwise embarrassing vacancy (Chandler and Morris 1984).

The Conservative Party

Locally, the Conservative Party does not have the structural uniformity that exists in the Labour Party. At the lowest level, the party is organised into branch associations which are formed in accord with the number of members attracted to the party within a particular area. Thus, the branch structure does not necessarily coincide with the pattern of local government electoral wards. On occasion, there may be more than one branch per ward or, in areas of little faith in Conservative values, a branch may cover several wards. At the next level is a constituency association, composed of delegates representing local branches. This body, as in the Labour Party, is primarily responsible for selecting and monitoring the activities of an MP or a prospective parliamentary candidate.

Most local authority areas will be shadowed by a Conservative Party organisation specifically created to consider the Party's policies and oversee selection of candidates and the conduct of local election campaigns for that area. The composition and procedures of the district or county Conservative associations are however not established to a standard formula. In Birmingham, the sovereign body of the city's Conservative Association comprises some 500 delegates nominated by branches. This body meets only twice a year and selects a smaller executive committee that still numbers over 100 delegates. Effective power lies with a small group of six officers elected annually by the Central Council and the permanently appointed party agent. This small group, which meets frequently, sends representatives to the meetings of the Conservative group of councillors (Newton 1976: 94–5).

The county and district associations of the Conservative Party are, in formal terms, much less influential concerning the policies of their councillors than is the case within the Labour Party. Tradition in the Conservative party ascribes the policy making role to the party leader at both national and local levels, although the practice of politics obliges most leaders to consult with potential rivals and lieutenants. The Conservative Party is more ruthless in ridding itself of its failed or pensionable leaders than its supposedly more divisive rivals. The party is not given to public displays of dissent and division, but relies on the influence of its respected leaders to call failed leaders to account. Although, in constitutional terms, the chairman of a district or county Conservative Association may have less power than his Labour Party equivalent, in practice, many incumbents of such a post are respected elder statesmen of the Party with the authority to suggest and secure the resignation of an insecure politician.

Candidate selection

The method of selecting Conservative candidates for local government is determined locally and practice varies widely. It is generally considered within the Party that candidates should apply for vacant posts of parliamentary or local government candidates. Many established district Conservative Associations will provide a panel of hopeful members who have expressed an interest in being considered as a candidate for election to the local council but normally no effort is made to prune the list and it is simply a guide to hopeful aspirants. There is rarely any obligation on branches to select candidates from the list and in some areas where there are either sufficient candidates in a branch, or none at all, no effort is made to construct a panel of candidates. Selection of candidates is made by the branches covering a particular ward, through a joint meeting if this is necessary. The executive of the branches concerned may draw up a shortlist of party members who have applied for the vacant post and then a full meeting of members of the branch will be held at which the shortlisted candidates are interviewed and a fortunate individual selected following a vote from those present at the meeting. There can, however, be startling variations in this pattern. In Sheffield, at least during the late 1970s, the executive of the district association exerted a very powerful influence over candidate selection by establishing a select panel of candidates who were to be the only individuals eligible for nomination to a safe Conservative-held ward (Chandler and Morris 1984).

The Liberal Democrat Party

In the mid-twentieth century when the Liberals were regarded as on the fringe of British politics, the party usually had little need for strongly developed organisations to deal with local political policy making and candidate selection procedures. In consequence of this situation, and also in keeping with a traditional support for local autonomy, the party established a federal structure in regard to local politics. This framework persists, despite the growth in importance of the Liberal Democrats in local politics. Even though the party has won control of several local authorities, including the cities of Liverpool and Sheffield, it still maintains a federal structure allowing considerable autonomy to local branches. Like the Conservatives, the Liberal Democrats establish local party groups in relation to the strength of the party in a particular area. If there are relatively few members, the grass roots meeting will be based on a parliamentary constituency, but in areas where party membership is more robust the constituency level may encompass a number of branch parties covering a single or two or three local electoral wards. The party does not usually form a formal party machine to cover a local authority area as a whole that would be similar to the district or county Labour Parties.

Candidate selection is generally a process determined by the local constituency or ward grass roots meetings, although they are obliged to submit their rules for selection for approval by the regional tier of the national party organisation. The usual format allows the local party to request applications from Liberal Democrats who wish to be considered for selection as a candidate. In some areas where there is competition to become a candidate for safe seats, as, for example in Sheffield, the local party may draw up a panel from which potential electoral candidates are selected. Selection procedures where there is competition for nomination usually require the candidate to address a selection meeting and the final choice is made by a single transferable voting system either by members at the meeting or, if the local party prefers, through a postal ballot.

It is difficult to make generalisations concerning the structures and selection procedures for local government within the minor parties. Unless a minor party has a very strong local presence, branches may well cover the whole of a constituency or even a local government area and there will be little need for any formal district or county party structures. Selection, in these circumstances, is almost certainly the result of an informal process in which an enthusiastic stalwart is wholeheartedly approved as candidate in the absence of any opposition or through a process in which somewhat unwilling members are cajoled by their party colleagues to put their names forward in order to help their cause.

The influence of the local party

In neither the Labour nor the Conservative Party does the local party machine in general greatly influence the policy of its councillors in any direct day to day basis. Indeed, it will most frequently be the case that it is the party group of councillors that influences the views of the district party, since councillors will usually be among the leading and influential members of the district party. In some areas, however, councillors may share some influence with a few powerful and respected party members who, whilst not elected to any authority, command leading positions in the local party organisation. In rural areas within the Conservative Party, these worthies once exerted and, occasionally, still exert very great power. A landed gentleman, perhaps with an hereditary title, can still retain some of the glories of the eighteenth century Whig aristocracy. In the Labour Party and, to a lesser extent the Conservative Party, considerable influence may accrue to able individuals who are disbarred from being councillors by virtue of employment. A school teacher or social worker can, for example, become the chair of a district party as an outlet for frustrated ambitions, in order to use this position to influence policy. Some active trade unionists may also choose not to serve as councillors and yet exert local influence. Richard Caborn, a Sheffield MP and Minister of State, when a local trade union official, was, as Chair of the District Labour Party, highly influential in Sheffield local politics even though he was never himself a local councillor.

The national machine

Gyford and James (1983), commenting on the consequences of the decline in the numbers of independent councillors observed a current of opinion fearing that

> The phenomenon of electoral nationalisation is but the first stage of a much fuller party political nationalisation whereby the energies of local councillors are harnessed to serve the national interests of the parties rather than local community interests (1983: 3).

Routinely there are channels for central-local consultation within the major parties. The Labour Party holds an annual Conference, lasting two days, for local government representatives who are usually delegates from council groups and district parties. The Conference is dominated by speeches from party leaders and debates issues of mutual interest, although the resolutions are not binding on the leadership and are simply a guide to local feeling. The principal purpose of the Conference is to generate publicity and allow councillors and district party politicians opportunities to meet colleagues from other parts of the country. The Conservative Party holds a similar Conference, where councillors fortunate enough to be selected as delegates may mingle with the great and the good and listen to speeches that will occupy some fragment of the headlines in the national press or television news.

More serious deliberation takes place in the Labour Party within a standing committee on local government which is, as if to stress local government's importance in the order of things, a sub-committee of a larger Regional and Local Government Sub-committee of the National Executive Committee (NEC). The Committee on Local Government has around thirty members selected by the NEC from its own ranks and from favoured local Labour Party politicians. The committee serves as a forum in which local party leaders may exchange ideas with the senior party policy makers on local government issues. The development of this committee was largely a consequence of the arrival on the NEC of politicians, such as David Blunkett, with strong local government roots. The Committee has not been without influence and is taken seriously. It will deliberate on Labour Party and NEC policy documents concerning local government and could not ignore strongly and widely held criticisms on policy from within the committee. Its function is, however, wholly in the area of policy making at a national level towards local government and it is not a forum for closely monitoring the policies of individual Labour groups or district parties. The strength of these committees to influence policy is also much greater when the party is in opposition rather than in government, when national party leaders as Secretaries of State receive advice primarily from civil servants and powerful interest groups rather than the party machine.

The Conservatives established in 1944 a National Advisory Committee on Local Government to advise the party on local issues. The Committee is large in size and includes delegates representing Conservative groups of councillors and a number of MPs with an interest in local politics. Many of its serious deliberations are ironed out in a smaller executive consisting of the Chairman and Vice-Chairman of the Committee and leading Conservatives in the local authority associations. The organisation is principally concerned with policy advice and bringing together prominent Conservatives concerned with local politics for an exchange of ideas. The body therefore has no authority to tell Conservative groups of councillors what they should do. Advice on local government policy is also available to Conservative councillors through the research department of the central office of the party and from the several right-wing research bodies such as the Adam Smith and the Policy Studies Institutes. It is difficult to discern how much influence radiates to localities from this source.

Both the Conservative and Labour Party central machines can provide advice and guidance to local councillors, but they have no mechanism for regular control of local government by the central party. Intervention by the national party offices may occasionally take place in the affairs of district and county parties or associations when local politicians are causing severe embarrassment to the national leadership. The Labour Party acted firmly in the 1980s to disband local parties in Merseyside which were seen to be infiltrated by Militant members and in 1995 suspended the local party machine in Walsall as left-wing councillors embarked on a radical decentralisation policy, opposed by the local MP and a significant number, although not a majority of the Labour group (Hall and Leach 2000). The action of suspending a local party organisation and controlling local Labour politics from the central and regional offices of the Party is to use a sledgehammer to crack a nut, but the occasional necessity for such action indicates the difficulty that the Labour Party has in controlling disaffected local party organisations. Given the even more federal structure of the Conservative and Liberal Democrat Parties, there is similarly in these organisations no effective machinery to steer local party policy in the direction that is favoured by their national party leaders.

Overt attempts to manipulate local government through the national party machine may end in disaster and embarrassment for the party. The attempts by the Blair machine within the national Labour Party to determine the outcome of the vote for the Mayor of London may well have taught national politicians to be cautious in seeking to control local politics through selection by the party hierarchy of candidates to stand as elected mayors. Many rank and file members of the London Labour Party resented interference in selection procedures by the party headquarters that were clearly aimed at undermining the chances of Ken Livingstone becoming the official candidate and, in the wake of much bad publicity, Frank Dobson, the choice of Blair was heavily defeated. A similar strategy to manipulate the choice of leader of the Welsh Assembly was successful only in so far as the chosen candidate, Alun Michael, was selected by the party with a narrow majority sustained by trade union and MPs votes. The chosen leader was obliged to resign as leader after less than a year in office, as he failed to gain any enthusiasm from his backbench Members of the Welsh Assembly.

It is only possible, at the time of writing, to speculate whether the Blair Government developed as part of its strategy to establish directly elected mayors in Britain, the hidden agenda that by manipulating the selection of candidates to these senior positions, they could ensure that the national party leaders secured fellow-travelling New Labour supporters to positions of control over major local authorities and regional assemblies. It remains to be seen in 2000, how, chastened by their experience in London, the Labour Party will arrange the selection of its candidates for elected mayor or leader of the larger cities.

The ideological influence of the national parties

Whilst there is no evidence of direct control over local party groups by the offices of the national party, the values of local councillors may be set by their deference to the ideas of their national party leaders. Dunleavy (1980) has argued that

> local policy making is in large part constituted by stereotyped ideological responses to issues and problems with relatively little distinctively local reference.

Dunleavy's argument is a proposition that it is difficult to substantiate, since there is always likely to be considerable coincidence of views between members of the same party who come together on account of shared values. There is, however, sufficient evidence of widespread divergence of opinion within both the Labour and Conservative Parties on local authority policy to suggest that some councillors, and local authorities, despite their party affiliations, are sufficiently free thinking to disagree with the views of their leaders. Within the Labour Party local socialist defiance of rate capping by some cities demonstrated different attitudes within some city Labour groups from those of the party nationally. During much of the 1980s, the radical defiance of Thatcher's policies by Labour-controlled local authorities such as Sheffield, Lambeth and Liverpool was widely seen as more decisively setting the tone of Labour Party policy than its rather supine national leadership. It is also clear from the formation of the Greater London Authority that not all members of the party in the metropolis are ardent enthusiasts for New Labour.

Within the Conservative Party there is also widespread evidence of local challenges to the new-right policies of the Thatcher Government. At its most extreme the councillors of West Oxfordshire resigned *enmasse* from the party in protest at continued cuts to local authorities. Few Conservative councils followed the pure Thatcherist policies of Wandsworth or Westminster and preferred to act as parsimonious paternalists who valued the need for some local public services in housing and social services. It must, therefore, be concluded that whilst the views of the majority of local councillors coincide with nationally held orthodoxy, not all local politicians are unthinkingly uncritical of their leaders and some are capable of generating their own local ideologies.

The many roles of councillors

There have been several attempts to classify councillors in terms of their motives and attitudes. Newton (1976), for example, developed a sixfold typology relating to their orientation towards policy making. The problem with such schemes is that they tend to consider but one aspect of a highly complex pattern. Councillors attitudes will be determined, in part, by their own character, by the type of authority in which they operate, their community, and the issues with which they are faced. Thus, a councillor who has won election to a Welsh unitary authority as an Independent is likely to have a wholly different orientation towards his role than the Labour leader of an MDC.

The parochial member

Most typologies identify members who may be termed the parochial councillor. They are predominantly motivated by a concern to represent their particular ward and to solve local problems on behalf of their constituents. The parochial councillor will see his or her task as listening to complaints and worries from local citizens about the state of council services and then seeking redress, either by action within council committees, or by galvanising local government officers into resolving the issue. The parochial councillor is, therefore, the member who hears about a hole in the road and then looks into it. He or she leaves major policy initiatives to others. An important element of the 2000 Local Government Act appears to enhance this vocation among backbench councillors by ensuring that they are free of many policy-making tasks and have time to listen and represent the local parochial concerns of the citizens of their local ward. In some authorities, in which independents are still predominant, the parochial attitude may not extend simply to backbench councillors. A chairman of the Housing Committee of a district council in Wales observed that his role was to channel tenants' complaints and demands to officers, and that, when a major decision had to be made on the building and design of a new council estate, the matter had to be left to his officers who were the experts on such matters.

The policy-orientated member

Policy-orientated councillors will try to steer the direction of the local authority as a whole or of some important element of its work. Although they will not necessarily ignore complaints from their constituents, such work will be seen as secondary to influencing the policy of the authority. Under the new arrangements for governing local authorities, such members when first elected will seek to gain positions on the executive of the local authority rather than remain tied to parochial tasks. The precise interests of such councillors will, of course, vary depending on political persuasion, interest and ambition. Some councillors acquire an overwhelming interest in some specific aspect of the work of a local authority. Before the advent of cabinet government, a councillor with modest, even parochial ambitions, might be put in charge of a minor committee and suddenly gain such enthusiasm for its work that she or he becomes an advocate within the authority for the expansion of that particular function.

Councillors may be motivated by predominantly political rather than administrative ambitions, in that they see their role on the council as a stepping stone to a major career in politics. They will be eager to develop policies and show managerial skills that gain them promotion within their authority and the applause of party colleagues at large. Other members may be motivated less by personal ambition but, more altruistically, by the desire to forward political aims and strategies. In Liverpool many Militant councillors were concerned to use membership of the local authority as a means of establishing a particular political viewpoint (Taaffe and Mulhearn 1988) and it is probable that some new-right activists are attracted into Conservative councils for similar, but ideologically wholly opposed reasons. In some authorities, policy orientated councillors may evolve strong ideological views that inform the direction in which they think their local authority should move. David Blunkett as leader of Sheffield City Council, or, from a wholly opposed perspective, Christopher Chope and Paul Beresford in Wandsworth, have all developed and practised innovatory ideas on the role of local government.

Many councillors are, however, naturally conservative, regardless of political persuasion, and yet ambitious enough to want a major role within their local authority. They may be motivated by personal pride, the desire to become at least a big fish in a little pool, or a feeling that they should make their mark on their community. For many politicians, especially among working-class Labour members, the responsibility of running a local authority presents an opportunity for job satisfaction that they could not dream of achieving in their ordinary working life. These members will be uninterested in radically new policies, but wish to ensure the retention of conventional techniques of local government management to ensure effective and efficient provision of local services and a growth in the local economy. It can be suggested that the greatest number of local authorities are controlled by councillors of this persuasion. Among the local authorities in Britain, only a very few adopt radical policies of either socialist or new-right persuasion. The majority pursue conventional aims and methods which, for the most part, accept the prevailing ethos of stewardship in relation to their dealings with central government.

The background and training of councillors

The most comprehensive surveys of councillors in Britain suggest, as shown in Table 8.1, that, as a group, they are drawn from what are normally regarded as the more privileged sectors of the population. They are predominantly male, 74 per cent in 1999 (Municipal Year Book 2000: 1629) which marks only a slight movement in favour of equality since the 1980s. They also tend to be middle class, and middle aged and are better educated than the average population. This tendency confirms the findings of most surveys of political participation in liberal democracies.

To some extent, the apparent discrepancies between the population and the background of councillors is not as great as it may seem. Many Labour and some Conservative councillors who have middle-class jobs will have been brought up in working-class backgrounds and cannot be presumed to have lost touch with their origins. Despite this caveat, there are, nevertheless, still serious areas of under-representation in town halls. The numbers of women councillors are increasing but the day when there is approximately equal male and female representation seems still to be distant. Evidence is not readily available on the extent to which minority groups in Britain are represented on local authority councils. It is probable, however, that the proportion of black councillors is considerably lower than their numbers in the population (Barron, Crawley and Wood, 1991: 24).

The working environment of councillors

An important factor that may deter many would-be councillors is the rigour of the job. Once elected, councillors spend a considerable proportion of their time

Table 8.1. *Characteristics of councillors*

		%
Sex	Male	81
	Female	19
Age	21–34	7
	35–54	44
	55–69	39
	70 +	10
Education	Higher education	31
	GCSE, A level or equivalent	46
	No qualifications	23
Activity	Working full-time	65
	Working part-time	7
	Unemployed	2
	Retired	16
	Full-time caring for household	7
	Other	3
Occupations	Professional	9
	Employers/ managers	32
	Intermediate non-manual	18
	Lower non-manual	10
	Skilled manual	16
	Semi-skilled manual	4
	Unskilled manual	1
	Armed Forces and not known	11

Source: Widdicombe (1986) Vol II 20, 21, 28, 30.

on local authority work. In 1985 it was found that councillors were occupied with the work of their local authority on average for some 74 hours per month and office holders, such as committee chairs, an average 80 hours a month (Widdicombe 1986, Para. 6:81: 126) which, given an 8 hour working day is over 9 working days per month. Representatives to larger authorities work even longer hours. This amount of time is clearly possible for retired or unemployed persons, but becomes extremely arduous for anyone who has a full-time job or is caring for children or the elderly.

Amateurs or professionals?

Council work was until recently unpaid, although councillors received an attendance allowance and compensation for lost earnings. There were many complaints about the allowances system on the grounds that it deterred people in full time work from becoming councillors and did not reward sufficiently leaders and chairs who spent most of their time working for their authority. In order to resolve some of these problems, the Labour Government appointed the Robinson Enquiry (1977) which recommended an annual minimum payment for councillors with a higher sum to be paid for financial loss. The recommendation was not accepted, although the issue was revisited by the Widdicombe Report which suggested a flat-rate salary for councillors, although the amount would vary according to the type of authority, and that special allowances should be paid to 'key' councillors.

A system of payment for councillors has subsequently been devised based on an annual allowance with further sums payable for committee responsibilities. Initially the maximum allowance was set by the Government, but since 1995 local authorities themselves determine how much should be received by their members. The 2000 Local Government Act allows payments to some leading councillors to be pensionable. Most authorities have consequently substantially increased the payment to councillors. Sheffield City Council, for example, in 2001 provided each councillor just short of £8,000 as an allowance with extra payments being made to members with responsibilities ranging from a further £2,000 to £13,000 for the leader. It became in the 1990s possible for a leading councillor to secure a living wage, although the resultant standard of life was still not what would normally be expected from someone with responsibility for an organisation employing several thousand workers. It will be expected that, with the adoption of cabinet government, the members of the executive will be mainly professional councillors and it is even more probable that all directly elected mayors will be full-time salaried politicians. Nevertheless, for the majority of backbench councillors, financial rewards will be small and they will still be in work, be retired or rely on the earnings of their wives or husbands.

Even before these changes to councillors' remuneration, there were professional councillors. The demands made on the leaders of a city council are such that it would be difficult to undertake the task and, at the same time, seriously be involved with another profession. The restructuring of the policy process has, in part, been motivated by the argument that if substantial power were given to a small group of local authority policy makers, they could be paid substantially for their work and involve themselves full time on local authority work. It is also hoped that higher salaries and greater responsibility will also attract better qualified candidates to these positions. However, it remains to be seen how far these hopes can be realised particularly when the lot of most councillors will be to remain poorly paid part-time politicians serving as rather weak petitioners to the small coterie of powerful professional local politicians on behalf of their constituents.

Training

Not only do councillors receive little financial reward for their efforts, they also are generally ill-prepared for their work. There is no system of formal, nationally established training for councillors. This may be argued to be undesirable since it could be feared that any compulsory training scheme might deter would-be candidates and more seriously be a means whereby ideological values and assumptions about the role of local authorities were inculcated into otherwise open minds. However, it is equally a matter of concern if local councillors have little idea as to their legal status, the structure of the local authority and of some of the basic technical issues that may confront them in committees. In some large authorities the political parties attempt to rectify this problem through careful sifting of candidates and by organising training courses for candidates to ensure they are aware of the basic structure and organisation of their local authority.

> Although little training is provided for British councillors, this situation is little different from other liberal democracies where it is also rare for newly elected councillors to gain a formal grounding as to their duties or the workings of a local authority. Generally, it is often a function of party membership that apprenticeship in local campaigning provides intending local representatives with the practical education necessary to be a councillor.

Apart from this rather sporadic element of basic training, councillors receive few opportunities to gain more specialised understanding of the operation of the services which they are required to govern. On occasion, a councillor may secure funds from his committee to attend conferences or short courses organised by a professional body or college into some new technical innovation or change in legislation. In general, however, local councillors are expected to find out how their authority operates and the requirements and potential of their technical services through their own and unaided initiative. Many will, therefore, be educated as a result of personal, and on occasion, painful experience, through talking to fellow councillors, and probably, most extensively as regards technical issues, from officers of the council.

Political ambition or civic duty?

The motive for becoming a councillor will rarely be for immediate financial gain and perhaps more frequently to take on a worthwhile task outside a dull job or in retirement, but for many it is also for the pursuit of political power. It is not infrequently alleged that any prominent councillor is motivated by the thought of becoming an MP rather than serving his locality, perhaps eventually emulating the Prime Minister, John Major, who was once a London Borough councillor. J.S. Mill (1975: 379–80) argued that this was a highly creditable motive and that service in local government was a valuable training ground for national politicians. It is, of course, difficult to ascertain how many councillors harbour thoughts of political progress, but it is undoubtedly the case that many of the most active and prominent council leaders have an eye on a national political career.

> It is unfortunate that the nature of the British political system, contrary to France, makes local government service a stepping stone, rather than an addition, to a role in national politics. A political structure that more closely integrated local and national politics might not create tensions between service to the locality and to the nation.

Whilst the desire for a political career may motivate some ambitious councillors, their aspirations are usually framed in local terms. The parochial politician is often concerned to genuinely aid his community and provide himself with a worthy purpose, at the same time as helping others. Many local politicians still believe in ideals of service to the community. For some councillors labouring in menial jobs, the responsibilities provided by council work stretch their abilities and interests way beyond what they could have received from a less political life. These motives may be self-interested, but are rightly self-interested, since they are motivated not only towards self-fulfilment, but the achievement of a better life for others.

The competence of councillors

It is argued that many of the ills of local government stem from the quality of councillors, 'people of such modest abilities . . . controlling such large organisations' (Henney 1984: 326). This view has a long pedigree. J.S. Mill wrote in 1861 of the 'low calibre of men in local government'. Dame Evelyn Sharpe, as Permanent Secretary to the MHLG, mourned the absence of councillors 'from business, from industry, from agriculture, from the professions' (Clements 1969: 14). This long-established view was one of the factors behind the pressures to reform local government structures that culminated in the Redcliffe-Maud Commission and the 1972 Local Government Act. It was hoped that by reducing the number of councils and therefore the number of councillors, local government would be served by more competent members. Such hopes do not appear to have been realised by official circles. The Audit Commission believes

> that a reduction in the number of elected members would be desirable, combined with an enhancement of their terms of service. Without such a change the worrying reluctance of well-qualified citizens to serve as elected members will grow and councils will increasingly face rapid turnover of young and inexperienced members. (1988: 9)

This attitude has, as indicated earlier, also been a significant factor motivating the Blair Government's restructuring of local decision making.

Given the demographic data on the background of councillors outlined in Table 8.1, it appears that arguments on the quality of councillors must revolve around judgements of value rather than demographic fact. Councillors clearly are drawn from what are popularly regarded, as the better strata of society, are better educated and have more prestigious jobs than the majority of their electors. A naive proponent of representational democracy could argue strongly that this data suggests that councillors, as a group, are inadequate since they do not mirror the populations they serve.

The source of the established complaint concerning the quality of councillors has its roots in utilitarian theory and, in particular, the writings of J.S. Mill. Liberals turned to democracy with some reluctance, since they feared what Mill described as the tyranny of the majority. There was, they felt, a serious danger that the uneducated masses would overrule wiser counsels of the more educated and perceptive few. In countries in a state of barbarism where they could discern none of the cultured values of Western civilisation, some form of benevolent despotism was the only answer. Mill, and many of his fellow liberals, were sufficiently confident in levels of education in Britain to believe that in a democracy the masses would select the better educated and intelligent to positions of power. He would not be disappointed as far as central government is concerned.

The reasons for the disappearance of the notable from local politics has been analysed in Chapter 6. The nineteenth century roots of the critique of councillors lie in distaste for parish government, but more recently, it is an expression of concern over the departure of capitalist elites from local government and their replacement by labouring stock. The complaints concerning the unsatisfactory quality of councillors must be viewed in the light of the consequent development of central government's ethos of stewardship towards local authorities. Absent from these criticisms of the quality of councillors is any thought for the role of a councillor as a community representative. The humble parochial councillor who is concerned to articulate the worries and complaints of her or his constituents is not to be despised. Many grievances concerning local people can be forestalled through their timely intervention. Indeed, it may even be tentatively suggested that some of the violent tensions that disfigure present-day society, from race riots to child abuse by parents housed in appalling conditions, could be assuaged if there were more, rather than fewer, councillors who could be closer to their electorate and more capable of dealing with their needs and complaints.

The criticism of the quality of local councillors is also dangerous, since it implies a serious critique of democracy. If councillors are of poor quality, then this must be a reflection of the choice of local people who must therefore appear to be unfit to make informed political decisions. In essence, it is a class-based critique which Stanyer rightly berates as

> impertinent, because it tells people what they ought to value, and undemocratic, because it denies that local elections should fulfil the role ascribed by the system of government to them. (Stanyer 1976: 278)

Further reading

The role of local parties is considered most fully by Gyford and James (1983), whilst Bulpitt (1967) still has considerable relevance and reference can usefully made to the Widdicombe Report's (1986) deliberations on this area, especially research Volume II on councillors. Hall and Leach (2000) produce useful case studies of conflict within local Labour Parties and conclusions on the relationship between district Labour Parties and the Labour groups.

One of the most recent studies of the working conditions of councillors is provided in Barron, Crawley and Woods (1991) and there is also much of value to be found in the Widdicombe Report (1986)

The study of councillors, officers and interest groups is particularly enhanced by community studies of local government that cut across many themes and issues. These studies are often easily read and enjoyable. Among studies of Britain, an early but excellent study is Birch (1959) which looks at a the rather non-political small town of Glossop. Another influential early study is Bealey, Blondel and McCann (1965) which looks at Newcastle-under-Lyme. Perhaps the most important British studies are Dearlove (1973) on Kensington and Chelsea, and Newton's (1976) study of Birmingham, which has a clear theoretical interest in democratic theory. Lee (1963) is a valuable study of the decline of notables in county government and more recently Goss (1988) considers the rise of the Labour Party in Southwark. Other interesting studies include Hampton (1970) on Sheffield and, from a disgruntled right-wing perspective, Green (1981) on single partly politics in Newcastle-upon-Tyne.

9

Bureaucracy and employees

The size of local authorities and the diversity of their tasks ensure that in comparison with most private sector organisations in Britain, local government is big business. Birmingham City Council spent £1,977 million in the financial year 1999/00. The Chief Executive has an exacting and powerful position with a capacity to influence greatly the social and economic development of an area of over one million inhabitants. He is paid accordingly a little over £100,000 per year, although few in the private sector may consider this is appropriate to the responsibilities incurred by the post.

Since local authorities in Britain are very large relative to those of other liberal democracies, they are much more complex bureaucracies and employ far more staff than in most local authorities in other countries. The small communes of France may have very few if any workers, as many of their services will be contracted out to private companies. Similarly a small United States city with a population of a thousand or less may employ a police chief and a deputy and perhaps a clerk and a few workmen, but rely mainly on contractors to undertake their tasks. However, in large cities or the state governments, the number of employees and complexity of the bureaucracy may be as equally large and labyrinthine as in Britain.

The structure of the local government service

The local government service will inevitably attract controversy, given its size and diversity. It is not a unified service in that each local authority appoints its own workforce and there is therefore no national employing organisation. In 1999, British local authorities excluding the police employed nearly 1,743,000 people (Office for National Statistics, 2000a). This extensive service encompass numerous skills and professions and includes several occupations such as

138

teachers, traffic wardens or probation officers who are not always thought of as local government employees.

Despite its diversity, the local government service has been based on several traditional understandings. It is divided, like the British army, into officers and the other ranks. The officers have white collar jobs and are considered to be middle class or upper working class. The manual grades are blue collar, working class, involved in one of the many skilled or unskilled labours of local government. The officers start work at 9.00 in the morning and go home around 5.00 in the afternoon, if not employed on flexitime, where, within prescribed limits, they can set their hours of work. Manual workers, unless on a round the clock shift rota will tend to begin work at 8.00 a.m. and end at 4.00 p.m. enjoying fewer holidays, generally lower pay and poorer working conditions than officers. Between the officers and the manual workers is a considerable coterie of clerks and typists who enjoy officers' conditions of work but not their salaries.

There are also sharp horizontal divisions among local authority employees, who are usually not transferable to other departments. Officers tend to be specialists, qualified and trained specifically to undertake the work of their department. Thus, chief education officers began their careers as teachers, directors of social services must be qualified social workers and chief constables began their working lives as police cadets. This feature of the local government service contrasts sharply with the generalist ethos within the higher levels of the civil service which is based on the belief that general administrative competence is more crucial than specialist knowledge. The specialist statistician, economist or engineer is kept in a compartmentalised hierarchy within the civil service and is not usually called upon to undertake leadership and policy-making roles at the higher levels of the organisation. At this level, a broad-minded intelligent administrator is considered to be essential to put specialist interests within a wider social and political context. The specialist is on tap but not on top.

The specialist, as opposed to generalist, structure of the local government service emerged in the nineteenth century and is in part a reflection of the technical tasks performed by the local government system. In its formative years, the local government hierarchy included specialist chief medical officers who had to be qualified doctors and borough surveyors who needed to be qualified engineers. However, the division is to a considerable extent engineered by central government. In as much as the value of local government to the centre was to ensure that detailed managerial and technical tasks were implemented to suit central needs, the proper functionaries to carry out these tasks were technicians rather than general administrators with a policy advisory role. This ethos was then conveyed through the then existing central-local links in the late nineteenth century and later imposed by statutory demands which required certain functions to be filled by professional qualified personnel.

A further division among local authority staff is the distinction between professionals who work in the field, providing services directly to the public, and those who work largely in the town hall or its satellite offices, undertaking tasks that service the needs of the local government system. The outworking professionals who include school teachers, social workers, fireman and policemen and women may often pay little attention to their status as an employee of local government and feel that their allegiance is, respectively, to a school or a police division rather than the town hall and its councillors. Although these field workers are part of the local government system, their working conditions often have little or nothing to do with what goes on in the town hall. These issues are determined at a national level through bargaining between local authority associations, trade unions and the government. Internal administrators such as auditors, solicitors or council tax clerks will, on the other hand, feel themselves closely concerned with the politics and society of town or county hall. Their working practices will bring them into close contact with the operations of the local authority and, whilst their rates of pay may be determined by national negotiation, their chances of promotion and better working conditions will require them to have good friends among chief officers or councillors.

Management and leadership

Within each sector of local government there are numerous stratifications that determine the status of personnel and their attendant pay and conditions. The typical ranking for non-technical and professional staff working in general administrative or managerial roles is illustrated in the following list.

- Chief Executive . . . Chief Officer to the Authority
- Chief Officer . . . Head of a Department
- Deputy Chief Officer
- Assistant Chief Officer
- Principal Officer
- Senior Officer
- Administrative Officers
- Clerical Officers

The chief executive and senior officers

The most senior position in the local government bureaucracy, following the recommendations of the Bains Report in 1972, is the chief executive of the authority. The post strengthened the powers held formerly by the town clerk or county clerk who was, as the most senior legal officer, usually but not always regarded as the senior officer for the authority. The town clerk did not, however, normally have direct line management control over other chief officers. The post of chief executive, at least in theory, established an undisputed head of the local government service in each local authority, to whom all officers outside the police and fire services would be responsible.

The chief executive is appointed by the senior councillors and in the new structure by the elected mayor with the help of his or her cabinet or by the leader and his or her cabinet. In consultation with senior councillors, the chief executive will then have a strong voice in appointing the senior officers in charge of each particular service department. In arrangements where a directly elected mayor appoints a city manager, who effectively has the chief executive role, the appointment of the chief officers will largely be the manager's responsibility.

In most European countries there is a post equivalent to the chief executive heading the administrative system. In the United States, the city manager usually takes this role. However, in France, Italy and Spain, the second tier of government is run by the centrally appointed civil servant, the prefect. In Ireland, the central government rather than local councillors appoints the chief executives of its local authorities.

As the senior officer of the authority, the chief executive will usually be instrumental in determining the management structure of the authority, although his or her ideas will require the approval of the senior councillors. It is expected that the chief executive will preside over a management team of senior officers, who would include the treasurer, who is the head of the local authority's financial services and usually the head of personnel/human resources and the heads of major services such as housing and education. In recent years, many local authorities have restructured their management arrangements to create smaller senior management teams in which a few very senior officers co-ordinate policy over a range of services. Thus, the Executive Board of, for example, Kirklees MDC, comprises the chief executive and three executive directors who strategically guide a range of portfolios such as leisure and education.

Chief executives are increasingly being seen as managers of large bureaucratic organisations who have a role in steering the policies of the authority to create a uniform strategy that brings together the disparate elements of the local authority, but also to forge partnership links with other agencies involved in local governance. The chief executive may, therefore, be the key leader in ensuring the enabling strategy for the local authority (Norton 1991). The position is, however, still predominantly staffed by individuals who have risen through the ranks of local government rather than through other local governance agencies, the civil service or the private sector. Norton in 1991 (152–5) found that the predominance of lawyers holding the old position of town clerk had not been fully extinguished as more chief executives (43 per cent), came from the legal professions than any other background. However, the post is not now a preserve solely for lawyers and is likely to be increasingly occupied by managers from a wide range of professional backgrounds.

Rank and file

Below the level of senior officers, the administrative staff of most local government departments are graded as indicated in the list above (p.140) according to a structure devised, initially in the 1930s, in what were known as the Whitely Councils, through negotiations between the trade unions and representatives of the local authorities. Within each grade are numerous scales of remuneration and status that form endless sources or argument, grievance, elation and gossip in the daily soap operas of local government service. Other local government employees such as teachers, the police and fire officers are governed by separate scales of remuneration developed by negotiating committees for each service composed of the appropriate trade unions or professional bodies representing these particular careers and suitable representatives of the local authorities. Manual staff, similarly, negotiate their career structures through joint trade union-local authority committees, although the differing circumstances and requirements of individual local authorities leads to much local bargaining on regrading and local working practices.

Although the local government service is not a national service, in that, unlike the civil service, there is no one employer for local government workers, there is, nevertheless, considerable standardisation in the pay and conditions of service in local authorities as a consequence of the influence of central government. Teachers, for example, are paid standard rates agreed by a national negotiating body made up of teachers unions and local authority representatives. The negotiating committee can, however, only recommend increases in teachers' salaries, which is the largest single item of any county council budget, if the government agrees to provide the extra grant income to pay for the rise. In effect, therefore, teachers, or similarly the salaries of lower grade staff or manual employees, are determined as much by a government confronting trade unions as by the local authorities themselves, who may become impotent bystanders in trials of strength between national trade unions and central government.

Professionalism

The world of many local authority officers is circumscribed not only by their position within the hierarchy of the authority but also by their profession. These are organisations composed of members who consider that they have common skills and interests. They behave in some senses like trade unions in that they safeguard the quality standards of their members work, although they may not necessarily be concerned with negotiating wage levels or conditions of service. The more powerful professional groups such as the British Medical Association, however, effectively take on this role. In other respects, their influence may exceed some of the wildest ambitions of trade unions in determining work practices. A professional association that achieves widespread recognition can be accepted as a self-regulating guardian of entry into, and conduct within its sphere of labour.

> The role of professionals is less prominent in may European States, where smaller authorities, such as the French commune, leave many basic tasks to the mayor. More specialist legal or technical help within a commune may be provided by the bureaucracy headed by the departmental prefect, who is a civil servant controlling a considerable bureaucracy of civil servants trained, through the civil service, in particular specialisms. In Italy until recently, many local officials owed their position as much to political contacts rather than professional training. In the United States professionalism established outside a civil service framework resembles more the British pattern and city managers themselves form an established professional group.

Many senior positions within local authorities are only open to members of specified professional associations. The most influential professions ensure that anyone practising in its area of competence has been trained to standards that it considers acceptable. The influence of the association may then continue throughout an officer's career. The profession will hold regular conferences and produce newsletters to keep their members up to date with the latest developments relevant to their work. The strongest professional associations establish detailed codes of practice for the benefit of their members and any officer who strays from the security of these commandments may be liable to serious criticism if not disciplinary procedures.

CIPFA is an example of a powerful profession within local government which can be assured of a near monopoly on all senior financial posts in local government. Long-standing practice, reinforced since 1989 by legislation, requires that the chief financial officer of a local authority must be a professionally qualified accountant. CIPFA is the accountancy association recognised by local government, as it is concerned primarily with the public sector. To become an officer of any importance in a county or district treasurer's department it is necessary to have taken a series of professional examinations set and marked by representatives of this association. For local government finance officers, the several volumes of CIPFA work practice, a document continually updated by the professional body, is their constant companion, at least in the work place. Since senior members of a professional body are likely to be influential members of promotion panels, career advance will also be influenced by the concerns of the professionals. With its headquarters in London, senior officers of CIPFA will be asked to advise not only local authorities but also central government on issues of public accountancy.

Given the importance of professional bodies, control over these organisations can assume important consequences for local government. In theory, professional associations are democratic societies whose members vote for a council or delegate conference to serve as its governing body. As the delegate meeting is usually too unwieldy to meet frequently, an executive will be elected to deal with policy issues in between the meetings of the sovereign body. Crucial to the operation of a large professional association will however be its elected officers and senior professional staff. The senior officers of an association will be elected by the membership and be recognised as being among the pre-eminent authorities in their field. In associations with a specifically local government remit, senior members will usually be chief officers of major local authorities.

In addition to the elected officers, an association will appoint a secretary or an equivalent officer who will be the head of a small team of professional servants to the association. Although subject to the policy of the association, the professional staff may be able to exert a powerful presence within the organisation and their general secretaries can sometimes be seen by the public as their principal spokesperson. Noel Hepworth, a former Director of CIPFA is, for example, the author of one of the most authoritative textbooks on local government finance (Hepworth 1984). Recruitment to full-time posts in professional associations can be through a slow process of rising through the ranks, but often the highest posts are awarded to individuals who hold senior professional appointments, for example, in a local authority.

Although some professional bodies may appear to be present at the birth and death of a local government officer's career, the extent to which they exert an influence over their members varies widely. Whilst some professional associations, such as the Law Society, which regulates solicitors, or CIPFA, have an effective monopoly over entry into their area of expertise, others have only some of the attributes of the favoured few. In certain sectors of local authority work, membership of the professional body can be a distinct advantage, but is not essential. Officers in housing departments may be members of the Institute of Housing, but membership of the organisation is not vital for promotion, since members of other professional groups such as the Royal Institution of Chartered Surveyors can be employed as housing managers. Laffin (1986) charts the slow and painful moves towards recognition of the Institute of Housing which, although established in the 1930s to co-ordinate the work of senior officers in local authority housing departments, has never attained the status of the most powerful professions.

Some local government posts are scarcely touched by organised professionalism. The relatively new, but expanding, sector of economic development has recruited personnel from a wide variety of backgrounds including experienced industrialists, social economists and town planners. There is no set qualification or examinations necessary for obtaining posts in this field and there are only the glimmerings of co-ordinated organisation among economic development staff. Another more established area, municipal catering, has developed its own association to represent members interests, but the organisation does not include the majority of officers working in this field and cannot impose its rules and standards on local councils.

Trade unions

Local government is a heavily unionised organisation and almost all levels of the service are represented by at least one and, in several areas, a veritable bouquet of trade unions. Manual workers in local government who have no professional bodies to serve their interest are particularly reliant on their trade unions to safeguard their working conditions. There are three principal unions representing these workers, the General, Municipal and Boilermakers Union (GMB) formed from the amalgamation of several smaller unions, UNISON and the Transport and General Workers Union (TGWU). Most manual grades such as refuse collectors, parks attendants or caretakers will join one of these unions, depending on individual preference or the number of fellow members in a particular department. Bus and van drivers will tend to opt for the TGWU. Some more specialised manual workers will, however, join the appropriate trade union dealing with their trade. Thus, builders will be members of the Union of Construction and Allied Trades and Technicians (UCATT) whilst a weights and measures technician may join Manufacturing, Science and Finance (MSF).

The clerical and officer grades were, until the 1970s, almost exclusively represented by the National Association of Local Government Officers (NALGO), although dissatisfaction with the nationally somewhat conservative demeanour of this Union led some junior officers to join either National Union of Public Employees (NUPE) or MSF. Unlike the unions for manual workers, NALGO was formed in 1906 as a very respectable association and it was not until 1964 that it recognised that its work lay in the same realm as manual workers and joined the Trades Union Congress (TUC). In conformity with a trend towards fewer but larger unions, NALGO merged in 1993 with NUPE and the health service union Confederation of Health Service Employees (COSHE) to form UNISON, now the largest trade union in Britain. The union represents white collar workers, not only in local government, but also the privatised utilities and the health service and continues the more militant tendencies of its parent organisations.

Local government manual trade unions have historically never been the most militant, reflecting a view that whilst work for the local council was relatively low paid, it represented a secure and socially respected job. The ethos of service before self and the honour of serving the community has, however, ceased to be widely cherished and also the security of employment is far more akin to that of the private sector than it was fifty years ago. Appeals to local government workers not to strike because of their service to the community could not easily be sustained when the gap between private and public sector became ever greater and the prestige of the service ever smaller. Local government workers during the 1970s and 1980s frequently spearheaded major strikes that had strong political implications. These included much of the industrial unrest in 1978 and 1979, christened by the press 'the winter of discontent', that did much to undermine the Callaghan Government and brought Mrs Thatcher to power.

The subsequent confrontation with trade unions by the Thatcher Government greatly reduced the influence of trade unions in general and those representing local authorities in particular. New legislation making it more difficult to call strikes, along with far higher levels of unemployment, ensured that many trade unions found little support among their workers for militant action. Within local government, the development of CCT ensured that blue collar unions had a further reason to avoid militant action, since they would run the risk that their local authority would lose the contract to supply a service and their members might not be re-employed by the new private sector contractor or, as is frequently the case, may be re-employed on even worse conditions of service. The process of contracting out has also tended to weaken union strength, as some private employers may be less inclined to recognise the trade unions accepted by the public sector, although such a trend is by no means universal (Doogan 1999).

Paradoxically, during the 1980s the white collar unions became more militant as conditions of pay and government support for public sector work seriously declined through the competitive individualist policies of the new-right Government. Values also changed, as local government began to attract radical and militant-minded graduates who saw public service as a career untainted with capitalist values and hence worthy of an uncompromising socialist. Some left-wing local authorities attracted as officers militant political activists who were not loath to turn against their political masters when they were forced to retrench their activities by the Government. However, in the 1990s with the introduction of CCT for many professional and clerical services and the decline of left-wing militancy, much of the white collar radicalism in some UNISON branches has melted away.

Training and socialisation

The professional associations have had major importance in many of the long-established spheres of management and service provision through their monopoly over recruitment and training in these fields. By the 1920s, almost all senior local government functionaries had joined the local government services from school at either fourteen or sixteen years of age and reached positions of influence through part-time study towards professional qualifications and practical experience of their work acquired in the workplace by 'sitting next to Nellie'.

In comparison with the senior levels of the civil service, the formal educational achievements of local government officers were until recently generally modest. Up to the 1950s, apart from the education service and medical officers, few local government officers were graduates. Most were recruited into a local government department after leaving school with acceptable General Certificate of Secondary Education (GCSE) ordinary or advanced level grades and set to work in junior capacities (Poole 1978: 150). If they showed any promise and ambition, their senior officers would enter them for appropriate professional qualifications and they would be expected to grind through several levels of a painstaking vocationally orientated courses leading to a professional qualification through either attendance at a further education college or late night sittings over a correspondence course. The curricula for most professional exams emphasised a need to acquire a meticulous grasp of facts and legal procedures rather than any ability to think innovatively. The emphasis on competence rather than understanding and innovative capacity within the new National Vocational Qualification (NVQ) qualification thus exerts a considerable attraction for more pedestrian local authorities.

The recruitment and training pattern reproduced the tradition that local government officers were specialists rather than generalists. Senior officer were usually well versed in the technicalities of their functions, but had no training in how to manage their department or appreciation of the political and social consequences of their work. In certain areas of activity, lack of social awareness has arguably had disastrous consequences. Had borough surveyors, planners and architects had greater understanding of social attitudes and values, they might not have so enthusiastically turned to high-rise housing developments. The emphasis on specialism has further serious implications in the wider context of the role of local government in the British polity since, as was argued earlier, it fits the system into the framework of stewardship, the implementation of centrally determined policy, rather than a culture that perceives local government as the legitimate representative of local interests.

The recruitment and training policies within local government were subject to scrutiny by a government enquiry published as the Mallaby Report (1967) at the time of a promised expansion in higher education. The Report argued that brighter potential recruits to local authorities would be attracted to universities and, from the lofty eminence of graduation, regard themselves as too well qualified for service in local government. In response to this suggestion, many local authorities began recruiting from universities and, twenty years later, the service has become a major source of graduate employment. The higher education sector also responded to the Mallaby Report by establishing a number of public administration degrees within polytechnics to provide graduates with a generalist approach to service in the public sector. Birmingham University formed the Institute for Local Government Studies (INLOGOV) to provide postgraduate training for senior local government staff. Despite these moves towards graduate recruitment, professional training remains a crucial step for progression to senior posts in many public sector specialisms and, for the most part, these courses still emphasise a factual and legalistic rather than imaginative approach. The rethinking of local government training of the 1960s led also to the creation, through the joint efforts of the local authority associations, of a training board to monitor and encourage vocational programmes by local authorities. Among its varied functions this organisation, currently named the Improvement and Development Agency (IDeA) tries to ensure that local authorities seriously promote the educational and training needs of their staff.

Management training

Although the Mallaby Report argued that generalist administrators should study courses such as public administration, based on a range of social science subjects, the impact of the Thatcher Government's emphasis on business efficiency and profitability has moved local government personnel departments to favour management training developed largely for private sector enterprise. Courses leading to a Master in Business Administration (MBA) have been particularly popular with aspiring senior managers in local government. The development of management training in local government is, at one level, to be welcomed as helping to secure more economic, efficient and effective service delivery. The innovation does, however, have serious limitations when it seeks solely to imitate training that seeks to sharpen the '3Es' of efficiency, economy and effectiveness cherished by private profit-making organisations. Such an approach recognises the 'price of everything and the value of nothing' by giving a limited appreciation of what generalism or efficient management entails without regard for the ethical, democratic and representational role of public service. Given the narrow curricula of most management education in Britain, the value of a generalist outlook is, once again, lost to the public service. The analysis of ethical, political and sociological problems that forms a basis for most public administration courses is not replicated in the study of business management in Britain (Kingdom 1986; Chandler 1988), although a successful manager and administrator must think about the social and ethical environment in which they work rather than simply about how to administer their tasks more efficiently.

The power of officers

The extent to which senior local government officers rather than the councillors determine the policy of their local authorities is a much debated subject. It has been argued by Patrick Dunleavy (1980) that some professional bodies representing local government officers are highly influential in determining local policy outcomes, but Laffin (1986) argues that, although some officers are certainly influential, many professionals have little impact on the policy process. It is a question with no set answer, since different local authorities will foster very different administrative cultures. Potentially, local government officers have a number of powers they can use to gain their own way, many of which are not unique to local government, but are available to any professional bureaucrat who is theoretically subservient to elected lay politicians.

Local government officers are full-time employees and therefore have more time than most councillors to devise policy and influence its implementation. A senior officer can spend many hours supported by subordinate staff drawing up a watertight report supporting his or her views, whereas a committee chair, who may have a full-time job in an unrelated field, will have scarcely the time even to read the final document. Officers are also specialists, more so than their civil service equivalents, and can argue strongly that a particular course of action is either imperative or unthinkable for technical reasons. Few councillors will, for example, be able to challenge an architect's report alleging that a building is unsafe due to the failure of concrete beams. Since local government officers are permanent employees protected by trade unions from arbitrary dismissal they can, on occasion, act with a measure of insubordination without much fear of adverse consequences. A decision of Sheffield City Council to ban corporal punishment in schools was undermined when, either deliberately or by error, officers informed schools that this was a policy for consideration by school governors and not a firm commitment of the local authority.

Whilst these resources of power are open to officers in most bureaucracies, the traditional structure of the local government system provides bureaucrats with further means of controlling their councillors. In contrast to civil servants who serve only the government, the local authority officer is a servant of the full council and not just its majority party. Thus, they advise not only committee chairs but any councillor, including the opposition spokesperson and can insist that information embarrassing to the party in power is made known to the opposition. The new executive arrangements for local government policy making will, however, tend to draw officers closer to the cabinet of the authority and, if opposition parties are excluded from this circle, they are likely to be less able to gain information from officers in their position as backbenchers. In the more adversarial climate of scrutiny committees, officers may be less inclined to reveal issues that the executive policy makers would prefer to be hidden.

In some circumstances, officers have a statutory duty to act contrary to the demands of their councillors. A chief executive and city or county treasurer must warn the full council if they are spending or raising funds illegally. Should they fail to provide such a warning and publicly repudiate the council's policy, these officers will be regarded as legally culpable for the decision as the councillors. The 1989 Local Government and Housing Act further entrenched these powers by requiring that some senior employees are designated as monitoring officers. These officers have a duty to inform all councillors and, in the case of financial issues, the district auditor if they believe a decision of the council will be unlawful or a case of serious maladministration.

The influence of councillors over their officers is further diminished by the networks linking professional interests within local government. Many local councillors will receive their understanding of the role of a department from professional officers and hence, like the officers themselves, be highly susceptible to receiving as gospel the values according to a well organised professional body. A professional body may be so influential that it can persuade not only its members but the Government to accept its values. Patrick Dunleavy (1981) demonstrated that enthusiasm for high-rise tower blocks began within Royal Institute of British Architects, who infected not only local authority architects but also the senior civil servants in the MHLG with their enthusiasm. Government ministers consequently provided such generous offers of grants to build tall that councillors could not refuse, even though many may have in their bones had no wish to create such impractical and untraditional housing.

Limits to bureaucratic power

Although it is possible to pile argument onto argument in support of the power of chief officers, it is essential to keep many of these points in perspective. Councillors are not necessarily naive uncouth amateur politicians. Even in the 1930s, no one considered Herbert Morrison, the Leader of the London County Council who later became one of the most senior members of Attlee's Government, could be easily fooled by his senior officers. Local politicians tend to be better educated and informed than the general public and some will be able to devote many hours to local authority work. Although it is difficult to measure factors such as ruthlessness or cynicism, many councillors who reach the position of a committee chairman are not likely to be made of the stuff that accepts every advice tendered or is unwilling to accept a political fight if their personal views are opposed.

Simplistic assumptions about the power of professionals are now seriously outdated and may become even more redundant with the advent of cabinet government and professional elected mayors. The leaders of many of the larger city authorities and several of their committee chairman are effectively full-time councillors and spend probably more time on local authority work than their chief officers. Many councillors enter the local authority with some measure of professional expertise, given that a greater number of graduates and professionals are occupying council positions. Once on the council, members specialise and can within a few years achieve a considerable expertise for example, on housing matters or social services. Indeed, they may assume a role which, in central government, is argued to be an ideal administrative attribute for a permanent secretary, the capacity to intelligently grasp the implications of technical knowledge and relate this to the wider needs of community and the prevailing political climate.

The advent of senior professional local politicians may well lead to the majority of councils to operate rather like central government in Whitehall, where a full-time secretary of state or the Prime Minister receives advice from an established permanent secretary. In local government, the relationship that develops between the leader or elected mayor and the chief executive or city manager can be supportive, but the two individuals may be in frequent conflict and the officer will be prepared to use his or her resources of biasing information, hiding awkward facts from the politician and acting without his or her consent that may typify, as in 'Yes Minister', difficult relationships between civil servant and politician. In local government, however, the politicians may have greater control than the government minister, as the local government profession lacks the prestige, resources and *éspirit d' corps* of the civil service and thus recalcitrant senior officers are more likely to be dismissed from office than awkward permanent secretaries.

The greatest policy tensions have emerged when a local authority changes its political control, leaving a cautious chief executive in charge of a radical policy or a radical officer stifled by conservative politicians. The new-right London Borough of Westminster obliged its Chief Executive to resign largely on account of his reluctance to endorse policies that are now subject to criticism from the press and the local authority auditors. Derbyshire County Council in its local socialist phase during the 1980s similarly forced the departure of senior officers who had policy differences with the council leaders.

In the United States, city managers are very vulnerable to sacking by the mayor and senior councillors and have a tenure in office not unlike that of a football coach. If this pattern were replicated in Britain, elected mayors and leaders would normally have the final word on policy decisions. Frequently an American city manager who loses a job in one city gains re-employment in another and hence loss of a post is not necessarily the end of a career, so that confident city managers may not always worry to much about losing the mayor's confidence.

The relationship between a councillor and chief officer is ideally and in practice rarely an adversarial contest, with each side seeking to gain the advantage over the other. Committee chairs and their senior officers will usually be aware that they need to work in a close harmonious relationship using each other's abilities if they are both to extract the best possible results for their department. If a chief officer and his or her committee chair cannot agree on policy, then it is probable that their department will fail to develop convincing policies or be in a strong position to gain and defend its resource base. Because of the need for such a relationship, councillors usually try to ensure, when appointing a chief officer, that the incumbent will be politically attuned to the values of the local authority. The relationship between the councillor and chief officer can, therefore, at times be so close that it is not only impossible but rather meaningless to discern who actually devises policy initiatives. Laffin and Young (1990: 110–12) identify four roles that emerge from the accommodation of professional values to the differences in policy and management style in local authorities. These are controllers who are powerful figures determining a parsimonious and orderly operation of a department, enablers who, in contrast, use their expertise to facilitate the policy objectives of the politicians, professional advocates who seek to pursue the objectives associated with their profession and finally policy activists who are rarely appointed to senior posts and are professionals with a strong view of how they wish to shape the development of their local authority or department.

Since councillors have the ability, except perhaps in case of the chief constable, to appoint chief officers, they will often secure the degree of co-operation and ideological viewpoint from their leading professionals that they deserve. Local authorities can and often do select chief officers who are sympathetic to their political views. Conversely a committee chair who has no wish to radically overturn established policies will choose a chief officer who will take complete control of his or her department and maintain the generally conservative mainstream tenure of his profession. In many of the predominantly Conservative rural counties and districts, where councillors do not become involved in the day-to-day running of the authority, chief officers tend to be cautious managers of the authority's affairs. Apparent domination of a local authority by its officers may be fully acceptable to the councillors and is not necessarily a product of some victory for bureaucracy in an internecine strife between officer and councillor.

Bureaucracy in restructured local government

The role of local government officers has been subject to substantial change as local authorities have increased in size in the second half of the twentieth century. Rather than being highly respected professionals working, in may cases, in relatively small organisations, the local officer is now part of a large organisation steered as much by professional generic managers as by dedicated professionals. At the highest level of chief executive or the senior officer of a complex department, it is necessary to be a generalist who can co-ordinate many different professional interests and, consequently, adopt many of the characteristics of a politician. Professionals are increasingly becoming subservient technicians to advise not just the politician but also the public sector manager and therefore take a role that is perhaps analogous to the relationship in hospitals of the administrator and the medical consultants.

Following the 2000 Local Government Act, the professional faces a further upheaval in working relationships, although it remains to be seen how local authority bureaucracies will adjust to the change. Most challenging for officers will be the establishment of powerful full-time professional politicians, either as elected mayors or leaders and their cabinet colleagues, who will be a very different foil to professional values than were the part-time and often deferential councillors on a sub-committee of an authority. Senior officers will be required to work alongside politicians who will expect to be as much involved in the operation of the authority on a day-to-day basis as the professional bureaucrat. The senior officer will be required to work in partnership with a senior politician, but also become the advocate for both professional values and the needs of his or her staff. There may yet, however, be some authorities that adopt the mayor and city manager structure and should this framework emerge as a significant feature of local governance a rather different role for senior bureaucrats will have to emerge. Under such a framework there may emerge a cadre of well paid but vulnerable politicised general managers expected to secure, on pain of dismissal by the elected mayor, the performance standards for services that are required by central government through the best value framework.

Further reading

Basic factual information on the local government service is provided in K.P. Poole (1978), whilst Martin Laffin has provided valuable studies in the areas of professionalism (1986) and trade unions in local government (1989). Laffin and Young (1990) analyse the growth and development of professionalism, although it is too early to reflect on the consequences of executive government in local authorities. Doogan (1999) discusses the changes in local authority employment brought about by CCT. Norton (1991) provides an extensive survey of the changing role and background of Chief Executives. Dunleavy (1980) presents a challenging scenario on professionalism, which he extends in his study of high-rise housing (1981). There is also much information on local government officers in community studies.

10

Management and ethics

Local authorities have been shown in the last chapter to be big business. They have a large financial turnover, employ several hundred and in many cases thousands of workers who are responsible for providing important services to a large customer base. It can be argued that a business differs from a local authority in that it must make a profit, whereas a local authority can operate its services inefficiently and simply make up any shortfall through taxation. However, as will be discussed in this chapter, the days when this myth could be argued to have some substance are now long past. Local authorities are required to make a profit on some of their services and must for all their services ensure that, even if they do not make a surplus, they avoid a loss and can show that they are making the most efficient use of public resources.

A more substantial difference between private sector business and local government is the overall aim and objectives of each enterprise. Most private sector firms have as their principal mission the aim of making money for their shareholders and have responsibility to society in general only in so far as the pursuit of profitability does not damage public welfare and ethical codes. A local authority, however, not only must demonstrate it uses resources efficiently but also it must have as its mission the concern to care for the economic, social and environmental well-being of their community. As a democratically elected public organisation, the local authority is also subject to realising these goals in accordance with the wishes of the populations they serve. Local authorities must therefore perform a difficult task of both reconciling the need for business efficiency and effectiveness with the demand to improve the well-being of the community that they serve on a wide range of issues which may be difficult to balance and reconcile with one another. This chapter will discuss both the demands on local authorities to ensure efficient, cost-effective management and the corresponding pressures this requirement places on what are essentially democratic organisations.

Management pressures

There has not been a time during the last century when local government has not been subject to pressures to use its resources effectively. The requirement that local authority accounts are subject to audit emerged in the early nineteenth century and by the 1850s the modern structures for local governance had to be careful to account for how they had spent the money they received in taxation and grants. By the 1950s, however, the financial probity of local authorities may have been of a generally high standard, but increasing concern was being voiced that money used by public bodies was being spent inefficiently.

By the 1950s, a new discipline of management as an applied social science had taken root in the private sector. Its classic founding theories were developed early in the twentieth century by businessmen such as F.W. Taylor and Henri Fayol, who believed that it was scientifically possible to produce greater efficiency and profitability in private businesses. These ideas led to the generation in the 1920s of time and motion work-efficiency studies and the acceptance of hierarchical line management, in which each individual was given a specific, clearly established range of duties to be undertaken under the supervision of a higher manager. These ideas were never wholly acceptable to the public service values of either the civil service or local government in Britain which were much influenced by the management theories that argued that the volume of output was not the only measure of the worth of strategies for the delivery of public services (Thomas 1978). Democratic theory argued that should a local authority waste money through inefficient management, aggrieved local citizens would replace poor councillors with a more effective team. There was, however, little faith in democratic safeguards when local government was dominated by nationally based political parties, whose councillors were elected less on local issues and more on the back of national swings favouring the major parties.

These views crystallised in the 1970s into a strong new-right critique of the efficiency of public services that greatly influenced the Conservative Government and also had sufficient resonance among voters to secure eighteen years of new-right Government. There was a growing popular disillusion with local government. It was widely believed that local authorities employed too many workers who had too little work and were also appointing far too many officers to check on the activities of their subordinates, creating a framework that stultified innovation and change.

One of the most trenchant critiques of the efficiency of the public sector that swept into Conservative Party thought stems from the ideas of a group of United States economists who are seen as the founding members of public or rational choice theory. They argue that it must be assumed that individuals are rational and seek to maximise their own self-interests. Politicians and public officials, therefore, have a vested interest in building bureaucratic empires that are far larger and more costly than are needed to provide a necessary public

service (Niskanen 1973; Niskanen 1973a; Tullock 1975). This is partly a consequence of the rational self-interest of individual bureaucrats who gain better
pay, chances of promotion and personal aggrandisement through the growth
of the public sector. The theory also suggests that government bureaucracies
expand in size because politicians win votes by promising greater expenditure
and thus build up increasingly large financial commitments which they find
impossible to reduce. There is, therefore, a ratchet effect of incrementally
increasing budgets. Local government, as a public organisation, will therefore
provide services with less efficiency than the private sector which is exposed to
market competition and forced to give value for money. The crude nature of
democracy, requiring voters to support packages of policies rather than express
opinion on individual programmes, prevents the ballot box from becoming a
successful device for restraining mismanagement.

The rational choice critique of bureaucracy was directed towards public
management in general rather than local government specifically, but several
writers, including the former Secretary of State for the Environment, Nicholas
Ridley, have applied these ideas specifically to local government (Henney 1984;
Ridley 1988). The solution to enlarged self-interested local bureaucracy was
the 'enabling authority'. As outlined in Chapter 3, local government should not
build huge bureaucracies to deliver services, but contract out its services to
private companies. The enabling authority has a few councillors and senior officers responsible for determining public needs and drawing up, awarding and
monitoring contracts with private sector bodies who will supply these services.
The local authority is therefore a body purchasing services for the public and as
such needs only a small number of largely white collar staff.

A central pillar of enabling concept as established by the Thatcher and Major
Governments was the principle of CCT. Legislation required local authorities to
draw up contracts as purchasers of services that they required for their community and then were compelled to invite sealed bids from any organisation
that wished to operate the service, including not only private firms but the local
authority's itself. The contractor who agreed to fulfil the local authorities
requirements at the lowest price had to be awarded the contract. Initially established to cover manual tasks such as refuse collection, the Major Government
widened the framework to encompass professional roles such as legal and
financial services, but before contracts in these sectors were fully developed the
Government fell and the CCT regime was replaced by the Best Value strategy of
New Labour.

Considerable empirical research, particularly in the United States and to a
lesser extent in Britain, has attempted to verify the validity of the public choice
critique of bureaucracy and the value of enforced competition to ensure service
improvement. George Boyne's (1998) study of this research found, however,
that whilst the majority of studies suggested competition saved costs and
improved technical efficiency of service delivery, most studies were flawed, in
that they did not take into account wider considerations of the cost of establish-

ing a competitive framework or the extent to which any savings were actually retained by the local authority. He concludes there is as yet no convincing evidence to support the public choice case. However, adoption of this strategy probably has more to do with ideological favouritism towards private sector provision and lessening government intervention in economic provision than the pursuit of better and more efficient public services.

New public management

In addition to the creation of the enabling authority, local governments were urged to adopt styles of management for those services that remained under their control which followed what were argued to be established techniques in use in the private sector. Christopher Hood (1991: 4–5) provides one of the most referenced definitions which has been refined by R.A.W. Rhodes (1991: 548) as

1 a focus on management, not policy and on performance appraisal and efficiency;
2 the disaggregation of public bureaucracies into agencies which deal with each other on a user pay basis;
3 the use of quasi markets and contracting-out to foster competition;
4 cost cutting;
5 a style of management which emphasises *inter alia* output targets, limited term contracts, monetary incentives and freedom to manage.

The concept involves a number of differing management issues and techniques, many of which require grafting newer ideas onto older practices. Thus, as Vivien Lowndes (1999: 37), shows, within local government 'management change is a non-linear process, involving continuities between old and new processes, movements forward and backwards and change at different levels'. Local authorities that grasped some of these ideas not only sought private contractors to manage many of their services, but also established internal structures to ensure that where possible a small group of staff devise service specifications as purchasers/customers for a team of officers who implement the service within tight budgetary demands set by the purchaser team. The London Borough of Brent restructured its administration to reflect a private business structure by replacing large bureaucratic departments with smaller business units which were required to trade as separate enterprises by selling their services to other business units that compose the authority. Local authorities are also encouraged to look at many of their activities as potentially profit-making businesses. The City of Bath, for example, can generate considerable income from tourist charges to historic monuments and ensures that the managers responsible for these facilities provide monthly information on turnover and profit.

Considerable impetus behind the new public management approach in Britain stemmed from the influential study of public sector management in the United States, *Reinventing Government* (1992) by Osborne and Gaebler. They suggested that public sector bodies should be operated as a business and praised those that made money from entrepreneurial risk taking. Such action whilst possible for many United States cities is generally ruled out by existing legislation in Britain that restricts local authorities from profitable trading unconnected with the central duties of a local authority.

Best Value

The Blair Government, rather than turning its back on the values that under-lie new public management (NPM) and CCT, has evolved these initiatives into a strategy for securing better standards of service provision which they have labelled Best Value. The completed blueprint for this strategy was announced in the 1998 White Paper and became legislative reality in the 1999 Local Government Act.

The central principle behind the idea of Best Value is that local authorities should set, or have set for them, performance targets for the efficient delivery of services and be required to maintain these standards or lose the capacity to run the service. The performance targets are many and varied, depending upon the particular service concerned. In some sectors such as education these are set by the national government and comprise, for example, targets for the numbers of children at key stage 2 of the national curriculum achieving an acceptable grade in their standard attainment tests for literacy or numeracy. Whilst the government sets the standards for sectors such as education or social services, the standards for many less crucial services are established by the local author-ities themselves and will encompass factors such as the extent to which council houses are fully occupied or the administration costs for dealing with each housing benefit claimant. The targets, although set by the local authority, will have a generally common structure, so that it is possible, for example, for local authority attainment on refuse collection to be compared with data available for a neighbouring authority of similar size. Thus there is effectively a compet-itive element built into the strategy to ensure that authorities which deliver ser-vices at a lower level of efficiency or quality than other comparable authorities can be identified and pressured into improving performance.

The appropriateness of the standards set by the authority, its attainment of the required targets and its strategy for dealing with failure to maintain the required level of performance are monitored by the Audit Commission, or in the case of some sectors, the appropriate national inspection agency; for education this is OFSTED. Should a local authority fail to set or consistently attain accept-able standards in relation to a service, the Audit Commission or an agency such as OFSTED can, following a series of inspections, recommend to the government that the service to be taken over by another organisation. this could entail contracting out the service to a private sector business chosen by the government or to a neighbouring authority.

The Best Value strategy replaced the CCT regime established by the preceding Conservative Governments, but has not abandoned the view that many local services can best be supplied by the private sector. Local authorities are encouraged in the White Paper to develop partnerships with private sector bodies and other agencies in order to supply services as efficiently as possible. Demands that sealed bids should be made for contracts to run specific services and that the cheapest offer be accepted have been abolished and the local authority can accept or reject private contracts with reference to the quality, trustworthiness and effectiveness of the contractor as well as the price offered for the contract. Local authorities will not, however, so easily be able to revert to in-house service provision, as it may for example be impossible for them to provide efficient and cost-effective refuse collection services in comparison with a local authority that contracts the service to a large-scale refuse collection agency which can operate more efficiently through economies of scale.

Involving the citizen

An important factor in the development of Best Value targets is that they should be secured through widespread consultation and their performance monitored at least in part through measures of public support or criticism of the service. Many local authorities have anticipated the need to ensure better consultation with their community in order to monitor the effectiveness of their services and to rectify serious problems. Consultation by local authorities sparked off the Citizens' Charter initiative of John Major. York City Council and the Scottish Region of Lothian established schemes in which members of the public could phone officers if standards set by the authority were not met. The Government's Citizen's Charter initiative which required public bodies to establish standards of service provision and provide compensation for customers who did not receive the promised service was taken up fitfully by some local authorities but is now, at least as regards local government, incorporated into the Best Value idea and, therefore, made redundant as a strategy.

The means of ensuring citizens' views are incorporated into the standards set by local authorities and schemes to ascertain public opinion are now widely operated and have a considerable level of sophistication. Survey methods include regular consumer surveys of public attitudes to services, usually conducted on a regular basis by private polling agencies. Much praise has been lavished by the Minister for Local Government Hilary Armstrong on the use of citizens' juries, focus groups and similar exercises in consultation with selected members of the public. Such schemes enable citizens to discuss at some length with pollsters and sometimes officers and councillors of an authority, their opinions on services or unfulfilled needs that can be met by the local authority.

Decentralisation

Although the Blair Government has, with the aim of enhancing local democracy, enthusiastically changed the policy-making structures of local government, it has shown little enthusiasm for decentralisation of power, which is the most significant policy established by local authorities themselves to achieve this aim. Restructuring of the policy making and bureaucratic implementation of policy to decentralised area committees or teams of officers has been energetically pursued by a number of local authorities since the 1980s, but received little attention in the 1998 White Paper which commented that

> The Government wants all councils to consider how they can bring decision taking closer to the people – to make government easier to access and easier to understand. Decentralisation is a valuable way, but not the only way to achieve this. The Government will encourage councils to consider . . . whether such arrangements would be desirable in their political circumstances. (Para 3.52)

The 2000 Local Government Act subsequently provides for local authorities wishing to decentralise to establish area committees, which they were able to do prior to the Act, and little further encouragement for a strategy to ensure in such large authorities that decisions are made within communities.

Decentralisation has evolved into two interlinked but essentially separate strategies. On the one hand, some schemes are concerned to improve service delivery by empowering local managers and breaking down long bureaucratic chains of command that stretch, for example, from a small housing estate to the director of housing in the town hall. A frequent complaint from citizens is that bureaucracy is far too remote. Decisions on behalf of the members of the public take far too long to be made and get lost in a labyrinth of committees. A simple enquiry may result in a caller being passed through a bewildering chain of offices as members of staff may not know who is responsible for a particular task or believe the task is someone else's responsibility. A second element in some decentralisation strategies is to pass power from the town hall to the communities who are affected by relatively localised decisions.

> Decentralisation is not widely practised in European or the United States local government systems, largely because there is no need for such action, given that most local authorities have a community-based tier that effectively can represent a small community.

The managerial advantages of decentralisation became apparent in the 1960s with a number of housing and social services schemes that gave greater powers to local officers in the field. Walsall MDC succeeded in rescuing a number of decayed housing estates by establishing within them a local housing office equipped with the means to re-let and renovate vandalised property and to have on hand a neighbourhood housing officer with a social worker role to deal with problematic tenants. The scheme was, however, killed off largely on account of cost when the Conservative Party took control of the Council in 1982 (Seabrook 1984). Decentralisation was also pursued by a number of social service departments which in the 1960s developed a patchwork system of management in which small teams of social workers dealt with all the problems of a small community. This system, which was given official accolade by the Seebohm Report, was extended by some local authorities such as East Sussex to the extent that each area team had responsibility for its budget and working strategy, leaving the central officers to determine the overall framework of the system and monitor the progress of each patch.

Some of the ideas behind these strategies that concerned a single service have been followed in the 1980s by authorities wishing to decentralise a range of services. In Harlow and South Somerset, devolution of service delivery to area committees has been accompanied by a rationalisation in the numbers of staff at the centre, through the adoption of flat management structures in which the traditional departmental structure with its chief officers has been abandoned and three or four senior chief officers co-ordinate a much wider tier of heads of section, thus removing two or three tiers of senior management.

Schemes to decentralise management soon were linked with parallel arrangements to decentralise decision making. One of the pioneering authorities in establishing a decentralised structure as a central element in its organisation is the London Borough of Islington, which established an area housing and social work office within a quarter of a mile of every resident in the Borough. Policies on housing, the environment and some aspects of social care are decided in each neighbourhood by a committee of ward councillors and representatives from local interest groups meeting in public. Their policies are then implemented by the neighbourhood offices which are administered by a senior officer and his or her subordinate staff. The scheme has been much admired, apart from its considerable costs (Burns *et al.* 1994; Hodge 1988). Bedford County Council initiated a scheme in which they transferred some powers to larger town councils or consortia of parish councils. Perhaps the most ambitious essay in this field was developed by the London Borough of Tower Hamlets, which decentralised almost all its services by transferring their management, budgeting and many aspects of their policy making to seven neighbourhood councils. These councils not only implemented policy, but also made major political decisions, since neighbourhood policy was devised by the councillors elected within each of the seven areas. The scheme was established under a Liberal Democrat controlled council which allowed several of the neighbourhoods to be controlled by Labour Party members. However, once the Labour Party returned to power in the Borough in 1994, the experiment was brought to an end. Despite such setbacks most decentralisation schemes have continued to flourish and it was estimated in 1994 that over half the local authorities in England and Wales were involved in some form of decentralisation (Chandler *et al.* 1995).

It can be argued that some vaunted decentralisation schemes are in reality, devices to aid local politicians and officers overcome political or managerial difficulties than genuine attempts at deconcentration of power. It has been argued that decentralisation of social services in East Sussex was as much a means of resolving problems of control over field units in the Department that had inherited different working practices from the centre from the time when they were controlled by another local authority, prior to 1974 (Tree 1989). In some cases devolution schemes do not hand power to any obvious community. Sheffield, for example, prides itself on community housing and yet its area housing offices do not encompass natural communities, but extend over more than one electoral ward making them almost as a remote from individual citizens as a centralised town hall. Several schemes seem to have stalled on the problem of reconciling the need for local consultation with demands for cheaper and more efficient local administration. Birmingham City Council had ambitious ideas to establish decentralised parishes within the City but these arguably came to grief as councillors could not decide on the correct priorities for such a scheme.

Despite some problems, decentralisation remains an important initiative and, at a time when local authorities are getting ever larger, it is one of the few means to ensure that government at any level in Britain is in touch with communities. Given the problems, to be discussed in Chapter 13, of securing greater empowerment for communities under recent legislation, it is unfortunate that more government attention has not been directed to these schemes.

Post-Fordism

The trend towards creating smaller bureaucracies through privatisation and new management techniques has been argued to be part of a trend followed by states entering a post-industrial era. Writers such as Jessop (1988) suggest that capitalism is moving away from ever-larger industrial giants producing goods in bulk for a general market to smaller productive units geared to producing goods or services tailored, through advertising and research, to particular demands. These techniques cut down waste and oversupply and, by using small productive units, curtails the potential power of a large semi-skilled work force acting through trade unions. The term post-Fordism has been used to differentiate this new method of production from the system of mass production pioneered by the American car manufacturer Henry Ford. Stoker (1989) has applied this theory to help explain the development of local government management in recent years. If the theory is valid, local government will become smaller, at least in terms of its workforce, as many tasks are contracted out, whilst councillors and officers will be concerned to listen to their more pressing and articulate 'customers' and tailor their policies to their needs.

The theory clearly can help to explain some of the development occurring within the management of local government, although it seems less effective in explaining the attitude of Westminster and Whitehall to the overall structure of local government. Whilst local authorities may be decentralising services and improving techniques for customer care, the Government is currently fostering ever-larger local governments that will be further removed from the suggested pattern of small productive or servicing units tailored to the interests of particular groups of customers.

The ethical dimension

A criticism of NPM is that concentration on the 3Es of efficiency, economy and effectiveness plays no regard to a further and more important 'E' word, ethics. Any business, whether private or public, let alone a democratically elected organisation, must require its policies and the conduct of its policy makers and employees to be completely justified in terms of the established moral standards of the society in which it operates. Unlike its Conservative predecessors, the Blair Government cannot be criticised for ignoring this dimension of local politics within its reforms of the policy and management machinery of the system. The Government has established a range of new procedures to deal with ethically questionable practices in local authorities.

Corruption

The need to establish new arrangements for rooting out corruption within local authorities emerges from errors of the Major Government, which placed the issue of corruption in public life to the forefront of political debate, so that the issue could not be ignored by a successful political party in the 1997 election. Corruption has been endemic within local government although, given the numbers of councillors and local government personnel, is not a particularly widespread problem and was less of an issue in the 1990s than corruption among MPs and central Government.

In the 1970s there were, however, several well publicised and very serious cases of corrupt practice within local authorities. The most serious evidence of systematic malpractice came to light in the 1972 when a firm of architects created by John Poulson was subject to investigation due to bankruptcy. Enquiries revealed that Poulson had secured a large number of contracts with local authorities through advancing bribes, such as expensive holidays, to councillors and senior officers in a number of large authorities and also to some civil servants. Leading national politicians were also implicated in the scandal. The most high profile local authority miscreant was the then well known leader of Newcastle City Council, T. Dan Smith, who was a central figure in the Poulson corruption circle and was subsequently imprisoned for his complicity in such behaviour. The Poulson issue led to a Government Enquiry under Lord Salmon which, among its recommendations, suggested that councillors must declare any personal financial interest in matters being discussed by their authority and also enter their outside financial interests in a publicly available register.

The Poulson scandal did not mark the end of corrupt practices in local government. In the 1990s, the most sensational case involved Lady Porter, former leader of Westminster City Council, who was accused by the District Auditor of arranging the sale of council houses within the Borough so as to fortify the Conservative vote. The courts have so far upheld this ruling. Other major authorities have had their share of less-political scandal that has been more concerned with the Poulson style of gaining bribes for securing planning permission.

A measure of corruption in local government for political or personal ends is unfortunately likely to be endemic within a complex system. There are, however, several means to assuage corruption, such as independent scrutiny of accounts through the Audit Commission, the designation of Monitoring Officers, and the openess of the system to public and media scrutiny. Inevitable human failings and the impossibility of scrutinising every action will facilitate continued and for a time successful unlawful behaviour. However, the conduct of local authorities, business is not regarded as universally corrupt and mal-practice is the exception rather than the rule. The Salmon Enquiry observed that

> We have heard no evidence to give us concern about the integrity and sense of public duty of our bureaucracy, or to suggest that it is common for members of the public to offer bribes . . . in the day-to-day administration of central and local government . . . (1976, Para. 35: 11).

Corruption is endemic in European and United States local governments, at least as much as in Britain. Problems can range from the serious accusations that the President of France, Jaques Chirac, used his position as mayor of Paris to squirrel away funds to support his political party, to the established tradition of political favouritism being the basis for selection as a local government officer within Italy or in some cities of the United States.

Codes of ethics

The Blair Government has made provision in the 2000 Local Government Act to ensure a more clear and co-ordinated set of ethical rules to guide councillors and mayor. The Act allows the Secretary of State for the DTLR to establish a model set of ethical rules to be adopted by local authorities and requires each local authority to adopt the code with suitable modifications that may be necessary to relate to the individual circumstances of the authority. Each councillor must sign a declaration agreeing to abide by the code once it is adopted and if they refuse to accept the document they would lose their position on the authority. The Government propose that they will work closely with the LGA in devising the code, which will cover a wide range of issues including the councillors' duties to their constituents and the proper handling and stewardship of public funds. Local authorities will establish standards committees to develop their individual codes and monitor and discuss any possible breaches of its rules. The committees will include backbench councillors, but not members of council cabinets and must also include some members who have not been elected to, or work for, the local authority. Under earlier Acts, each local authority has to appoint monitoring officers, usually a very senior officer such as the chief executive, to review the conduct of councillors and officers and draw the attention of the Audit Commission and now the standards committees to failures to uphold the ethical code.

The development of the code and investigating cases which may have breached the code will be the work of a Standards Agency, which will have regional subgroups whose members are appointed by the government with the advice of the LGA. The Agency will have full-time investigatory officers who may look at accusations of dubious practice in detail and receive papers or call witnesses from local authorities to help with their deliberations. The Agency can also refer complaints to other investigatory bodies, such as the police or the Ombudsman. If the Standards Agency finds that there has been a breach of ethical codes, this will be reported to the monitoring officer of the local authority concerned who will put the issue to the authority's standards committee. The committee will have powers to censure or suspend the erring official or councillor.

Checks and balances

Liberal democratic theory requires not only that policy makers should be elected, but also that their decisions are subject to public scrutiny and comment.

Checks and balances are an element of the liberal democratic tradition, more honoured in the United States than Britain, where nationally no one segment of government has absolute power, but each element should be subject to checks from other independent sectors within the formal governmental system. In local government within the United States, such arrangements are established in systems where the mayor is elected separately from the council.

Compared with central government, the local political system in Britain is more effectively endowed with these attributes and the new structure of the local government system builds in an even greater measure of checks and balances than was already implanted into the system. It has been shown in the preceding chapters that the central government has many powers to resource, check and monitor the actions of local authorities. The work of the Audit Commission discussed in Chapter 4 is central to ensuring the funds have been properly raised and applied effectively to deliver local services. In Chapter 5, attention was drawn to many inspectorates that review specific local authority services. Best Value and the creation of standards committees has added yet further procedures to check the behaviour of councillors. In addition to these powers, a number of other procedures have been established to ensure local authorities can be open to public scrutiny.

Local government has in recent years become a much more open structure, whose inner workings can be revealed and brought into the light of day. All meetings of a full council and its sub-committees are, by law, open to the public, although the 2000 Local Government Act does allow local authority cabinets to meet in private. The 1986 Local Government Access to Information Act ensured that all documents relating to the meetings of a local authority should be made available to the public. The contrast of open local government to that of the capricious and arbitrary secrecy of the 1911 Acts that shelter central government from scrutiny suggests no little element of hypocrisy in recent government criticism of local democracy.

Institutionally, local authorities are fully open to influence by interest groups. There is no barrier to the freedom of association and communication at the local level, provided the groups involved are not indulging in slander or meeting for some criminal purpose. The rights of association at local level are not differentiated from nationally set restrictions on forming societies and groups or assembling for protest marches and rallies. The right to communicate dissent is in practice less restricted at the local level. Central government can prevent publication of what they regard euphemistically as 'sensitive' material through the use of the Official Secrets Act and the convention of 'D' notices, through which they inform the press that certain issues ought not to be published. Local authorities do not enjoy these powers of protection and have no formal powers to restrict press comment on their actions.

Ombudsman

Should the many schemes for testing public opinion and evaluating efficiency still break down, especially in relations to the problems that may be faced by the individual citizens, there remain important structures to ensure some redress can be secured. Citizens still have the capacity to take their local authority to court, should they feel that the negligence of the local authority has caused them injury or loss of income. If a local government does not act within the boundaries of its statutory competence or legal obligations, it can be taken to court. A council must also abide by more general legislative requirements and legal obligations to provide a safe environment for the public. A local authority may, and many are, sued by citizens who have fallen and suffered injury as a result on uneven paving or providing contaminated food in a café and can be subject to judicial proceedings if a citizen considers that a school has wrongfully excluded their child.

The new ethical code is not meant to replace the functions of the Ombudsman, which is the office designed to deal with cases where local authority officers or councillors may have acted within the moral code, but have made serious errors of judgement or failed to act effectively.

Such cases, referred to as maladministration, can be referred to the local Ombudsman or, to give the position its official title, the Commissioner for Local Administration. There are three such Commissioners in England who work on a regional basis and one each for Scotland and Wales. The office was established for England and Wales in 1974 and two years later in Scotland. The institution followed in the wake of the establishment in 1969 of the Parliamentary Commissioner to investigate complaints against the civil service. Any citizen who considers she or he has been unjustly treated by a local authority as a result of maladministration may complain to the appropriate Commissioner, in the first place through their local councillor, but if this individual will take not take up the case, then directly to the Commissioner. The office received over 17,000 complaints in the year 1999/00 and found that the local authorities should amend their action in over 2,500 of these (Local Government Ombudsman 2000). The largest number of cases relate to failures in planning permission.

The system has a number of serious flaws which are also present in the national Ombudsman system. Access is initially through an elected representative and so the office is not well known or very readily approachable. Even more seriously, the Commissioners have no power to investigate failings themselves, or to prosecute or compel authorities that have acted unreasonably to mend their ways. The Commissioner issues reports on its investigations which are communicated to the erring local authority and can be made public. Most local authorities take notice of the complaint and compensate the aggrieved citizen but they can, and on occasion do, sit out the criticism.

> In contrast to Britain, the Swedish Ombudsman, the office which was the model for the idea, can prosecute authorities that have neglected their duties and investigate cases on their own initiative or as a result of a direct approach from an individual or interest group.

At local and national levels the government established an office designed more to give the appearance of concern about redress, more than the substance.

Management and democracy

The brave new world of New Labour presents an image of a modern local authority led by a directly elected mayor, or at least a visible leadership which is obliged to meet high standards of performance and efficiency on behalf of its citizens whose opinions are constantly monitored through opinion polls and more in-depth focus-group-style analysis. This may then be democracy as we know it, but is it democracy as it should be? In the following chapters of this book the issue of local democracy will be further analysed.

Further reading

Management practices in local government have a long established literature and major studies on corporate management are referred to in Chapter 7. New ideas of management developed in the 1980s can be approached through Walsh (1995) and Hood's (1991) article is important in Stoker (ed) (1999), defining the idea. Boyne (1998) is the most comprehensive study of empirical work on the results of new-right management theory. The application of these ideas more specifically to local government has an extensive literature. A useful guide is provided by Kerley (1994) and also of importance is Leach, Stewart and Walsh (1994). Clarke and Stewart (1990) and Stewart (1986) develop an influential framework for citizen focused management, although their views are not in the new-right perspective of NPM. Stoker (1999) provides a number of valuable articles on recent changes in the management process. Chandler (1996) and Prior (1995) contains material on the citizen's charter and local government.

  Decentralisation is analysed in several studies, with Hoggett and Hambleton (1988) being a pioneering study, but the most comprehensive work is Burns, Hambleton and Hoggett (1994).

11

Interests, business and the media

The policies and the delivery of local government services are not determined solely by the interaction of councillors, officers and central government agencies. Neither at national nor local levels is a government 'an island pure and entire unto itself' but operates as an actor amidst a maze of voluntary and business organisations that reflect the many interests and enthusiasms of individuals and communities. Traditionally, it has been routine to depict these external aggregations of interests as pressure or interest groups that seek to influence government policies without themselves taking power and responsibility for services. In the 1960s and 1970s, academic studies of interest groups in local government were greatly stimulated by a theory of pluralist democracy, based on the view that electorally successful politicians achieve popularity by listening to the many voices of disparate interests and then steering a policy direction that successfully satisfies as many of these interests as is possible.

R.A. Dahl in his classic study of pluralism *Who Governs?* (1961) studied the power of the mayor in New Haven, the city in which the University of Yale is established, and argued that the position required the mayor to mediate between numerous interests within the town so as to secure the policies that best fulfilled the demands of numerous complementary and conflicting interests. Thus democracy was secured, as decisions generally reflected the most strongly supported policy outcomes.

Studies of power in communities in Britain in the 1970s (Dearlove 1973; Newton 1976; Hampton 1970; Green 1981) generally argued that pluralist theory, especially where local government was concerned, was misleading and only a few well-connected wealthy groups were ever successful in influencing local policy.

Over the last thirty years, this pattern has substantially changed. It may still be true that the great majority of interest groups seeking to influence local

169

authorities make relatively little headway but, largely through government pressure, local authorities are required to work in partnership with external interests. These groups are usually business interests that develop partnerships with local authorities for operating services or promoting economic development or major voluntary organisations that have an increasingly important role in the operation of social welfare and housing services.

The range and diversity of groups

Since interest groups comprise all organisations involved at some time in political action, apart from the institutions of central government and political parties, their numbers are scarcely calculable. Most groups are formed for purposes other than political representation and only become incidentally involved with governments. A football club may become an interest group if it discovers that the local authority are about to grant permission to a large multi-national firm to dig up its playing field. Similarly, the large chemical manufacturer will be an interest group if it attempts to persuade the local authority to allow them to build on the council-owned playing fields beloved by the football club. In addition to sports clubs and large firms, local authorities will receive demands from groups as varied as chambers of commerce, the National Society for the Prevention of cruelty to Children (NSPCC), neighbourhood watch schemes, ratepayers' associations, anti-road lobbies, Greenpeace, local radio stations or women's shelters.

Newton (1976: 38) attempted to assess the number of groups active in the City of Birmingham and reached the figure of 4,264 before he stopped counting, whilst a new count of Birmingham interests reached 5,781 (Maloney, Smith and Stoker 2000). The majority of Newton's groups had not however been involved in political activity, at least in the two years preceding the survey, and hence only around one-third could be classified as political interests. However, groups that are politically active frequently relate to the local authority and Maloney, Smith and Stoker (2000: 807) found that 82 per cent of voluntary and community groups believed that Birmingham City Council was an important source of information. Dearlove (1973: 157) observed that in 1968/69 the London Borough of Kensington and Chelsea funded some 50 interests, sent representatives to over 80 non-Council organisations and had a list of nearly 200 groups.

Types of interest group

Groups require some classification if sense is to be made of their political characteristics and influence. Most basic theories of interest groups make a distinction between those that are formed to fight against a particular cause or issue

and those that represent an on going interest. Single-issue groups include committees formed by irate home owners threatened by a road development or a
group seeking to prevent dumping of nuclear waste in their community. Once
the group has succeeded or irrevocably failed, it will disband or have to restructure itself around some new cause. Because of the usually limited nature of
their concerns, single-issue groups are not usually as important as the more
numerous promotional groups representing an ongoing interest. These include
organisations as varied as trade unions, trade associations of employers, religious bodies and community groups. They are formed to represent the concerns
of groups that have an interest in promoting or pursuing an activity that will
continue for the foreseeable future.

Classification of such groups must be arbitrary, since the complex diversity
of human interest does not lead to neat logical packaging of interests. Newton
assigned groups into thirteen functional categories (1976: 38), Stoker (1991:
115–17) has suggested a fourfold classification into producer groups, which
encompass businesses and trade unions, community groups, cause groups and
voluntary groups. However, such one-dimensional classifications do not do
justice to the complexity of the relationship between government and interests.
The subject area of a particular group needs to be considered alongside its attitude towards local policy makers. Frequently, established groups may behave
differently towards the local authority on certain matters and take a different
approach on other issues. Larger, more powerful groups often tend to be multi-
purpose organisations, conducting a range of activities which may lead them
to oppose and criticise a local authority on one particular issue whilst in
another area they may be actively working in amicable partnership with the
local authority. A business may, for example, work in partnership with a local
authority on the delivery of a service but also attack the authority over its policy
on car parking or tourist promotion.

It is therefore necessary to develop a classification based not only on the
broad subject area of the interest group, but also of its relationship of interests
to local authorities. This has been portrayed as a simplified relationship matrix
as depicted in Table 11.1.

Single-issue groups and campaigns

A glance at a local newspaper often suggests that the majority of interests are
groups protesting about some aspect of local authority policy. This impression
is, however, misleading. Whilst not a few groups oppose a particular policy of
the local authority the most visible are often not the most successful. Examples
are numerous and include groups opposing building developments, closures of
local authority facilities such as a school or an elderly persons' home or protests
from groups enraged that the local authority may have not clamped down on
'rat running' through a residential neighbourhood or kerb crawling in a red-
light district. A not untypical issue is campaigns by local residents to oppose the

Table 11.1 *Interest group and local authority relationships*

Attitude to local authority	Single-issue group	Community group	Business and economic interest	Voluntary welfare group
Hostile	Xville bypass protestors	Xville residents group against the bypass	Xville Chamber of Commerce opposing high council tax	NSPCC criticises Xville social services
Supportive	Xville bypass supporters	Xville residents group for the bypass	Xville Chamber of Commerce for the local authority trade fair	MIND praises social services for help to mentally ill
Partnership	The Xville bypass supporters and local authority working group	The Xville residents and local authority area committee	Chamber of Commerce and local authority promoting a trade fair and SRB bid	Xville Housing Association builds sheltered housing for mentally ill on local authority register

construction of a large supermarket in their community which would cause even greater congestion on an already overcrowded road. A few campaigns gain national prominence, such as attempt to prevent the extension of Manchester Airport, which included colourful 'moles' such as Swampy.

Often the more successful groups campaigning over a single issue are less visible than some less efficacious groups, since they can ensure that the local authority is fully in agreement with their cause and deals with the problem. They, therefore, have no need to further publicise their concerns and work to support rather than oppose the authority. On occasion, alliances on single issues between the local authority and campaign groups develop when both organisations are in agreement over their opposition to policies of the central government or a large business group. In the 1980s several left-wing authorities with the co-operation of the Campaign for Nuclear Disarmament (CND) declared themselves nuclear-free zones as a gesture that had little practical impact but gave publicity to the cause of CND. Local authorities in South Yorkshire have sided with local residents' campaign groups against open-cast mining in their areas.

Community groups

An important class of interest groups that affect local authorities more than central government are the numerous community groups that are established to look after the mutual concerns of people living in a specific locality or representing a particular group of city-wide residents who have a common set of values. Often such groups are the source of single-issue campaigns and their interest in a particular area or community of interests ensures they will constantly refer issues to the local authority. In Sheffield for example, residents of the Nether Edge area may voluntarily join the Nether Edge Society, which issues a regular newsletter informing its members about the history and personalities of the area but in political terms has much to say on building development and road improvements in the area and may be important in forming local opinion on, for example, replacement of council-owned trees on the local streets.

Community groups representing localities within a local authority are a necessary creation of the growth of local government units into what are effectively sub-regional rather than genuinely local organisations. In towns, professionals living in leafy suburban communities are governed by the same authority as the unemployed residents of a run-down council estate. Both groupings may have reason to support and defend their localities, but will make very different demands on the local authority. Within rural districts encompassing an area of many square miles there will be many small towns and villages that have interests that are wholly different to the residents of other villages that may be many miles distant. The interests of villages and towns may be taken up and promoted by the parish or town council and many of these minor authorities can effectively act as local community interest groups by pressuring the local authority to respond to their needs. In cities, these groups are replaced by an informal network of community associations and, on occasion, decentralising authorities such as York City Council or Islington have created local area consultative committees to facilitate better liaison with communities,

There is a further sense of a community as incorporating people of similar interests and background, even though they may not live close to one another. Thus, many towns have city-wide communities, for example of particular ethnic minorities, homosexual groups or the elderly. Ken Livingstone, when leader of the GLC gave particular prominence to such groups as he sought to provide support to many London-wide minority interests. On occasion, a local authority may even create groups in order to gain an insight into the needs of a particular community. Most local authorities foster the development of tenants' associations or advice centres as a valuable means of gaining feedback from citizens, even if this may at times be highly critical of their actions. Large authorities often provide considerable financial help to such groups.

The success or failure of single-issue and community groups

The likelihood of single-cause groups achieving success depends on factors that affect the majority of interests, although many single-cause groups have far fewer resources to help them secure their goals.

Newton's (1976) study of Birmingham was an attempt to evaluate in a British context the pluralist theories established in Dahl's earlier writings. He concluded that the most politically active and influential interest groups tended to be those which have a larger membership and substantial financial resources and staff, and that these factors tended to cluster together. This finding confirms most national studies. A group with a large membership will be more likely to have an electoral impact. Many members provide a higher income and a greater ability to pay for professional workers and expert advice. Professionalism and an ability to recruit expert help allows interests to research their argument fully, and present their ideas in a clear well-documented form. These factors will, in turn, ensure that leaders of the better resourced and supported interest groups are more likely to get the attention of policy makers.

Perhaps the most crucial factor is the nature of their cause and the values held by the policy makers within the local authority. A group that seeks support on an issue that is consistent with local authority policies and values is likely to find it far easier to succeed than a group, for example, seeking to ban fox hunting over council-owned land by a county council governed by 'sporting' knights of the shire. It is also important for the group to show that it is representative of opinion and that its views are not likely to be opposed by a significant number of individuals or interests. Dearlove (1973) adds that the success of a group may also depend on its campaign strategies. Councillors will not enthuse about groups that seek to coerce and politically embarrass them. Dearlove shows that councillors in Kensington and Chelsea preferred to be approached through ward councillors or committee chairs, whilst actions such as demonstrations or complaints through the press were frowned upon.

If the two sectors promoting success are put together, it is clear that groups led by well-educated middle-class activists campaigning on an issue likely to gain the sympathy of councillors and senior local government officers will be most likely to have their concerns considered sympathetically. Within such a framework lies a further crucial characteristic of a successful group: the ability to have close personal links with senior policy makers. As will be demonstrated in the next section in relation to business, voluntary and professional groups, the most effective interests work within the local authority through close linkages with senior officers and councillors and usually have little need to campaign against the authority. These links form what is often termed a policy network.

Local authorities and the business community

The most influential groups are arguably businesses that command extensive financial resources and expertise and have a major influence on the local economy. Large firms and their representative groups at the local level, the chambers of trade or commerce, can develop highly effective networks with senior councillors and officers of a local authority that are important in shaping the pattern of local economic development. In the late nineteenth century, when civic pride was as it its zenith, most industrial cities were effectively controlled by local businessmen. Although municipal entrepreneurs had almost disappeared by the 1920s, there remained some business links with local councils. An important area of co-operation developed in tourist resorts. Blackpool was effectively created as a centre for 'fresh air and fun' by businessmen who used local authority help to aid their developments. The Borough has, since its creation from a small village, continued to devote substantial local authority funding to provide holiday attractions and infrastructure and also widely publicise the delights of the area. Many other resort towns followed Blackpool's lead in self-promotion. Such close co-operation between a major business and a local authority was not, however, often replicated for other industries. The growth of business on a national scale and the emergence of the Labour Party removed these links, and by 1950 connections between the business community and local government were, with few exceptions, a rather formal affair. Businesses were aware of local government through payment of rates and if they wished to plan new buildings or as trading organisations that had to conform to public health and weights and measures inspection. Outside this framework, business and local government interests seemed to rarely trouble one another. A standard response from businessmen to local government was that, as an institution, they charged too high a rate.

Behind this ill-considered view, there were, however, far more connections than was often realised and, rather like the man who discovered he was talking prose all his life without knowing it, businessmen have always had a considerable number of working relationships with local authorities. The demands for goods and services by local authorities make them major customers of industry. Many firms have been reliant on local authority contracts and some are almost wholly dependent on local authority support. There are, for example, firms specialising in orders from public libraries and, until recently, manufacturers of dustbins and refuse sacks were largely dependent on the orders of cleansing departments. John Bennington (1986), when Director of the Employment Department of Sheffield City Council, calculated that the authority purchased £80 million of goods in a year and spent £84 million on construction work of which a large proportion went to local firms.

Public–private partnerships

Since the 1980s there has been a considerable revival in the links between business and local government which results in co-operation beyond the boundaries of attacks on high rates or even the customer–supplier relationship. The economic slump of the 1980s, which followed a decade of decline in the rate of economic growth gave great impetus to new schemes for local economic development that promoted many new public–private co-operative ventures and, for many businessmen, shifted their stance of sullen indifference to local government.

The most dramatic schemes for employment creation were, in their initial stages, predicated on a generally hostile attitude to the public sector, and have been outlined in Chapter 3. Whilst much attention was focused on the left-wing authorities, less radical councils promoted economic regeneration through developing partnerships with the private sector. Bradford City Council established an economic development unit with powers to negotiate relocation and expansion packages with incoming firms that included the ability to shorten what could often be protracted negotiations on planning permission. St Helens Borough Council, in partnership with Pilkington Glass, developed an enterprise workshop estate to provide employment for redundant glass workers (Moore and Richardson 1989). Birmingham City Council built and maintains the National Exhibition Centre in partnership with the city's Chamber of Commerce, with each body appointing half the management committee (Englefield 1987). By the second half of the 1980s the radical Labour authorities that had attempted to regenerate the local economy, in spite of private sector capitalism, realised that if you cannot beat them you must join them and many turned to more conventional means of attracting new businesses.

The Thatcher and Major Governments required local authorities to consult with local businesses concerning their budget and poll tax charge and also encouraged the formation of Business in the Community (BIC), a predominantly private sector-led organisation that sought to develop a greater sense of social responsibility in industry through links with groups such as chambers of commerce, trade union and local authorities by establishing new enterprise agencies. Further Government-inspired impetus towards public-private partnerships were created through CCT legislation, which obliged local authorities to work with private sector contractors. Relations between contractor and client can be stormy, but in other cases a private company has forged close links with the contracting local government officers and effectively arranged its activities to suit local needs as well as its own. Where major contracts are involved, the links may allow the local authority to extract important concessions from the contractor. Sheffield City Council, for example, allocated many of financial services such as the collection of property taxes or distribution of housing benefit to a private company which, as part of the deal, agreed to establish its principal office in the City of Sheffield and so employ local people.

Further links have been forged through the distribution of central government, European and lottery commission grants for capital development, which require that all proposals must involve matching funds from the private sector or involve strong private sector partnership in the operation of developments. City Challenge and the SRB for allocating development funds, for example, require local authorities to develop schemes for funding the resurrection of areas of industrial decline through plans that involved a substantial element of private sector support. Similarly, European Union regional aid usually requires an element of private sector involvement in schemes. Lottery money can also only be received by organisations that match the funding offered from donations from other sources.

The development of strong business and local authority links have also been forged during the last decade through the Major and Blair administration's policies on urban development that, as described in Chapter 3, require local authorities to secure SRB funding for schemes that require a partnership arrangement with private or voluntary sector bodies. In keeping with the Government's vision of a local authority being more an enabling strategist rather than delivery organisation, local authorities are encouraged to promote schemes for economic regeneration that attract private partners and substantial private funding.

In the United States, links between business interests and city governments are generally much closer and in some cities, such as San Antonio, Texas, the government of the city is predominantly controlled by business representatives. More often, as demonstrated by Clarence Stone (1989), in his study of government in Atlanta, Georgia, city politics revolves around the co-operation between business groups and community, based interest groups.

Employment groups

In the preceding chapter, the role of one of these sets of groups, those concerned with employment interests, the professional and trade union organisations, was discussed at some length and requires no further analysis here, apart from pointing out that such groups are in effect interests promoting a specific community just as much as a neighbourhood group or cause group. The success of these groups are also promoted as with other interests by factors such as the cohesion of their members to the profession, or union, the resources at their command and also (and crucially) the extent to which they can be seen as legitimate and supportive interests by the local authority and hence the extent that they can forge close networks of interests, that work closely with the authority, a concept discussed in more detail later in this chapter.

Voluntary or third sector organisations

Local authorities are dependent, not only on the activities of business but the work of what are popularly seen as voluntary charitable groups. To some extent, there is an image of voluntary groups as small well-meaning organisations run on rather amateur lines by teams of enthusiastic volunteers. Whilst there are many local charities based on purely voluntary help that enhance the sense of local community throughout the country, the largest voluntary organisations, although often using unpaid help, are major public service organisations employing full-time professional staff. Many of these groups have a crucial role in filling the 'gaps' within the welfare state by providing services that have not been fully met by the State at both local and national levels. For example, an organisation such as the NSPCC investigates cases of child abuse that would otherwise be the province of local authority social service departments. Such bodies are not, however solely involved in humanitarian and welfare activities, but now permeate other areas of local activity. The large-scale not-for-profit organisations that fill important gaps in state provision are frequently referred to as third sector organisations, as opposed to voluntary agencies. They differ from private sector businesses as they do not aim to make a profit but, as they are not controlled by statutory governmental bodies, they are not public bodies.

Frequently it is essential for the professionals of a welfare organisation such as the NSPCC to work closely with local government professionals. A social services department will be aware of the cases of child neglect being investigated by the society and may often have cases referred to them for longer term care by the NSPCC or ask the organisation to investigate families where there are concerns about child care. Effective co-operation creates a close partnership between local authorities and the voluntary agency.

The Conservative Government encouraged the growth of third sector, organisations in many public service sectors, in order to gradually supplant public sector and particularly local government activity in these areas. As shown in Chapter 3, this was a central aim of the Thatcher Government in relation to housing where the Governments reinforced the previously rather small sector of rented housing provided by housing associations to the point where the majority of publicly owned housing is now constructed by housing associations rather than local government (Malpass 2000). The role of the local authority housing department is to work with housing associations in identifying those in need of subsidised housing and there has been discussion, even within the Blair Government let alone the Conservative Party, on the possibility of transferring complete responsibility for subsidised public housing to the third sector housing associations.

Policy networks and communities

As emphasised in the preceding paragraph, the most important interests affecting local government policy and service delivery have no need of mass demonstrations or petitions, and but work quietly but effectively behind the scenes. It is misleading to depict these efficacious interests primarily as adversary organisations locked in internecine strife with the government or public sector agencies. Confrontation requires a considerable expenditure in energy and stress and is far from the most effective means of gaining power. Successful groups do not have to resort to expensive strategies of confrontation, but achieve their aims through the development of close working relationships with officers or members of a local authority. Successful interests permeate the thinking of local government actors and may often be involved in the day-to-day operations of some aspect of local government work.

The patterns of frequent interaction between interests and government and political parties can be complex, since it is far from being a one-way process of an isolated group putting pressure on government. In practice, influential groups may modify their actions as much as politicians so as to co-ordinate their interests for mutual benefit, and groups may often interact with one another to achieve their goals. These intricate patterns have been described as policy networks, to demonstrate the presence of many interlinking relationships between organisations that devise and deliver policy (Rhodes and Marsh 1992). On many occasions, these networks become well-established stable relationships that form the arena in which policy is made and are referred to as policy communities. Some writers argue that such communities tend to revolve around powerful wealthy interests that exclude other more pluralist groups from influencing policy. Cawson (1978, 1985) among others refers to this relationship as corporatism.

Some of the most important examples of policy networks within local government have already been analysed in discussing the professional interests of officers. A professional association is an interest group acting on behalf of its members, even though it can be deeply involved in the day-to-day decision making of a local authority and exert its authority on a number of levels. A professional body such as CIPFA will influence a local government through the ideas of its members, who will be senior officers in the authority, through recommendations and reports that it issues nationally, through its influence on central government policy towards local government finance and its influence on other associations such as the local authority associations or the Society for Local Authority Chief Executives (SOLACE). CIPFA will, however, itself be subject to influence from all these sources.

Trade unions may also enjoy an important status in policy communities and expect to be regularly consulted on matters concerning the working conditions of their members. Many trade unions and especially those representing manual workers have, moreover, a special relationship within the Labour Party as affiliated members with the right to send delegates to constituency and district parties and nominate members as candidates for the council. They can therefore be influential in forming party policy, especially where a particular union dominates the local workforce. However, there is rarely a concerted effort by a trade union to control a local authority and in many cases where leading councillors are also prominent members of a trade union, it is impossible to determine whether they act as union members, councillors or Labour Party members (Barker 1982).

Many cases of local authority funding of interest groups, such as tenants' associations, are designed to foster corporate links between consumers and producers of a specific service. Most housing authorities with established tenants' associations will grant the officers of these groups privileged access to councillors who will be able to have early notification of grievances and an opportunity to solve problems that may otherwise snowball into serious public discontent. Similar efforts are made to cultivate minority group representation in the larger cities.

The politics of influence

Although policy communities reflect co-operative mutual adjustment of interests between politicians and leaders of interest groups, securing such a position may be the consequence of more submerged and invisible powers that are potentially in the hands of the successful group. If a powerful interest did not enjoy close consultative status with a local authority, it might be able to damage local authority policy and credibility either by withdrawing jobs and services from the area, gaining mass publicity or using its influence with central government to change local policy. Local authorities compete vigorously with one another to offer concessions that will attract large firms into their area and thus provide greater prosperity for the community. An established firm that reverses this process, and threatens to leave an area if it cannot secure favourable conditions such as planning permission to expand its factory, will also present the local authority with a challenge it may be unable to refuse.

In addition to action over a specific interest, powerful groups will attempt to influence a local authority on more general issues. Chambers of commerce representing local businesses are never reticent about using the press as a means of putting pressure on local authorities concerning the rates. Until the Government took over the task of setting the business rate, most local newspapers in larger high-rated cities ritually contained statements from local firms predicting bankruptcy or threatening to relocate when the council came to the time of year for setting the rate.

The most powerful interests in Britain do not, however, operate solely on a local level, but influence politics through close working relationships with government ministers and senior civil servants. Groups can secure such a favoured status because of their economic importance to the nation. These comprise the large multi-national firms and banks and insurance companies. They may also be groups with a monopoly of expertise and authority in a particular area, such as the British Medical Association or the Law Society, or organisations that share strong ideological links with a political party, such as the trade unions enjoy with Labour Governments or business interests with the Conservatives. If a local authority chooses to thwart the interests of any of these powerful groups, they may not only have to contend with direct local pressure from the offended interest, but also with pressure from central government acting on behalf of that interest.

> The effectiveness of interest groups in comparative terms is also dependent on deeply ingrained attitudes within the political culture of a nation. Whilst in Britain and the United States there is a widespread acceptance that interests negotiate with each other and central government to secure policy change, in France there is far greater suspicion of interests, with the result that disaffected groups such as farmers are more likely to resort to direct confrontational action than negotiation to achieve their aims.

It may be concluded that the most successful interests enjoy close working relationships with one or a combination of local government officers, councillors and political parties. The influential group may have members who are also powerful councillors or officers; they will have ready access to local government policy makers and may be organisations actively delivering services to the public on behalf of the local authority. Once securely placed within a network that helps determine policy, a group will not operate as an adversarial group pressurising the local authority through threatening actions, but operate as a partner of the authority. However, the groups that secure such a role have achieved this status largely because they have skills and knowledge crucial to the local authority and if ignored could make policy making an awkward and hazardous process.

Critics of these arrangements argue that the development of corporate relations between local authorities and big business is an inevitable consequence of the capitalist system. Even in the most left-wing local authority, the interests of capital will oblige a local authority, to follow its own interest and co-operate with business. Cynthia Cockburn's (1977) study of the rise and fall of local authority funded community associations in Lambeth suggests that the good intentions of local councillors to consult residents on their future could not be sustained against pressures by big business to redevelop large areas of the Borough. A combination of economic power and influence by business at local and national level defeated any attempt by community associations to assert their individuality. It may be suggested, therefore, that local authorities can play a partnership role with industry and commerce in local economic development, provided they swim with the interests of the private sector partner and provided central government does not see fit to impose a national solution to local economic problems.

Communication and the media

The press and local radio and television have an important role in the interaction of interests and local government. The media can be a very powerful interest in its own right as local newspapers or radio stations may have decided views as to the activities of the local authority and forward these ideas as part of their editorial policy. They also act as an important means of communication between councillors, local interests and the electorate.

The national media

Local government is of interest to television, radio and the national press, largely in so far as it has an impact on national government. Thus, local electoral contests are reported and monitored on national television, usually late at night, and normally as a form of opinion poll on the rating of the national parties. Similarly, major issues affecting local government, such as the poll tax, are reported not so much because of their local consequences, but in so far as they are issues that divide the parliamentary parties and affect national voting opinions. Even when the reported local issue appears to concern a single local authority, the subject is used to discredit national political tendencies. In this context, therefore, the national media is an important factor, undermining any value for local government as the representative of specifically local opinion.

The local media

Locally, the most potent communicators of local politics are the press and local radio. Since the range and scope of these media are varied, there is a considerable variation in the coverage of local politics. In a large city, such as Birmingham or Leeds, there are local daily and evening newspapers that will have a significant coverage of local political issues. In recent years, the established press is being rivalled by free newssheets geared to maximising advertising revenue, but many of these will include local political comment. Some local authorities are seeking to emulate this tendency by issuing their own periodic newssheets to households in their areas. A city will also have at least one, and increasingly several, local radio stations. It is normal for most BBC local radio networks to devote some attention to local authority issues and they will frequently interview leading councillors and their opponents concerning major issues before the authority and will also cover local election campaigns. The political coverage of independent stations may be minimal or as extensive as the publicly owned stations.

In the United States, where there is far more substantial development of local television largely through cable channels, it is possible to gain far more detailed coverage of local politics and in some towns the local cable television company will each week show live the proceedings of their local city councils for the benefit of the community.

Whilst there are many sources of local information in urban centres, the coverage of local issues in rural areas may be much less thorough. Before 1939, most small towns or groups of neighbouring villages had a local weekly newspaper which reported extensively the proceedings of local authorities in their areas. There has been a steady decrease in the number of local weekly papers as a consequence of amalgamation and closures. This trend has, however, paralleled an increase in the size of local authority areas, so that it is not infrequent for a weekly newspaper to cover one county or district area. In as much as this takes place, it is more by coincidence than by design. For many parts of the country there is no particularly local press and hence district and county council issues are reported either in special editions covering a particular area or, more usually, as local items that are often given relatively little detailed coverage. J.M. Lee reflected on this fragmentation in Cheshire

There were no newspapers that thought in 'county terms'- no county society existed to buy them – and a considerable amount of anti-ministerial feeling directed against county officials sprang from ignorance occasioned by this lack of publicity. (1963: 205)

It is difficult to assess what impact reporting of local politics may have on the fortunes of a local authority. There appears to be a strong coincidence of local and national voting behaviour, which has led several analysts to argue that local policy making is not determined by local interests. This is, as is argued in

Chapter 12, a doubtful assertion and there is plenty of evidence to suggest that able local politicians are usually concerned to cultivate the electorate by working through the local media. It is also argued that variations in national and local vote can occur, but these are too little researched to evaluate the effect of the local media in this process.

Evidence on the attitude of councillors to the media is, rather than vague, clearly conflicting. John Dearlove (1973: 182), comparing the attitudes of councillors in community surveys, showed that few councillors thought the press was a major source of influence as regards the needs of their electors. In reality, councillors' opinions on the media will be determined by its political stance. Where, as in Kensington and Chelsea, the press was not regarded as politically supportive of the local authority, the councillors would be negatively influenced by the media and hostile to its reportage. In many local authorities where the press is at least tolerated, leading councillors will try to form good working relationships with favoured editors, journalists and broadcasters. Thus, a council leader will be prepared to provide news to a local editor, provided he reports the issue in reasonably balanced and fair terms.

Mutually self-interested but cordial relations between local leaders and the press are, however only sustained where the local media support, or at least tolerate the policies of the council. In some cases the press may be seen by councillors as unhelpful and can therefore be ignored, presumably with the hope that no one would seriously read the offending rag. It is probable that such a breakdown of trust between the press and councillors will be more likely within Labour rather than Conservative groups. Although some newspapers are favourable to the Labour Party, it takes money to run a newspaper or local radio station and those with money tend to support the Conservative cause.

Further reading

Whilst many community studies and textbooks refer to interest group activity in local government there is no substantial work solely dedicated to reviewing this field. However, Newton (1976) is of crucial importance and contains important research on the role of local groups, and Saunders (1979) is also invaluable in the case of powerful economic interests as is Cockburn (1977). Studies relating to professional groups and trade unions were considered in the previous chapter. Hain (1976) provides some useful case studies. There are few studies of the relationship between racially united groups and local government, with the valuable exception of Ben Tovim *et al.* (1986).

There is now a considerable literature on local authorities and business partnerships which touches on the role of interest groups. Of interest is Moore and Richardson (1989), whilst Chandler and Lawless (1985) is beginning to date in a rapidly changing era, but should still have useful material.

12

Patterns of government

One of the most fascinating aspects of the study of local government is that it deals with a diversity of elected organisations that demonstrate differing tendencies and behaviour. Despite the pressures from central government, local authorities can pursue divergent policies. During the 1980s, the politics of a radical left-wing authority such as Lambeth differed sharply from the neighbouring new-right London Borough of Wandsworth and both these radical authorities were highly newsworthy subjects. However, at the beginning of the twenty-first century, differences between the policies of local authorities do not seem as sharp as they were in the 1980s. This may be a reflection of several possible issues. Has local government ceased to interest the media because increased restraints by central government on local authorities have driven them to adopt similar policies? Alternatively, has the third way agenda of New Labour presented a satisfactory compromise between the Old Labour and Thatcherism that has been adapted by all local authorities to the extent that policy differences are too insignificant to be worthy of much comment?

Democratic theory maintains that the political values of a local authority, in so far as it may act within the confines of centrally determined rules, must be a reflection of the values of its elected representatives, the councillors who in turn represent or respond to majority opinions within the electorate. It should therefore be expected that local politics in Britain is predominantly a function of party politics. At its most simplistic, this view leads to the generalisation that residents of rural areas and the affluent suburbs of large conurbations are largely Conservative, whilst the inhabitants of inner-city areas support the Labour Party. This is, however, misleadingly simplistic.

Table 12.1 demonstrates that it is by no means easy to characterise the politics of most local authorities as stable or as clearly definable with reference to the class of its electors. Over half the local authorities of Britain have experienced changes in political control during the last ten years and many have no single dominant party, whilst a significant few have a majority of councillors professing no political allegiance.

Table 12.1 *Party control of local authorities (1979–98)*

	1979	1989	1995	1998
Conservative	262	169	13	28
Labour	79	163	206	210
Liberal or Liberal Democrat	1	12	51	44
Other parties	39	12	4	19
Independent majority	57	32	23	19
No overall control	77	127	157	148

Source: The Municipal Year Book (1979 and 1989) *Municipal Year Book*, London, Municipal Journal Ltd; *Local Government Chronicle* 13 May 1995; Llewellyn (1999).

The independent council

At the beginning of the twentieth century, the majority of local authorities, especially those covering rural areas, were non-partisan, in the sense that councillors did not stand under party labels but as unaffiliated individuals. The fully independent councillor thus voted on issues without reference to any political leader. In practice, however, independent councillors are often supporters of a political party, particularly the Conservatives (Holliday, 2000: 168), but they do not believe that at a local level their views should be marshalled into a particular direction by a party machine. During the century there has been an insidious erosion of the capacity of councillors to stand as independents. This is due to many factors, such as the growth of the more organised Labour Party at the beginning of the century which required non-socialists to organise in opposition to its success, the disappearance of smaller local authorities, where individuals could be known by many in the community, and the growth of national media focus on party politics. Only a few independent authorities therefore remain and as Table 12.1 indicates, their number is declining.

Whilst there are but a few obviously independent local authorities, there are probably many others that are in practice non-partisan. As Bulpitt (1967) found in Lancashire and Cheshire, local elections were often fought on party lines in smaller authorities, but once councillors were elected the party groups did not co-ordinate the policies of their members or expect them to vote at all times with their party colleagues. It is, however, probable that, in terms of day-to-day decision making, there is far greater non-party political dealing than appears to be the case from the numbers of independent councillors. Decision making in a non-partisan authority is likely to be achieved through shifting alliances between councillors. Birch (1959) relates how a debate on finance in Glossop, a largely non-partisan council, produced divisions based as much on length of residence in the area as party stereotypes on spending preferences. In some cases, the lack of party values may lead to much greater reliance on the opinion of officers.

Does party politics matter?

Although many local authorities are firmly partisan, there has been considerable debate about whether, at the local level, party politics has any bearing on the policies adopted by local governments. The concept of the 'end of ideology' developed by Daniel Bell (1960) promoted the idea that the stability of mature capitalist systems meant an end to class polarisation between left and right and that the ideological differences between parties were increasingly of little relevance. Political rivalry in these circumstances becomes a contest between parties claiming to be better managers of a nation's economy and social well-being rather than a conflict over ideology. Considerable evidence was marshalled in the 1960s to back up this view. In Britain, electoral studies of the major political parties argued that they were less and less divided in terms of ideology (McKenzie 1963).

Surveys of local government policy output at this time did not, however, support this thesis. A study by Noel Boaden of spending by county boroughs in England and Wales showed that

> As predicted, Labour councils were more active in services with a significant impact on the overall role of government. They were bigger spenders on the bigger services. In addition they were more active where the service appeared to benefit sections of the community supporting them. Even where these two factors were less operative, there was a tendency for Labour to favour higher standards in the broadest sense. Our evidence suggests very clearly that party affects the priorities established between services. (1971: 112)

Boaden also indicated that Labour authorities tended to be more partisan and less accessible to the public than those under Conservative control. These findings were later supported in a major study by Sharpe and Newton, which looked at both cities and county councils and concluded that 'Parties are a much more potent factor in influencing governmental outputs than much of the previous output research has recognized' (1984: 215).

Studies of individual local authorities led by the 1970s to a received wisdom on the characteristics of Conservative and Labour controlled authorities that still has some resonance today. These will be described in the following sections, although the arrival of Thatcherism and her onslaught on many of the traditionally accepted roles, values and freedoms of local government led to serious schisms within local parties of both the left and the right and established a radicalism in local government that had not previously been apparent, at least since 1945. The following discussion of the characteristics of differing values within local government must explain the rise and fall of these movements.

Conservative local authorities

The Conservative Party historically has its roots in the Tory Party, which emerged in the seventeenth century as the party of the monarchy and the Anglican Church, although the modern party also includes the radical new-right that owes its values more to early nineteenth-century liberals who were at the time bitter opponents of the conservative Tory tradition. The Tory Party emerged as a movement for smaller landowners, the village squires, who, although relatively wealthy, did not have the resources to modernise their farms as did the larger, generally Whig, aristocratic landowners and feared their possible Whig commercial power over their land. The Tory, therefore, opposed rapid social and technological change and believed that society should evolve, if at all, through slow incremental steps. The squire should remain, with the parson, the focus of village life and receive respect and deference from the lower bred tenant farmers and labourers. However, the squire also had duties towards his inferiors and, at least in theory, protected the lower classes in his domain from the disasters of infirmity and economic misfortune.

Many of the old Tory values, although modernised in the nineteenth century by leaders such as Peel and Disraeli to fit an industrial age, remain within Conservative thinking. This element of the Conservative Party prefers gradual rather than radical change and does not seek to overhaul the political system by following some prefabricated ideological blueprint. The party values an hierarchic class-based society in which the better bred and educated should lead the economic development of society through a predominantly free market system. Such leaders have, however, a duty to the less fortunate and must establish the means whereby they can receive decent education, housing and social security. It was, therefore, not impossible for the Conservative Party to accept and foster the ideals of the welfare state as it emerged after 1945.

The Tory tradition of the nineteenth century valued community government. The parish represented an organic unit of order in which the squire and parson were dominant and the lower orders provided the minor offices according to their station and degree. The more dominant landowners were JPs who met to co-ordinate their work and supervise parishes in the quarter sessions of the county court. These local worthies frequently socialised together in house parties and on the hunting field and formed the elite county set. This Tory tradition still falteringly survives in mainstream Conservative local government, especially in the rural counties and districts. In general, however, the decline of the local notable has replaced the landowners with local professionals who have, from often relatively humble origins, gained local political prominence in the Conservative cause. Many of these political activists accept many of the old Tory values, partly as a consequence of socialisation into the ethos of local party politics and also because of the importance of Tory paternalism in national politics.

Conservatives in local government who accept this strand of thought govern their communities with a light, paternalistic hand. Many Conservatives supporting traditional values tended to stand as independents, arguing that party politics was not relevant for community government. However, this school of thought has seriously declined and those whom Holliday (2000: 171–3) describes as the 'a-political' Conservative are now standing as mainstream Conservatives using the Party label to denote their political affiliation. The Tory councillor does not seek to develop radically new policies within his or her authority and is usually willing to defer to accepted professional practice, provided this does not lead to policies that are particularly radical or expensive. Many shire counties, which are usually Conservative controlled, consequently have a three-month cycle of meetings which leaves much detail in the hands of officers and are not geared to promoting radical restructuring of policies. The Tory council does not choose to spend large sums of money or substantially raise taxes, since they are opposed to policies that would redistribute resources to the extent that the privileges of the affluent are levelled down to the benefit of the poor. Boaden (1971) and Sharpe and Newton (1984: 209) showed that Conservative local authorities tended to set lower taxes and spend less than Labour councils. Nevertheless, such authorities are not opposed to the principle of paternalistic welfare and accept that it is important to provide educational opportunities and social services to all deserving families. The local authority also has an important duty to maintain law and order and funding of this sector is seen as an important function.

The typical Tory shire county is, therefore, generally officer-led, not because of the intellectual incapacity of its Conservative leaders, but because they accept the cautious professionalism of their officers. On the basis of a study of a traditional Tory shire county council, Cheshire, J.M. Lee summed up the relationship between policy maker and officer

> It is misleading to think of the County Council primarily as a body of elected representatives who make decisions on policy and then order officials to execute them ... It is better to regard the system of county government as a body of professional people, placed together in a large office at County Hall, who can call upon the services of representatives (the councillors) from all places throughout the area which they administer. Some of these representatives by sheer ability and drive make themselves indispensable to the successful working of the machine; others merely represent points of view which come into conflict with it. (1963: 214)

A similar illustration of the cautious, unexciting and steady tenor of Conservative local administration is provided by J.D. Dearlove in the context of an urban Conservative controlled authority, the London Borough of Kensington and Chelsea (1973: 225).

The new right

The term new right has been used to describe a portfolio of overlapping, but by no means identical theories, that have had a dominant influence in the Conservative Party since the 1970s. In reality it would be better to describe the theory as neo-liberal, since this approach revives the beliefs in individual competition as a means of progress that were developed by classical liberals such as Bentham and Adam Smith. They argued, in opposition to Tory traditionalism, that the government should only interfere in the lives of individuals to prevent one person from harming the happiness of others by causing physical injury or unlawfully appropriating his property. Government would, therefore, be limited to keeping law and order and defending the realm.

These beliefs have been reasserted in the context of twentieth-century capitalism by philosophers such as F.A. Hayek and Robert Nozick, and the economist Milton Freidman and the public choice theorists. They differ on many points concerning, for example, the role of welfare provision in society, but all generally accept that during this century the state has grown out of control and now interferes with so much of the lives of its citizens that there is little individual freedom and scope for personal initiative and progress. It is, they argue, essential that the power of the state is diminished along with self-interested restrictive bureaucracies that have become useless parasites on individual entrepeneurship and thus a barrier to progress. The welfare services produced by the state also diminish the potential for innovation through high taxation and by forcing the poor into an inescapable cycle of servitude, as they are given no incentive to develop their lives through productive work.

The extent to which these ideas were accepted by the Thatcher and Major Governments is a matter of debate. There is little evidence that these theorists were bedtime reading for Conservative ministers but, through their policy advisors and a few more philosophical politicians, such as Sir Keith Joseph or Nicholas Ridley, there was a recognition of the principal substance of the new-right argument. The Thatcher Governments operated on a premise that the government of Britain was too large, was corrosive of individual freedom and inimical to progress and that welfare services needed, at least, pruning for all but the elderly or infirm. These values have led to the concept of the enabling authority, whose values were outlined in Chapter 3. This authority would have the much diminished role of ensuring that services necessary to the community were undertaken by the private sector.

In Chapters 5 and 6, it was shown how these values help prompt the Thatcher Governments to attack local government as part of the over extensive apparatus of the state. These attacks led to protests not only from Labour authorities, but, in more veiled form, from the many Tory-led shire counties and districts that found these ideas inimical to their own ideology. Whilst interested in thrift, the Tory councillor also values as a duty the welfare role of his or her local authority. Although supportive of private provision for education, housing or homes for the elderly, the Tory recognises that there will always be poorer people in society who need their support to protect them in times of adversity. Such politicians cannot accept the dismantling of local authority provision for social need. The leaders of shire counties were also much influenced against neo-liberal values by their professional officers who would, in general, see the destruction of their departments and transfer of their resources to the private sector as a threat to their very existence. The scale of changes required by the new right also perturbed Tory leaders nurtured on a cautious approach to change and the sanctity of tradition.

Mrs Thatcher was probably very disappointed that her radical new-right values were not widely accepted by Conservative local authorities but, whilst the values of the new right had resonance among fortune seekers in the foreign exchange, insurance and stockbroking offices of the City of London, it had far less appeal to the older Conservative of the shire counties who entered local politics partly as a duty required for membership of the 'county set' and a charitable desire to support good work in the community. The brash, ambitious individualist, of the new right will be more likely to seek their fortune in business and national politics and if they enter local government, it will be to shake up the municipal empire and to make a name in doing so.

There are, therefore, only a handful of major Conservative authorities that seem to have wholeheartedly accepted a new-right direction. The flagships for new-right values are the London Boroughs of Westminster and Wandsworth, which began pursuing elements of new-right theory when Conservatives won control from the Labour Party in 1978 and, against the tide of national electoral opinion, have held onto the Boroughs in successive elections. A scattering of smaller district councils, such as Southend, and for a brief period in the late 1980s before losing control to Labour, the Metropolitan District of Bradford also adopted new-right values. Among county councils, Kent has flirted with new-right policies and for a time the Conservative Group of Wiltshire was bitterly divided between traditional and new-right Conservatives. However, by the mid-1990s, the crushing defeat of the Conservatives in county council elections left only Surrey under overall control by the party and hence, at least temporarily, removed any chance of the new right forwarding their values in what were once the party's local strongholds.

The strategy adopted by these local authorities has been to reduce their expenditure through ensuring that all their services are either abandoned in favour of private sector provision or, if they must be provided by the public sector, opened to competition with the private sector. Thus, in Wandsworth, its former leader, Paul Beresford (1987: 6) described his strategy as

1 The efficient management of services: to cut waste; to ensure high quality and to test all Council services, where possible, against the private sector and to contract out, where appropriate.
2 A vigorous sales policy involving: a) the sale of land and buildings where such

action proves economically efficient; and b) the sale of houses to families on low incomes, thus breaking up enormous housing estates and providing a stimulus to the maintenance of such housing.

3 Major capital investment, using capital receipts from sales and capital allocations to rebuild the local commercial and industrial infra-structure.

This policy has led to a major reduction in expenditure by the authority and, with the help of favourable government manipulation of grant, for a time the lowest local taxes in London. It has also resulted in a major reduction in the number of employees and a substantial decrease in the number of council houses and land held by the Borough.

It can be questioned whether these policies are pursued in line with new-right theory or whether, as Beresford argues, they are the product of 'ordinary common sense'(1987: 5). There is, in at least some supposed new-right authorities, a strong business ethos that does not so much denigrate welfare provision, but the manner in which it has been provided by traditional local authorities. Councillor Pickles who led the radical new right of Bradford City Council in the late 1980s maintained that he has little interest in new Conservative philosophy and received little help from the Conservative Central Office as to how to manage his Authority. His principal attack was against an over large inefficient bureaucracy and he saw his role as that of a management expert seeking to oust waste and inefficiency from a stagnant private business in order to improve the welfare of the City (Smitham 1991).

There is insufficient research on the ideas of the new-right authorities to make any definitive statement on their values and, indeed, it may be shown that, as in the case of local socialist authorities, there are many different variants within this category. The evidence that does exist suggests that whilst these authorities are not particularly ideological in outlook, they are led by ambitious and enthusiastic political activists who do not accept the traditional Tory values of gradual change and deference to authority and expertise. It may be suggested that the proponents of new-right values at the local level, as in central government, represent a relatively new type of Conservative attracted to the party, not as the upholder of tradition and privilege, but as the best means of forwarding individual progress rather than collective welfare through ruthless business efficiency.

Labour local authorities

The Labour Party gained control of seats in local authorities almost as soon as it was formed in 1900 and by the 1920s party members controlled a number of city councils. Many of the early Labour Party activists, especially Fabian intellectuals such as the Sidney and Beatrice Webb and Bernard Shaw, motivated local councillors to secure socialist objectives through the municipalisation of productive and welfare services. Thus, they sought to buy out gas and electricity companies and extended transport undertakings as well as enthusiastically embracing new powers and financial resources to build houses. Attempts to become involved in the productive and commercial economy were, however, soon blocked by a Conservative Parliament which refused to sanction the private bills that would enable the development of municipal socialism. Expansion was, however, possible in the provision of welfare and many Labour authorities led the way in the development of council housing.

Following the reconstruction of local government functions by the 1945 Labour Government, much of the innovatory enthusiasm of Labour controlled authorities appears to have run into the sand of the professionalised routines of their Tory rivals. The moderacy of many Labour authorities stemmed in part from a desire to demonstrate to the electorate that the Party was not, as claimed by many Conservatives, a hot-headed revolutionary body, but instead a respectable, efficient and prudent Party that was fit to govern. Many Labour authorities were, after their initial years of expansion, also imbued with the values of professional officers. The largest Labour-held local authority during the interwar years, the London County Council, under Herbert Morrison's guidance recruited able professionals who pioneered many innovations in education, housing and social services. It would be unreasonable to suggest that Morrison was controlled by his officers. It can, however, be argued that he preferred and fostered their more cautious values rather than more radical policies that, for example, had been advocated by George Landsbury. Both Morrison and Clement Attlee, the future Prime Minister, then mayor of Limehouse, distanced themselves as much as possible from Poplarism (Branson 1979).

The values held by Morrison were not untypical of most leading Labour Party councillors at least until the 1980s and not a few of these cautious Old Labour stalwarts still stalk the corridors of city halls. They support the existing range of services held by local government with its emphasis on education, housing, social services and recreation and seek the development of these activities as public welfare services which should be exclusively designed and controlled by the local authority. Labour leaders of this school of thought are suspicious of alternative methods of delivering these traditional local services as undermining the centrality of their local municipal empires and throwing open public welfare to what they see as the vested interest of the private sector. Like their traditional Tory counterparts, they tend to be deferent to professional advice. Both Old Labour councillors and professional officers have a stake in the *status quo* of incremental expansion of municipal welfare.

The conservatism of many Labour authorities before the arrival of local socialism was also a consequence of the ageing of such councillors and their domination by long-established leadership cliques. There are a number of studies that attest to a decline in Labour Party membership and activity since the 1940s. Hindess (1971) argued that in Liverpool under the leadership of the Braddocks, most working-class wards dwindled to a tiny membership of ageing stalwarts who had little impact on their community. David Green observed that

> The Labour party in Newcastle . . . was large neither in terms of total membership nor in terms of active membership. The party was kept going only by the energy of a few individuals. The selection of electoral candidates the most important function of the party was carried out in such a way that the vast majority of Labour councillors were assured of continued reselection more or less regardless of how well they performed their duties. (1981: 34)

In such circumstances, the mainstream Labour authority was not greatly given to innovation. The Morrisonian Labour leader accepts the subordinate role of local authorities in the British constitution and many leaders of Labour authorities at the time of the rate-capping conflict in 1985 refused to support the radical socialist leaders and reluctantly accepted that at a time of cuts and restraint on revenue they had to cut services.

Local socialism

Since 1945, no commentary on Labour Party politics could seriously suggest that the major ideological innovations in the thinking of the party emanated from local rather than national sources. The largely conventional social democracy of most major authorities controlled by the Labour Party placed them in the mainstream of party thought. In the late 1970s, even before Mrs Thatcher came to power, there was, however, growing dissent among younger councillors in some cities against the established oligarchies that controlled city politics. The generation of radical younger councillors coincided with Thatcher's attacks on local autonomy at a time when the national leadership of the party was so riven with conflict it provided little leadership for party supporters. The energy with which the radical socialist local authorities attempted to challenge Thatcher, therefore, earned their leaders great respect and support among ranks and file party members. The older oligarchies of Labour politicians were in a number of cities swept aside by younger radical councillors. David Blunkett became leader of Sheffield City Council in 1980, Ken Livingstone was elected leader of the GLC in 1981 immediately following local elections that had not only returned Labour councillors in sufficient numbers to overthrow a Conservative majority but also a new generation of radical councillors prepared to replace a more moderate leader of the Greater London Labour Party. Further successes for the left took place in Lambeth, Islington and Hackney. Radical socialism was, however, only partially successful and many cities continued to be dominated by more moderate politicians whilst some Labour Groups, as in the City of Manchester, were torn apart by a bitter struggle between new and old styles of leadership.

Local socialism was not, however, a consistent phenomenon and there are marked differences in policy. Radical Labour authorities followed or paralleled each other's example, not so much by always imitating the actions of fellow travelling authorities, but by a preparedness to rethink traditional policies and innovate into new areas. A consequence was not uniformity in the policies of the socialist local authorities but often a diversity of ideas. Thus, Sheffield City Council and the GLC placed much effort into seeking ways of redeveloping their local economies through establishing funding agencies for new co-operative business. Islington in contrast concentrated more on the innovation of decentralisation and popular participation in local policy making. South Yorkshire County Council emphasised its strategy for subsidised public transport. Liverpool attempted to alleviate unemployment and homelessness by a major house-building programme.

Many of the strategies adopted by the local socialist councils, although vilified in the British tabloid press as products of a 'loony left', were policies that had long been established in many European countries. For example, many German and Italian cities substantially subsidise public transport to develop highly efficient integrated bus and tram services and many European, let alone United States, cities were active in promoting local economic regeneration before this became a major issue pioneered by local socialist authorities in Britain.

A maverick exception to the strategy of Sheffield, the GLC and some London Boroughs was the City of Liverpool, whose moribund party machine had been captured by the Militant Tendency. Militant was founded by two Trotskyists, Peter Taffe and Ted Grant, who, following several attempts to establish a significant political movement, developed a strategy of infiltrating the Labour Party by gaining converts within its ranks (Crick 1986). Its aims were radically different from those of Ken Livingstone or David Blunkett, since it aimed to overthrow the capitalist state through populist revolution to form a classless society. Militant strategy in Liverpool sought to revive the local economy by large-scale public spending on housing and defeating the Government through embarrassing public confrontation. In 1984 they appeared to have gained a considerable victory when, following a threat to set a deficit budget, they gained more funds from the Government. The following year the Government were more determined not to give way and, after surcharging errant councillors, the movement went into eclipse. It was subsequently recognised as a danger by the Labour leadership and many of its leaders expelled from the Party by Neil Kinnock.

Although much has been written concerning local socialism, questions must, however, be raised as to whether this movement was but a flash of the decade. Following the rate-capping crisis of 1985, radical local authorities of the left were forced to retrench many of their more expensive policies and thus rethink their programmes. Sheffield, for example, effectively abandoned almost all of its radicalism of the early 1980s, and the cost of servicing debts incurred in the late 1980s by seeking to revive the fortunes of the City through ambitious projects such as hosting the World Student Games has eventually led to the local electorate replacing the Labour Party majority by Liberal Democrats. This change is replicated in other once left-wing cities. In Liverpool Militant not only lost control within the Labour Group, but the Labour Party lost control to the Liberal Democrats. The more turbulent London Boroughs such as Lambeth and Hackney have toned down their radicalism, whilst the Labour left lost control of Brent. Nevertheless, there remains in place an important legacy from this period. The local socialist authorities pioneered the strategy that local government should be a focus for local economic development and also spearhead campaigns to secure better welfare for women and minority groups.

New Labour

New Labour has, as described in earlier chapters, made major reforms in the structure of sub-national government in Britain through its policy of devolution and in the 2000 Local Government Act radically reshapes the policy-making framework for local authorities. The party, through its self-styled adoption of third way policies which supposedly take a middle road between the compassionate collectivism of Old Labour and the effective, but socially unjust managerialism of the new right, has also tried to forge a new political identity for the party. It is not clear how far Blair has nurtured strong roots of a new ideology even within the Cabinet and Whitehall, let alone in local authorities. There appear to be few local governments that would assert enthusiastically that they are New Labour as opposed to the local socialist enthusiasm of some authorities in the 1980s. Even if local Labour controlled authorities assert that they are New Labour, it is difficult to ascertain exactly what this may entail in terms of policies.

In practice, the role that the Blair Government has assigned to local government as organisations with a duty to care for the economic, social and environmental problems of their communities is not dissimilar from the goals that the local socialists established for themselves in the 1980s. These values were also acceptable to Morrisonian local party leaders from the 1930s to the 1960s, who were concerned that the local authority should be an exemplary employer, bring new business into their communities and deal with pollution through, for example, the development of smokeless zones.

The major difference between New and the traditional Old Labour authorities or the local socialists lies not so much in the goals of local government but the methods through which they are to be achieved. New Labour has accepted from the new right the message that public provision of services is not always to be preferred to private sector delivery and hence local authorities taking a New Labour approach are prepared to consider the merits of private or public service provision in relation to criteria of cost and efficiency. The archetypal

Blair authority will also be prepared to sweep away older pedestrian styles of decision making in favour a directly elected mayor and preferably a mayor who will govern through a city manager. In effect, this may parallel 'Old' Labour deference to the professional administrator. It remains to be seen how many local authorities enthusiastically take up such an arrangement but evidence so far suggests a preference for the cabinet-leader structure, which requires least change from previous practice.

The Liberal Democrat and local government

By the 1950s the Liberal Party had almost disappeared from local politics as they had from the national Parliament. They had once been a dominant force in local politics, particularly in the cities, but were upstaged by the Labour Party, and clung to enclaves of support in the West of England, Wales and some areas of Scotland. The traditional Liberalism of the Celtic periphery of Britain stemmed from the party's representation of non-conformist religious values and regional aspirations that countered the Anglican centralism of the Tory Party. This was a set of values that did not adhere well with the utilitarian mainstream interests of the party as supported by urban manufacturers and added a further strain in the fissiparous movement. Support from the dissenting periphery, however, remained after Liberal interests in the cities had collapsed (Butler and Stokes 1974) and induced within the party by the 1950s a groundswell of support for decentralisation and community politics that was wholly absent from either Conservative or Labour thinking. The Liberal Party was, therefore, suggesting ideas such as Scottish and Welsh devolution long before its two major rivals considered that they had to have any thoughts about the issue.

The revival of Liberal electoral fortunes had little to do with their policies of devolution and community as opposed to their presence as a party which could gain the votes of Labour and Conservative supporters who had become disenchanted with their once favoured party. However, the development of Liberal interest in local community politics may have been considerably influenced by this strand of modern Liberal Party ideology. Liberal leaders began to emphasise the value of gaining support at the local level through attention to community politics. Jo Grimond urged his rank and file in 1960 that

> The Liberal Party should be the party to which the people look to reforms which affect their daily lives ... let us get things done and let us start in local government. (Bulpitt 1967: 106)

This prescription was enthusiastically endorsed in Birmingham by local activists. Wallace Lawler became a Birmingham councillor and then the Liberal MP for Ladywood in a surprise by-election victory in 1969, as a consequence of cultivating widespread, cross-party support for his efforts in helping local residents with their individual local problems (Cyr 1977: 260). Lawler's example was followed by a generation of later Liberals and culminated in the party gaining control of a number of local authorities. The most dramatic success for Liberal community politics has been in Liverpool, where it became the largest single Party in 1973 after holding just one seat five years earlier in a city which, even in the nineteenth century, did not have a strong Liberal tradition.

The Liverpool success was engineered by a local businessman, Trevor Jones, who perfected the techniques pioneered by Lawler. Stress is placed on ensuring that local residents are in frequent contact with Liberal activists who are prepared to act as a channel for their complaints. Liberal Democrat community politics is concerned with getting done many simple things that are important in people's lives, such as securing a new dustbin, ensuring council house repairs are properly carried out, or leading local campaigns for safer roads. These strategies were publicised by house to house canvassing, backed up by frequent community newsletters.

Whilst it is clearly evident that Liberal Democrat politicians have developed new campaigning styles in local politics, it is much less easy to discern the extent to which they run their local authorities differently from the other parties. There are too few Liberal authorities to provide any general evidence that they spend more or less than their rivals, although, from examples such as Liverpool City Council and more recently Sheffield, it appears that the party is much more inclined to prune budgets than Labour. In general, the party pursues different policies in different areas and is as prepared to collaborate with Labour as Conservative authorities in hung councils (Leach and Stewart 1992).

There is, however, some evidence to suggest that the localist campaigning of the Liberal Democrat Party inclines them towards a closer identification with strategies to disperse power from town hall. The Liberal Democrats in Tower Hamlets established a unique system of decentralising power to seven townships, allowing a number of these 'mini local councils' to be controlled by the opposing Labour Party. Apart from Tower Hamlets, other Liberal Democrat authorities such as South Somerset District Council and Rochdale MDC have pioneered structures for decentralised services. These authorities clearly take heed of the traditional localism that has been one of the more clearly characteristic policies of the Liberal Democrats.

Hung councils

Analysis of party values in local politics has been muddied in recent years by the increase in local authorities where no one party has had overall control. In such circumstances there have been a number of strategies for dividing power.

Table 12.2 *Types of hung council (1992)*

	Number
Formal coalition	7
Power sharing	8
Minority administration	53
No administration	8
Unidentifiable	4
Total	80

Leach and Stewart (1992) classified these councils, in terms of working relationships between parties. In the majority of hung councils, one party, usually the largest in terms of seats, is permitted to take the lead role and select the committee chairs. The party will, however, only secure enactment of its policies if it makes concessions to the opposing parties. Less frequently, in some authorities, two or more parties form an effective working coalition in which they agree to divide the committee chairmanships between them and form agreements on policy. A third category involves parties agreeing to share power by sharing out the committee chairs between themselves, but making no further permanent agreements on policy. Finally, Leach and Stewart identified a small number of local authorities where there was no agreement among the parties and no pattern of control emerged. In such a situation, committee chairs may be elected for each meeting and policy emerges, if at all, by a long and painful process of inter-party wrangling (Leach and Stewart 1992). They also noted that there were a few authorities where party discipline was low and hence the fact that no party predominated made little difference to the cross-party bargaining that had always characterised these councils (Leach and Stewart 1985). Leach and Stewart classified hung councils in 1992 as is shown in Table 12.2 (above).

It is difficult to generalise about the party composition of the alliances that underlie hung council in which a minority administration is able to govern. Surveys on these authorities have been regularly undertaken by *The New Statesmen* that suggest there is frequent change in relationships. Between 1987 and 1995, many hung councils are a consequence of the Conservatives losing control of authorities due to an upsurge in Liberal Democrat protest votes, so that the most likely arrangement is for Labour and Liberal Democrat Parties as the opposition to the Conservatives to form tacit agreements to increase local spending. However, other arrangements are not infrequent and Conservative support for the Liberal Democrats is not unusual. On rare occasions, as in Bradford in 1985–86, local Labour and Conservative groups have co-operated to keep the Liberal Democrats from office (Leach and Stewart 1992).

Managing local authorities in which no party has an overall majority is the expected rather than the exceptional pattern in many European cities. In Italy, the stagnation created by the competition between many opposing parties led to the creation of a system for directly elected mayors which has gained considerable popularity. The Mayor of Rome, despite having no strong party identification, has been suggested as a future Prime Minister of Italy.

Regardless of the combination of alliances, it is generally the case that hung councils develop policy through behind the scenes bargaining between parties that have developed some form of informal understanding between them. The result is the politics of compromise and accommodation. It is also a situation in which the ideas of senior officers may often be regarded as an important means of resolving differences. However, many chief executives prefer not to work with the uncertainty of a coalition arrangement which will also place difficulties in the way of any major proposals put forward by a chief officer as much as for a councillor.

Differences and similarities

A review of policy styles and orientation that stems from differing party ideologies must be treated with some caution. The idealised models of behaviour suggested under each category are not meant to precisely fit all local authorities. There are numerous variations on the basic themes. It can, however, be concluded that there is probably far more substantial areas of agreement between political parties in local government than substantial differences. Even in the 1980s, the majority of local authorities were neither enthusiasts of the new right or the radical left, but had similar 'end of ideology' values concerning the role of local government as an element of a mixed-economy welfare state.

At the beginning of the twenty-first century, there appears to be far less that differentiates local authorities than twenty years earlier. There are no authorities that appear now to be radically socialist pursuing policies centrally geared to achieving greater social equality. There similarly remains few authorities wedded to a new-right philosophy, although both Westminster and Wandsworth have continued under right-wing Conservative domination, despite the demise in the national fortunes of their Party. Effectively, with the Blair government pressing local authorities to adopt private sector contractors where this is found to be more efficient and with no effective relaxation on tight spending curbs on local government, it has been far more difficult for any local authority to follow the local socialist path of high local taxation to fund extensive subsidies to housing and transport budgets so as to benefit the poorer groups in the community. Thatcher ensured that socialist values could not be pursued by local government and the Blair Government has done nothing that effectively removes this constraint. The policies of the new right are still more open for local authorities, although Best Value may constrain some of the wildest shores of outsourcing key services should any local authority wish to pursue the path to the fully enabling but not implementing authority. However, sufficient remains of new-right values to ensure that all local authorities have been pushed to the right under Thatcher and Major and are being kept in such a position by Blair. Under such constraints, far less ideologically divides local authorities under different party controls than was the case in the previous century.

Any radical change in local government policies may lie not in the old framework of local government, but in the development of the role of elected mayors heading powerful executives. It is possible that, as in London, despite central constraints, a strong mayor supported by local party loyalists and the general electorate could place new pressures on central government by taking radical departures from centre-right policies. Such an eventuality was probably not anticipated by Blair, who hoped directly elected mayors could be controlled by the national party leadership. New Labour's leadership failure to impose their own candidate as Mayor of the Greater London Authority, as opposed to a populist figure such as Ken Livingstone, may be a taste of events to come.

Further reading

Community studies will clearly provide a profile of individual local authorities and therefore are a valuable background to this section. These studies have been summarised in Chapter 8. The importance of party politics in local government is broached by Bulpitt (1967) and considered empirically by Boaden (1971) and Sharpe and Newton (1984). Hung councils are analysed by Leach and Stewart (1992).

There are few general studies of the Conservative Party in local government, although recent work by Holliday (2000) provides a useful summary of the present situation, but there are valuable insights into the Disraelian tradition in community studies such as Lee (1963) and Dearlove (1973). Further reading on the new right was outlined in Chapter 3.

Local socialism received considerable attention when the movement was at its height with Boddy and Fudge (1984), Gyford (1985) and Lansley, Goss and Wolmar (1989) being particularly valuable and, although not always as incisive as it could be, Blunkett and Jackson (1987) is also important. There is much less writing focused on the attitudes of New Labour councillors but Hall and Leach (2000) provide a valuable introduction to the situation. Older traditions upheld in the values of Herbert Morrison are provided in his biography by B.

Donoghue and G.W. Jones (1973) and some idea of the indifference of other Labour leaders of this time to local government can be gleaned from works such as Williams on Gaitskell (1979), Pimlott on Dalton (1985) or Crosland on Crosland (1982), although I would not advise reading the whole of these biographies solely to discover the paucity of enthusiasm they demonstrate towards the subject of this book.

13

Local democracy

Local government has always had its critics, but from the 1980s was subjected to a vociferous largely new-right inspired onslaught on its democratic integrity. These views gained considerable currency in the Governments of Thatcher and Major. It was argued that lack of exposure to competition and the electoral system that created many one-party dominated councils established a closed club of councillors and senior officers who could isolate themselves from public opinion. The system was, consequently, overstaffed and inefficient and harboured widespread corruption (Henney 1984; Walker 1983). These arguments have been considered in Chapters 8 and 10 and need little further discussion here and do not, moreover, appear to be fully accepted by the Blair Government, which has developed policies to reward the most efficient local authorities by granting them 'beacon' status. However, the argument that the institutions of local government are, in practice, out of touch with their electorate and therefore essentially undemocratic is a view that does seem to be harboured by many within the Blair Government. A central theme of the White Paper *Modern Local Government: In Touch with the People* (1998, Para. 2.12) was to secure 'a bigger say for local people by'

- creating new political structures for councils;
- improving local democracy;
- strengthening local financial accountability;
- establishing a new ethical framework.

As a conclusion to this study it is important to consider whether the view that local democracy in Britain is in poor health is warranted, and whether the solutions to improving local democracy that are being taken by the Blair Government are appropriate.

203

The nature of democracy

The rationale for the argument that local government is not particularly democratic is not so much new right in character as founded on empirical studies that poured scepticism on pluralist theories of democracy developed initially in the United States, which were founded primarily on local government studies.

Pluralist theory

Liberal democracy emerged in Europe in the late nineteenth century and was soon challenged intellectually by theorists bent on asserting the credentials of fascism. Two Italian writers, Geatano Mosca and Villfrado Pareto, had argued that, for both psychological and organisational reasons, liberal democracies at a national level broke down into oligarchies of elite policy makers. They maintained that most individuals defer to strong-minded leaders and that those in power had the political knowledge and experience to persuade the public to follow their views. Organisationally, leaders could manipulate the disciplinary and financial machinery of the state or political party to rid themselves of those they failed to convince by persuasion or through deference. German sociologist Roberto Michels, formulated an 'Iron Law' that maintained 'who says organisations, says oligarchy (1958: 418).

These theories were to be influentially challenged by J.A. Schumpeter (1947), who argued that whilst no one could deny that small elites determined policy, it was nevertheless possible through democratic means to ensure that the elites that governed were sensitive to popular opinion. He defined democracy as

> That institutional arrangement for arriving at political decisions in which individuals acquire the right to decide by means of a competitive struggle for the people's vote. (1947: 269)

By competing for the popular vote, elites would be obliged to tailor their policies to the interests of majority opinion. Thus, democracy was achieved not as a result of individuals in power representing their electors, but because elected politicians had to respond to voters interests if they were to retain their support and therefore power.

This theory was not however supported by some earlier attempts to empirically evaluate the effectiveness of democratic institutions, which studied local governments as convenient and practical guinea pigs. Among the early influential studies was an analysis by R. and H. Lynd (1929) of political power in a middle-sized American town of Muncie, disguised under the pseudonym of Middletown. Floyd Hunter (1953) later investigated the structure of power in a number of larger United States cities, especially Atlanta, and concluded, like the Lynds some years earlier, that power within these cities rested with a small coterie of businessmen who could, on their own or through subordinate agents, dominate local decision making.

The reassertion of elitism by community research was countered by Robert A. Dahl, who revised Schumpeter's ideas in *Who Governs?* (1961), a study of power in the city of New Haven, home of the University of Yale. Dahl argued that, whilst authoritative decisions were clearly taken by the mayor of the city, this apparently powerful individual could only hope to remain in office if he or she accepted the demands of the more popular and least-opposed of the interest groups concerned with a particular issue. Interest groups acted as the intermediary between individual electors and the formal decision makers. They aggregated opinion and obliged leaders to devise policies that could best reconcile or co-ordinate the views of these groups. The successful politicians were those who could chart a course between numerous conflicting or complementary demands so as to generate a coalition of interests in their support. Thus, elites had to respond to popular opinion, not just at election time but continually in the day-to-day conflicts and debates of political life. For Dahl, a democratic system required not only that those in power were elected by citizens in regular secret ballots, but that there was a capacity to develop numerous interest groups in society that were able to challenge and replace those in power. Such an open society was termed a pluralist society or, as later formulated by Dahl, a polyarchy.

Following the publication of Dahl's theory, academics sought to confirm or destroy the pluralist theory in what became known as the 'community power debate'. Some researchers enthusiastically affirmed Dahl's ideas. R. C. Wood's study of New York entitled *1400 Governments* (1961) is typical of pluralist enthusiasm. Others, however, affirmed the Floyd Hunter view that the business elites controlling cities need pay little attention to interest groups. A particularly influential attack argued that no amount of empirical research could resolve the issue, since pluralism was only visible on issues that the elites preferred to put into the arena of public debate. Powerful politicians who controlled the political agenda could prevent widespread discussion of issues that were important solely to the general public. Many issues were therefore assigned to the category of 'non-decisions' that never became subject to public debate (Bacharach and Baratz 1962).

Dahl (1985, 1989) himself has become a stern critic of his theory by pointing out that the uneven spread of resources in the form of wealth, education and expertise means that large well-resourced groups such as multi-national companies have much greater access to power than a poorly endowed group of individuals. Democracy is imperfect and does not secure equality of power and influence. The critics of the original idea of pluralism, often termed neo-pluralists, nevertheless, suggest that despite its flaws pluralist democracy is better than autocracy and further reforms and better popular education as to its merits could lead to a more egalitarian and participative structure of power.

The neo-pluralist debate in Britain

A number of community power studies were undertaken in Britain during the 1960s and 1970s, some of which were specifically concerned to evaluate the Dahl thesis. In general, these studies were critical of the pluralist idea. Newton (1976) argued that, whilst there was evidence of interest group activity in Birmingham, the most effective groups were large organisations, usually operating in a national political context, and that, apart from these groups, councillors could insulate themselves from local pressure. Some later studies have been even more dismissive of pluralism. David Green's study of party politics in Newcastle (1981) attempted to show that the city was controlled by a tightly-knit coterie of council leaders. Marxist-inspired studies of community conflict such as Cynthia Cockburn's, *The Local State* (1977) have, from a different theoretical perspective, suggested that local authorities are insensitive to their electorate since they are inevitably controlled by capitalist interests.

There have also been a number of attempts to ascertain how much of the vote in local election will tend to reflect local as opposed to national interests. Newton, in his study of Birmingham, found that only 10 per cent of the variance in electoral results in the city could be attributed to local issues (1976:14–15). An analysis of the election of 1979, when local elections were held at the same time as the general election showed that there was little divergence between the vote for councillors and the vote for parliamentary candidates (Waller 1980). Summing up critiques of the pluralist model, Patrick Dunleavy argued that it was 'empirically inappropriate to local elections in Britain because local parties and elites fundamentally do not compete' (1980: 136). He maintained that pluralism did not work because most citizens cast their vote in local elections according to their views on the national parties and not on the performance of local parties. Aware of this, local party leaders can ignore popular opinion, since their chances of winning elections are not in their hands.

The Blair Government has clearly accepted these arguments, at least in so far as assuming that elected local councillors may operate inefficient local services and raise unnecessarily high local taxes without any fears that the local electorate will be sufficiently aware or concerned about the problem that they will vote the miscreants from office. The Best Value framework has been established on the premise that, should a local authority fail to meet nationally established standards for service delivery and economy, they must be brought into line by central government action rather than through the procedures of local democracy. Similarly, the Blair Government continues the assumption of the Thatcher and John Major that local electors will not reject local councillors if they raise what in their opinion may be excessive property taxes. These views indicate that, during the last twenty-five years, governments in Britain have had little confidence in local democracy. Local electors are, it appears, incapable of discerning when they are dissatisfied with their local councillors and are, therefore, incapable of removing them and securing for their better good more efficient services at a lower cost.

A critique of the isolationist theory

This argument that local government in Britain does not respond to local opinion is, however, subject to too many exceptions to be fully acceptable. It is, of course, hardly surprising that voters who favour a particular party in national elections will also favour that party in local elections. Their local vote may not be directly related to the current national policies of their favoured party, but on the belief that the values held by that party, both at local and national levels, reflect their values and beliefs. A staunch Conservative who believes in low rates of taxation and, whenever possible, private provision of welfare, will be motivated to vote for whichever party expresses this view and this is likely to be the Conservative cause both within the local authority and for the national government.

There is, however, evidence to suggest that it is possible for local election results to be radically different from that which would be expected on the basis of an analysis of the social composition of the electorate. The political fortunes of the City of Liverpool do not lend themselves to the thesis that predominantly working-class areas vote Labour nationally and will therefore return a Labour Council. Liverpool was dominated by the Conservative Party during the first half of the twentieth century because of religious, as opposed to class, differences as Protestants supported the party of the Anglican Church against the Liberal and later Labour affections of the many Irish Roman Catholic immigrants to the City. After 1955, it appeared that Liverpool had entered the conventional fold by returning a Labour majority, but this pattern was shattered in the late 1960s when the Liberal Party began winning many working-class seats in the City and by 1980 obtained majority control at the expense of Labour seats as much as Conservative ones. The Liberal hold was then broken in 1983 by the Labour Party which, under the influence of the Trotskyist Militant Tendency, had views that were considerably at variance with the national leadership of the Labour Party. However, following what turned out to be a brief socialist reign, the City returned to Liberal Democrat control.

The development of Liverpool politics cannot simply be ascribed to national trends. The Liberal success, in a city where they had never before been dominant, was at least in part, a consequence of the localist policy which, as devised by Sir Trevor Jones, became a blueprint for Liberals throughout the country. The party was able to oust the Labour Party from office by emphasising local rather than national issues. Not only did the Liverpool Liberals captured local control in the City but also later won parliamentary seats which suggests an example, not of the local vote following the national vote, but the national vote reflecting local concerns. The Liberals' success was, however, also a consequence of the moribund nature of the Labour Party in Liverpool where its dominant leader, Jack Braddock, had allowed many ward parties to deteriorate into small enclaves of elderly stalwarts supporting the views of their local leader and had, by the 1970s, neither the energy, imagination or the new recruits to fight the energetic Liberals with similar locally orientated policies (Hindess 1971).

There are many other examples of Liberal and Liberal Democrat success in areas that, on the basis of the socio-economic composition of the electorate, would be expected to support either Labour or Conservative candidates. Liberal Democrat control of Tower Hamlets, which was one of the most depressed areas of London, was in part attributable to the collapse of the local Labour Party and the community politics of an adventurous young Liberal Democrat Party, whilst failures in the local Conservative Party have led to Liberal Democrat control of Isle of Wight in the 1990s. In 1998 the City of Sheffield transferred from Labour control to the Liberal Democrats despite high levels of national support for the Blair Government, largely due to concern over local problems of local authority debt and urban decline. In Scotland, local opposition to the major parties has resulted in periodic victories for Scottish Nationalists as well as Liberal Democrats.

It may, therefore, be concluded that whilst correlation between national and local voting patterns is to be expected as a consequence of both parties and electors having similar values when operating in both a local and national context, there can be a breakdown in the relationship if locally a party fails to organise itself effectively and is faced with a concerted locally orientated challenge from a rival party. Councillors who learn from these cases soon realise that they may be vulnerable to challenge if they wholly neglect local opinion. Most political parties do take the local electorate seriously and do not assume that they can neglect popular feeling, but need to convince voters of their values. By far the most expensive item in the budget of any ward party or association is the cost of local elections which, unlike general elections, must be met predominantly from locally raised finance. Most urban and many rural parties are able to marshal the resources to distribute leaflets explaining their policies and many will actively canvass house to house in local elections. If, as Patrick Dunleavy suggests, this is simply 'going through the motions' (1980: 136), then it must be questioned why local parties bother to make the effort at all. In reality, party leaders and rank and file activists wish to believe that they have the support of their electorate and avoid dangers of a collapse in their support occasioned by neglect of their voters. This is not, however, proof that many local policies reflect the wishes of the majority of local voters, but it does indicate that the general coincidence of local and national voting patterns does not, in itself, show that local elites need never respond to local opinion, along the lines of the Schumpetarian view of democracy.

Research by Miller, Dickson and Stoker (2000) also suggests that the general public strongly support local democracy as a means of making collective decisions for a community and have a much greater preference for such a system of

Table 13.1 *Percentage voting turnout in local elections (1995–99)*

	1995	1996	1997	1998	1999	2000
London				35		
Metropolitan districts	34	31		25	26	26
Counties			73			
English districts (partial election)	40	37		30	33	32
English district (whole council)	42				36	
English unitaries	40	35	70	28	32	29
Scottish districts	45				59	
Welsh districts	49				50	

Source: C. Rallings and M. Thrasher (1994; 2000).

government than a structure based on appointed boards and agencies. Miller *et al.* found that the public trust their local authority more than other non-elected local public agencies and much more strongly than the national government (102; 169). The public also thought central government was more likely to waste public money than local government (161). Citizens were also more likely to have complained about political issues to a local councillor than their MP (164). Thus, despite low turnout in local elections, other indicators of democratic efficacy, such as the capacity to listen and respond to popular views and to gain the trust of the citizen, show local democracy to be in a healthier state than the national political system.

Participation and indifference

Even though local councillors cannot assume that, if their party is the national party of choice for their community, their electorate will vote for them however incompetent they may be, democracy at the local level is still an issue for the few rather than the many. It is argued by the Blair Government that a serious symptom of the malaise of local democracy in Britain is that it involves a minority within most communities, even at the level of simply voting. It is but a small part of the electorate that votes in local elections and central government has never been slow to remind local authorities that challenge their authority that in General Elections a much higher proportion of the electorate bother to vote than in local elections.

The proportion of the electorate voting in different types of local authority during recent elections is shown in Table 13.1 and compares with a 78 per cent turnout for the General Election of 1992 and 71 per cent in 1997. when local and national elections were held at the same time, thus accounting for the

Table 13.2 *Voting turnout in local elections in liberal democracies*

	%	Date of election
Denmark	80	
Finland	61	1996
France	70	
Germany	72	
Ireland	56	1991
Italy	85	
Netherlands	50	1995
Portugal	61	1993
Sweden	90	

Sources: Where election date given Loughlin (1999); Others: Rallings and Thrasher (1996: 64).

much larger turnout for local contests in that year. The data in Table 13.1 conceals, of course, a wide variation in turnout in local elections from ward to ward and authority to authority. In Sheffield MDC turnout in the 1995 election varied from 42 per cent in one ward to 22 per cent in the most indifferent electoral division.

Turnout in local elections is generally lower in Britain than other European Union countries as is indicated in Table 13.2. Turnout in local elections in the United States is, however, generally lower than in Britain, although this is also true for national elections and may reflect that in the United States voters must make an effort to register to vote rather than being legally obliged to register.

There are many factors that can affect voting turnout. These can include the number of parties in the contest, the socio-economic status of the electorate and even how near the election may be to a General Election. It is also generally found that low turnout is more associated with wards where one party predominates (Rallings and Thrasher 1996: 79), as voters may not consider it worth voting if the result is certain. The low turnout in local elections is the most obvious, but far from the only, indicator of a relatively high level of indifference to local politics (Commission for Local Democracy 1995). Local issues are not generally of such importance that a local candidate can pack out a meeting hall of eager voters concerned to find out the views of their candidates. Indeed, although most voters may know which party controls their local authority, the majority will be unable to name their local councillors (Hampton 1970: 127).

There is also relatively little enthusiasm to stand for local office. It may be easier to become a councillor than many citizens may think. There is often little contest within political parties for the party nomination in safe seats, let alone marginal and hopeless wards. In the 1981 metropolitan county elections there were, for example, in Merseyside, 99 vacant seats and only 109 names on the panel of candidates, whilst for South Yorkshire the ratio of candidates to seats was 2.6, which, if somewhat better, does not lend itself to strenuous conflict (Chandler and Morris 1984).

There is also little evidence of mass participation in local authority government, through interest group mediation. As was shown earlier, the more successful groups tend to be nationally based, highly professional organisations such as trade associations or trade unions that may have mass memberships but will be controlled by relatively small elites of full-time employees or highly active politically orientated volunteers. The many clubs, sports teams and welfare groups that enrich urban life are rarely and only incidentally involved in local politics.

The Blair Government's reforms: can they work?

The 1998 White Paper *Local Government: In Touch with the People* indicates through its title that a major element of its proposals concern greater citizen identification and participation in local governance. As described in Chapter 7, the Government has fulfilled these aims through the 2000 Local Government Act which requires local authorities to choose between three styles of government, the mayor and manager, mayor and cabinet or leader and cabinet, in order to focus power to make and implement policy more clearly in a small executive and thus free backbench councillors to pursue with greater leisure the tasks of working with their local constituents and holding the executives to account through scrutiny and standards committees. The local authority is also given more general powers to work for the economic social and environmental good of the community which may facilitate greater local freedom to produce innovatory strategies for the good of their community. Accountability has been strengthened by a new ethical code and committee structures to supervise the code and the Best Value framework that makes performance targets more visible and easily monitored.

It can be argued that concentrating decision making in the hands of a visible mayor rather than a wider group of councillors who make decisions in the closed room of party caucuses may provide local citizens with a figure who is visible and accountable to them. It is likely that directly elected mayors, if not the new style leader and cabinet members, will become a more visible target for the media and hence better known to citizens in general than the old-style leader of a local authority.

It is, nevertheless, difficult to see how many of these changes can effectively generate greater democracy by bringing local government closer to their electorate and stimulating greater participation. The impact of a move towards a smaller executive, in itself, does not suggest a move towards spreading power more widely within the community, but rather concentrating power in the hands of a few individuals. Political visibility does not on its own necessarily equate with greater democracy. Even in an open society, a single individual governing a large community is likely to be far less accessible than members of a larger collective group of decision makers. Elected mayors will have time to relate personally to only the most influential and powerful members of the public and are unlikely to deal with most ordinary citizens on a day-to-day basis. Unlike the mayor of a French village commune who is likely to know and meet frequently the citizens of his or her community, the mayor of a big city, whether in France, the United States or Britain will be, like British national government leaders, a remote figure seen by the population through the lens of media reporting rather than personal contact and experience. The elected leader will, moreover, especially if working in a mayor/city manager structure be likely to be advised by a coterie of individuals who will be selected as aides to the mayor and will not be directly elected or directly accountable to the population. A consequence of such a system may initially be to create greater interest in local politics, especially in cities where the media find much in the personality or earlier career of the mayor to interest readers. Interest will not however be translatable into power and influence for the individual, any more than readers of *Hello* magazine can influence the mind of the fashionably glamorous.

Whilst the elected mayor may be high profile but remote from most citizens, the ordinary backbench councillor who is supposed under the new system to be able to devote more time to his or her constituents is likely to be an increasingly marginalised and insignificant figure. National politicians have long been aware that the lot of a backbench MP is generally unglamorous and lacking any effectiveness (Kingdom 1999: 373). Such a system translated to local level will produce even more marginalised figures. Under the old system, a backbench councillor could busy themselves on what may, in terms of the local authority as a whole, be an unglamorous sub-committee such as markets or parks and gardens. Such a task can often fire the councillor with enthusiasm for their particular niche and give them a fulfilling role that generated real improvements in their community. Instead all councillors are expected to bring general issues from their constituents to the attention of the great and the good in the form of the cabinet or the mayor and manager who may wholly ignore their complaints and concerns.

It seems unlikely that the strategies open to the new-style backbench councillors will be adequate as a means to redress the likelihood of probable indifference of council executives to their work on behalf of their constituents. Select committees of the British Parliament are infrequently reported and it would seem even less likely that a local press will pay any attention to the cavils of well-meaning scrutiny committees, unless they uncovered some highly sensational scandal.

In many authorities citizens are attracted to politics and become candidates in local elections under the belief that they may be able to shape the development of their community, become a local person of consequence and perhaps reach senior political positions as leader of the council or, possibly using service on the local authority as a stepping stone to gain election as an MP. Under the arrangement of a directly elected mayor, there may, however, be far less motivation to become a backbench councillor as an entry point towards a national political career. If, as is possible, the senior post of mayor goes to nationally recognised politicians parachuted into the job by their national party leaders, service as backbench councillors will be a far less attractive apprenticeship for securing more senior political positions.

Whilst the Blair Government has focused power and management of local government in cabinet governments or mayors and appointed managers, it has done little to encourage local initiatives to secure closer contact with the electorate through devolving power to area committees or to parish councils. As shown in Chapter 10, the Government has not prevented schemes for decentralisation, but has also not seen such a move as central to its aim of reinforcing local democracy. This seems particularly strange, given the preceding argument that Britain with such large units of local governance is more in need of decentralised government than almost any other European State or the United States.

Democracy by opinion poll and focus group

A further element in the New Labour package to restore local democracy is the demands within the Best Value framework that local authorities continually test public opinion concerning the quality of their services through regular surveys of popular opinion. The Minister of State for Local Government in the 1997 Blair Administration, Hilary Armstrong, has frequently praised schemes in which local governments have ascertained public opinion on policy and service delivery efficiency through citizens' panels and focus groups. The methods for ascertaining public opinion involve techniques such as opinion polls, focus groups and citizen juries. In effect, these schemes use opinion polling strategies that have been pioneered by private businesses to ascertain how they may best develop and sell their products.

The pursuit of such opinion surveys is to suggest that democracy may be replaced by polling techniques. There are however serious dangers in this approach. Democracy is ideally not about elites responding to public opinion, but about popular active participation in policy making. Opinion polling and to a large extent citizen juries and focus groups can be devices that are easily manipulated in the interest of those who establish the questions and topics to be discussed in such forums. A questionnaire may include only those issues on which an officer or councillors wishes to ascertain public opinion, rather than issues which they wish to ignore. Moreover, the most open exchange of opinions between a panel of citizens and council or government leaders is subject to the interpretation that the council leaders will put on the responses and their willingness to accept that they should pursue the ideas that are being put forward. The democratic credentials of a citizen panel are also dependent on whether the assembled group is genuinely representative of the population and whether such a group may become far more favourable in their opinion to the local authority simply by virtue of being selected for comment. Even more seriously, it may be argued that effective democracy is not about responding to a few, but creating structures that enable the many, if they wish, to participate fully in all aspects of the political process that affects their lives. To understand this latter point, British political leaders need to absorb the theory of democracy as developed in the United States or some European countries.

Controlling the local authority

The level of democracy within a local democracy is not solely dependent on the democratic framework of the structures and internal decision-making machinery, but also on the extent that those who control the local authority are given freedom to govern through being given a high level of resources and political discretion by central government. The 2000 Local Government Act has granted local authority leaders and directly mayors at least some measure of discretion through clauses that define the broad purpose of a local authority to develop the economic, social and environmental well being of their communities. Such a step moves local government in Britain more towards a framework that is less restrained by the principle of *ultra vires*. However, removing some of the barriers to develop potential new powers still remain, in the hands of central government.

The Government, as indicated in Chapter 4, has not substantially changed many of the crucial limitations on local spending imposed by the Conservative Party in the 1984 Rates Act. Rate capping, although less visible, still remains a weapon in the Government's armoury. Determination of the extent of capital spending, although simplified, also remains in the hands of central government. The Blair Government has also increased its capacity to intervene in service delivery by local governments through the Best Value framework. Whilst local authorities do not now have to submit to the crude demand in CCT that they accept the lowest bid for the provision of particular services, local authorities are bound by central inspection to provide services of a standard that is laid down not by local views and values, but by the centre. There has also been no move to relocate the substantial powers to build and manage public housing away from the housing associations back to democratically elected local authorities, nor to restore some of the controls local authority held over education prior to the 1988 Education Reform Act. Similarly, the Blair Government has imposed ethical codes on local authorities which also ensure that should local opinion and the electoral process fail to undermine actions regarded by the Government as unethical, the Government itself can act. The increase in regulation of local government activities by the centre and the continued central imposition of financial restraints, does nothing to suggest that the Blair Government trusts local democracy and local government to be able to govern without central surveillance and regulation.

What is needed to secure local democracy?

It remains to be seen whether the development of cabinet government and directly elected mayors will increase the profile of local government. However, such a development does not seem to be the most obvious way of fulfilling the aim of the White Paper to ensure 'modern local government: in touch with the people'. If local government were to be brought closer to the people in Britain, it might seem more appropriate than creating elected mayors to encourage far greater decentralisation of decision making to bring the opportunity of making decisions that affect a local community down to the community level of village, town or district of large city. Whilst it may be inappropriate for any government to embark on yet another round of restructuring existing boundaries of local authorities, it would be possible to legislate that each local authority develops a strategy for decentralisation of policy making to neighbourhood committees or to parish councils and to develop a system of direct participation of citizens in such local decisions, as opposed to discerning public opinion through question-naires and focus groups.

At the opposite end of the spectrum of sub-national government, democracy would also be enhanced if a system of elected regional governments were created in England which would have powers to develop strategies concerning regional economic growth and also to provide a focus that secures public accountability for a wide range of regional services, such as the NHS or, perhaps, regulation of water, gas and electricity supplies which are currently governed at the regional level by *ad hoc* unelected agencies.

Serious democratisation, whether to the smallest communities or at a regional level, must also involve subsidiarity, in that effective powers and resources to implement policy are passed to the appropriate level of government. A system in which financial resources given to localities are controlled by the centre and in which most authorities provide services to a standard approved by the centre or subject to appeal to the centre from dissenting interests, is scarcely a structure facilitating genuine local democracy, but rather a system of local management of centrally determined strategies.

Effective local democracy must also entail that the local politicians, elected to make decisions for a community, county or region, should be accountable not to the national government but to the local electors. The procedures that have been particularly developed by the Blair Government that demand, through Best Value, minimum standards of service provision or the adherence of councillors and local government officers to appropriate ethical codes demonstrate a distrust by the centre of a basic premise of democracy, that the voters are the most appropriate determinants of what an area should require by way of services and the standards to be expected from its representatives. Moreover, if local government, as opposed to local management, means anything, it is that communities differ in their needs and demands and will, therefore, choose to have different types and levels of service delivery, different styles of government and different codes of conduct.

It would of course be wrong to move too far in arguing for local autonomy and no one should expect local governments to be independent of state controls. Whilst differences in service standards or ethical conduct may be acceptable and even expected at local level, there are clearly standards of morality that must be expected to be applied universally throughout a nation and certain services that must be made available to everyone in society, regardless of class, race, sexuality or ableness. Nevertheless, within such a framework most European States and the nations of North America generally appear to strike a far better balance between local and central power than has developed over the centuries in Britain.

> Britain differs from other European Union countries in its arrangements for local government in the size of its effective lower tier local government units and in moving towards single rather than two- or three-tier organisational frameworks. Britain also has in comparative terms much lower levels of participation in local politics. These factors should suggest to policy makers that greater participation in local politics may result from substantial decentralisation of power to small communities by creating a local government structure based on grassroots views of community, rather than a view from Whitehall.

Further reading

There are many important theoretical studies of democracy. One of the most important general works to appear in recent years is Held (1987). Lively (1975) may also be a useful shorter read. Specifically addressed to local government, Hill (1974) is still a useful text.

The community power debate may be followed through Parry (1969), but reference can be made to Dahl (1961 and 1971), whilst Newton (1976) is an important empirical appraisal of the idea. Dunleavy (1980) is a stimulating challenge to the Schumpetarian theory.

Concern for the decline in local democracy has been expressed by the Commission for Local Democracy (1995) and in several research papers written in connection with this campaign (Stoker 1994; Phillips 1994).

A valuable guide to some of the many issues concerning the theory of local democracy is provided by the contributors to King and Stoker (1996) *Rethinking Local Democracy* and from a more empirical position by Pratchett,

L. and Wilson, D. (eds) (1996) and Pratchett's (2000) edition of papers examining local democracy in Britain first published in *Local Government Studies* 25, 4,1999.

Public opinion concerning differing models of local governance is rigorously tested by Miller, Dickson and Stoker (2000).

Appendix: dates of major events concerning the development of local government in Britain

1832   Electoral Reform Act and the emergence of liberal values as a governing ideology in Britain

1834   Poor Law Amendment Act
Establishes poor Law boards, removing powers from individual parishes and setting up *ad hoc* amalgamations of parishes and also creating a central supervisory Poor Law Board

1835   Municipal Corporations Act
Gives larger towns and cities powers to create elected borough councils and, thus, lays the foundation for the modern system of local government

1848   Public Health Act
Creates *ad hoc* health boards to provide clean water and sewage systems from amalgamations of parish councils

1870   Education Act
Establishes requirement for compulsory education for children up to twelve years of age and that School Boards are created where no arrangement for administering public education exists

1871   Creation of the Local Government Board
The first government department specifically dealing with local government

1888   Local Government Act
Creates elected County Councils and removes the powers of JPs over county administration

1894   Local Government Act
Creates elected Urban and Rural District Councils based on health board areas and effectively transfers most parish duties to larger local government units

1899   London Boroughs Act
Restructures boroughs in London thus completing the modernisation of the local government system in England and Wales initiated in 1834

1919 Housing Act
Establishes financial powers to enable local authorities to build large housing estates

1919 Creation of the Ministry of Health which takes over the Local Government Board functions

1929 Abolition of poor law boards of guardians and transfer of their responsibilities to local government

1935 Creation of centrally controlled National Assistance Board ending local authority responsibility for alleviation of poverty

1946 National Health Services Act
Creates a national health service outside local government system

1947 Electricity Act
Nationalises electricity production and supply and removes this power from local government

1947 Town and Country Planning Act
Greatly extends local government role in town and country planning

1948 Gas Act
Nationalises and demunicipalises gas production and distribution

1952 Creation of a Ministry of Housing and Local Government

1960 Herbert Commission Report on local government in London published

1963 London Government Act
Creates the Greater London Council, 32 London Boroughs, and the Inner London Education Authority to come into force in April 1965

1996 Redcliffe-Maud and Wheatley Royal Commissions established

1969 Redcliffe-Maud, Wheatley Commission reports published and broadly accepted by Wilson Government

1970 Conservatives win general election in June and Heath as Prime Minister announces major modifications in plans to restructure local government

1971 Creation in October of the Department of the Environment which takes over the powers of the Ministry of Housing and Local Government

1972 Local Government Act
Creates new structures for local government in England and Wales which come into force in April 1974 following deliberations of a Boundary Commission to determine the exact arrangements for the new authorities

1973 Local Government (Scotland) Act
Restructures local government system for Scotland to come into force in 1974

1973 Water Act
Transfers municipal water and sewage disposal powers to unelected regional water authorities

1974   Labour wins the general elections of February and November

1975   Consultative Council for Local Government Finance created

1976   Layfield Report on local government finance published

1978–79   'Winter of discontent', major strikes by municipal workers

1979   Conservatives win the general election in May, Mrs Thatcher becomes Prime Minister

1980   Local Government Planning and Land Act
       Establishes new system for local government grants, creates enterprise zones and UDCs, required direct works departments to compete with private sector for building contracts

1980   Housing Act
       Requires local authorities to sell council houses to tenants

1982   Local Government Finance Act
       Further restuctures grants system, removes local powers to set more than one rate demand in a year and creates the Audit Commission

1984   Rates Act
       Provides the government with powers to cap the rates set by local authorities and, thus, effectively allows central government to determine local authority expenditure

1984   A Bill published to pave the way for abolition on the Metropolitan Counties and GLC

1985   From March until July some local authorities attempt to defy the provisions of the Rates Act but all are unsuccessful

1985   Local Government Act
       Abolishes from April 1986 the MDCs and GLC transferring powers respectively to MDCs and London Boroughs or unelected agencies

1986   Transport Act
       Deregulates public transport removing local government powers to subsidise bus services and also allowing competition between bus companies on the same routes

1986   Local Government Access to Information Act

1986   Local Government Act
       Prevents local authorities from publishing material critical of the government

1987   Widdicombe Report published

1987   Rates Act (Scotland)
       Creates poll tax system to replace the rates for Scotland

1988   Local Government Act
       Requires local authorities to put many services out to compulsory competitive tendering (CCT) and includes section 28 banning local government support to homosexual groups

1988 Housing Act
Facilitates the sale of council estates to the private sector or their transfer to Housing Action Trusts

1988 Rates Act
Establishes the poll tax for England and Wales abolishing the domestic rate and removes local control over rates to businesses with the unified business rate

1988 Education Reform Act
Allows schools to opt out of local government control, sets up the national curriculum and creates local self-management for schools

1989 Local Government and Housing Act
Further measures to increase council house sales, gives local authorities powers to develop their local economies but curtails their capacity to own and control businesses

1990 National Health Service and Community Care Act
Places responsibility for care in the community to local government

1990 Mrs Thatcher loses leadership of the Conservative Party in November and is succeeded as leader and Prime Minister by John Major

1991 Further and Higher Education Act
Removes further education from local authority control

1991 Consultative documents announced by Michael Heseltine propose a restructuring of local government to favour a single-tier system and directly elected mayors

1992 Local Government Act
Establishes a Local Government Commission under the chairmanship of Sir John Banham to restructure the local government systems for England. The Scottish and Welsh Offices conduct parallel studies

1992 Local Government Finance Act
Repeals the poll tax and replaces it with the council tax

1993 Local Education Act
Establishes a Funding Agency for Schools

1995 Elections for some of the new unitary authorities created by the Banham Commission but also concerns over some proposals and replacement of Banham as Chair of Commission

1996 New unitary and restructured counties following the Banham Commission fully established

1997 Labour Party take power with Tony Blair as Prime Minister

1998 White Paper *Modern Local Government: In Touch with the People* published

1998 The Scotland Act and Government of Wales Act set the framework for regional self-government in these areas

1998   Regional Development Agencies Act establishes the regional development agencies and regional chambers

1999   Local Government Act
        Creates the Best Value framework for establishing standards for local government service provision and systems to replace CCT in ensuring competition and partnerships between local government and private sector service provision

1999   The Greater London Authority Act establishes the Greater London Authority which begins work the following year

2000   Elections and opening of the Greater London Authority

2000   Local Government Act
        Gives new general powers and duties to local authorities, creates cabinet government and elected mayors or mayor/manager structures, establishes new role for backbench councillors, scrutinising committees and new ethics and standards committees

References

Ashford, D.E. (1981) *British Dogmatism and French Pragmatism*, London, George Allen and Unwin.

Ashworth, P.D. and Chandler, J.A. (1981) 'Perceptions of Politics in Stocksbridge', Unpublished.

Audit Commission (1988) *The Competitive Council*, London, Audit Commission.

Bacharach, P. and Baratz, M. (1962) 'Two Faces of Power', *American Political Science Review*, Vol. 56, pp. 947–52

Bailey, S. and Paddison, R. (eds) (1988) *The Reform of Local Government Finance in Britain*, London, Routledge.

Bains, M.A. (1972) *The New Local Authorities: Management and Structure*, London, HMSO.

Barker, M. (1982) 'The Relation between Trade Unions and the Labour Party in Sheffield', Department of Political Studies, Sheffield Polytechnic, Sheffield, unpublished monograph.

Barron, J., Crawley, G. and Wood, T. (1991) *Councillors in Crisis*, Basingstoke, Macmillan.

Batley, R. and Stoker, G. (eds) (1991) *Local Government in Europe: Trends and Developments*, Basingstoke, Macmillan.

Bealey, F., Blondel, J. and McCann, W.P. (1965) *Constituency Politics*, London, Faber and Faber.

Bell, C. and Newby, H. (1971) *Community Studies*, London, George Allen and Unwin.

Bell, D. (1960) *The End of Ideology*, Glencoe, The Free Press.

Benington, J. (1986) 'Local Economic Strategies: Paradigms for a Planned Economy', *Local Economy*, Vol. 1., No. 1., pp. 7–33.

Ben-Tovim, G., Gabriel, J., Law, I. and Streddet, K. (1986) *The Local Politics of Race*, London, Macmillan.

Beresford, P. (1987) *Good Council Guide: Wandsworth 1978–1987*, London, Centre for Policy Studies.

Birch, A.H. (1959) *Small Town Politics: A Study of Political Life in Glossop*, Oxford, Oxford University Press.

Blunkett, D. and Jackson, K. (1987) *Democracy in Crisis*, London, Hogarth Press.

Boaden, N. (1971) *Urban Policy-Making*, Cambridge, Cambridge University Press.

Boddy, M. and Fudge, C. (eds) (1984) *Local Socialism?*, Basingstoke, Macmillan.

Bowman, M. and Hampton W.A. (1983) *Local Democracies*, Cheshire, Melbourne, Longman.

223

Boyne, G. (1998) *Public Choice Theory and Local Government: A Comparative Analysis of the UK and the USA*, Basingstoke, Macmillan.

Bradford, M. (1988) *The Fight for Yorkshire*, Beverley, Hutton Press.

Branson, N. (1979) *Poplarism 1919–1925*, London, Lawrence and Wishart.

Bulpitt, J.G. (1967) *Party Politics in English Local Government*, London, Longman.

Bulpitt, J.G. (1983) *Territory and Power in the United Kingdom*, Manchester, Manchester University Press.

Burns, D., Hambleton, R. and Hoggett, P. (1994) *The Politics of Decentralisation*, Basingstoke, Macmillan.

Butler, D., Adonis, A. and Travers, T. (1995) *Failure in British Government: The Politics of the Poll Tax*, Oxford, Oxford University Press.

Butler, D. and Stokes, D. (1974) *Political Change in Britain*, 2nd edn., London, Macmillan.

Byrne, T. (2000) *Local Government in Britain*, (7th edn.), Harmondsworth, Penguin.

Cabinet Office (2000) *Civil Service Handbook 2000–01*, London, HMSO.

Castells, M. (1977) *The Urban Question*, London, Edward Arnold.

Cawson, A. (1978) 'Pluralism, Corporatism and the Role of the State', *Government and Opposition*, Vol. 13, 178–98.

Cawson, A. (1985) 'Corporatism and Local Politics', in Grant, W. (ed.), *The Political Economy of Corporatism*, London, Macmillan, pp 126–47.

Chandler, J.A. (1988) *Public Policy Making for Local Government*, London, Croom Helm.

Chandler, J.A. (1992) 'Three Faces of Intergovernmental Relations', *Public Policy and Administration*, vol. 7, pp. 47–57.

Chandler, J.A. (ed.) (1993) *Local Government in Liberal Democracies*, London, Routledge.

Chandler, J.A. (ed.) (1996) *The Citizen's Charter*, Aldershot, Dartmouth.

Chandler, J. A. (1998) 'Regenerating South Yorkshire: How the public sector dominates Business Partnerships in Britain' in Walzer, N. and Jacobs, B.D. (eds) *Public Private Partnerships for Local Economic Development*, Westport, Praeger, pp. 157–76.

Chandler, J.A., Gregory, M., Hunt, M. and Turner, R. (1995) *Decentralisation and Devolution in England and Wales*, Luton, Local Government Management Board.

Chandler, J.A. and Kingdom, J.E. (1999) 'MPs and Local Government: The Case of Sheffield' presented to the Political Studies Association Annual Conference, University of Nottingham.

Chandler, J.A. and Lawless, P. (1985) *Local Authorities and the Creation of Employment*, Aldershot, Gower.

Chandler, J.A. and Morris, D. (1984) 'The Selection of Local Candidates' in Bristow, S., Kermode, D. and Mannin, M. *Redundant Counties?*, Ormskirk, Hesketh Press.

Chandler, J.A. and Turner, R. (1997) 'Pricing and Local Authorities', *Public Money and Management*, Vol. 17, No. 2. April–June, pp. 37–43.

Clarke, M. and Stewart, J. (1990) *General Management in Local Government: Getting the Balance Right*, Harlow, Longman.

Clements, R.V. (1969) *Local Noteables and the City Councils*, London, Macmillan.

Cockburn, C. (1977) *The Local State*, London, Pluto Press.

Cole, G.D.H. (1947) *Local and Regional Government*, London, Cassell.

Commission for Local Democracy (1995) *Taking Charge: The Rebirth of Local Democracy*, London, Municipal Journal Books.

Crick, M. (1986) *The March of Militant*, London, Faber and Faber.

Crosland, S. (1982) *Tony Crosland*, London, Jonathan Cape.

Crossman, R.H.S. (1975) *The Diaries of a Cabinet Minister,* Vol. 1, London, Hamish Hamilton and Jonathan Cape.

Cyr, A. (1977) *Liberal Party Politics in Britain,* London, John Calder.

Dahl, R.A. (1961) *Who Governs,* New Haven, Yale University Press.

Dahl, R.A. (1971) *Polyarchy,* New Haven, Yale University Press.

Dahl, R.A. (1985) *An Economic Theory of Democracy,* New Haven, Yale University Press.

Dahl, R.A. (1989) *Democracy and its Critics,* New Haven, Yale University Press.

Dearlove, J. (1973) *The Politics and Policy of Local Government,* Cambridge, Cambridge University Press.

Department of the Environment, Transport and the Regions (1999) *Local Government Financial Statistics 1999,* London, HMSO.

DTLR (2000) *The Government's Response to the Environment, Transport and Regional Affairs Committee's Report: Local Government Finance,* www.local-regions.dtlr.gov.uk/response/lgfin/index.htm

DTLR (2000a) *The Single Regeneration Budget,* www.regeneration.dtlr.gov.uk

DTLR (2000b) *Modernising Local Government Finance: A Green Paper,* www.local.dtlr.gov.uk/greenpap, London, HMSO.

Dod (1994) *Dod's Parliamentary Companion,* London, Dod's Parliamentary Companion Ltd.

Donoghue, B. and Jones, G.W. (1973) *Herbert Morrison,* London, Weidenfeld and Nicolson.

Doogan, K. (1999) 'The Contracting out of Local Government Services: Its impact on Jobs, Conditions of Service and Labour' in Stoker, G. (ed') *The New Management of British Local Governance,* Basingstoke, Macmillan, pp. 62–78.

Duncan, S. and Goodwin, M. (1988) *The State and Uneven Development,* Oxford, Polity Press.

Dunleavy, P. (1980) *Urban Political Analysis,* London, Macmillan.

Dunleavy, P. (1981) *The Politics of Mass Housing in Britain 1945–1975,* London, Clarendon Press.

Dunleavy, P. (1984) 'The Limits to Local Government' in Boddy, M. and Fudge, C. *Local Socialism?,* London, Macmillan, pp. 49–81.

Dunleavy, P. (1991) *Democracy, Bureaucracy and Public Choice,* Hemel Hempstead, Harvester Wheatsheaf.

Dunleavy, P., Gamble, A., Holliday, I. and Peele, G. (1998), *Developments in British Politics 6,* London, Macmillan.

Dye, T. (1988) *Politics in States and Communities,* 6th edn. New York, Prentice Hall.

Elcock, H. (1991) *Local Government,* 2nd edn, London, Methuen.

Elcock, H. and Jordan, G. (1987) *Learning from Local Authority Budgeting,* Aldershot, Avebury.

Elcock, H., Jordan, G. and Midwinter, A. (1989) *Budgeting in Local Government,* London, Longman.

Englefield, D. (1987) *Local Government and Business,* London, Municipal Journal.

Finer, H. (1945) *English Local Government,* 2nd edn, London, Methuen.

Fraser, D. (1979) *Power and Authority in the Victorian City,* Oxford, Basil Blackwell.

Goss, S. (1988) *Local Labour and Local Government,* Edinburgh, Edinburgh University Press.

Gray, C. (1994) *Government Beyond the Centre,* London, Macmillan.

Green, D.G. (1981) *Power and Party in an English City*, London, George Allen and Unwin.

Greenwood, R. and Stewart, J.D. (1974) *Corporate Planning in Local Government*, London, Charles Knight.

Greenwood, J. and Wilson, D. (1989) *Public Administration in Britain Today*, 2nd edn, London, Unwin-Hyman.

Greenwood, R. Walsh, K., Hinings, C.R. and Ransom, C. (1980) *Patterns of Management in Local Government*, Oxford, Martin Robertson.

Griffith, J.A.G. (1966) *Central Departments and Local Authorities*, London, George Allen and Unwin.

Gustafsson, A. (1988) *Local Government in Sweden*, 2nd edn, Stockholm, The Swedish Institute.

Gyford, J. (1985) *The Politics of Local Socialism*, London, George Allen and Unwin.

Gyford, J. and James, M. (1983) *National Parties and Local Politics*, London, George Allen and Unwin.

Hain, P. (ed.) (1976) *Communities in Conflict*, London, John Calder.

Hall, D. and Leach, S, (2000) 'The Changing Nature of Local Labour Parties' in Stoker, G. (ed.) *The New Politics of English Local Governance*, Basingstoke, Macmillan, pp. 150–65.

Hampton, W.A. (1970) *Democracy and Community*, Oxford, Oxford University Press.

Hampton, W.A. (1987) *Local Government and Urban Politics*, Harlow, Longman.

Hampton, W.A. (1991) *Local Government and Urban Politics*, 2nd edn, Harlow, Longman.

Held, D. (1987) *Models of Democracy*, Oxford, Polity Press.

Hennessy, P. (1989) *Whitehall*, London, Secker and Warburg.

Henney, A. (1984) *Inside Local Government*, London, Sinclair Browne.

Hepworth, N. (1984) *The Finance of Local Government*, 7th edn, London, George Allen and Unwin.

Herbert, E. (1960) *Royal Commission on Local Government in Greater London*, London, HMSO.

Hill, D. (1974) *Democratic Theory and Local Government*, London, George Allen and Unwin.

Hindess, B. (1971) *The Decline of Working Class Politics*, London, McGibbon Kee.

Hodge, M. (1988) 'Central Local Conflicts: The View from Islington' in Hoggett, P. and Hambleton, R. *Decentralisation and Democracy*, Bristol, School for Advanced Urban Studies, Bristol University, pp. 29–36.

Hoggett, P. and Hambleton, R. (eds) (1988) *Decentralisation and Democracy*, Bristol, School for Advanced Urban Studies, Bristol University.

Hogwood, B. and Lindley, P.D. (1982) 'Variations in Regional Boundaries' in Hogwood, B. and Keating, M. *Regional Government in England*, Oxford, Clarendon Press.

Holliday, I. (2000) 'The Conservative Party in Local Government 1979–1997' in Stoker, G. *The New Politics of English Local Governance*, Basingstoke, Macmillan.

Hollis, G. *et al.* (1990) *Alternatives to the Community Charge*, York, Joseph Rowntree Trust and Coopers Lybrand.

Hood, C. (1991) 'A Public Management for All Seasons?', *Public Administration*, vol. 69, pp. 3–19.

Hunter, F. (1953) *Community Power Structure*, University of North Carolina Press.

John, P. (1989) *Introduction to the Community Charge in Scotland*, London, Policy Studies Institute.

Jones, B. (1995) *Local Government Financial Management*, Hemel Hempstead, ICSA Publishing.

Jones, G. and Stewart, J. (1983) *The Case for Local Government*, London, George Allen and Unwin.

Jessop, B. (1988) *Conservative Regimes and the Transition to Post-Fordism*, Essex Paper in Politics and Government, No. 47, Colchester, University of Essex.

Keith-Lucas, B. and Richards, P.G. (1978) *A History of Local Government in the Twentieth Century*, London, George Allen and Unwin.

Kellas, J.G. (1968) *Modern Scotland*, London, Pall Mall

Kerley, R. (1994) *Managing in Local Government*, Basingstoke, Macmillan.

King, D. (1987) *The New Right*, London, Macmillan.

King, D. and Stoker, G. (eds) (1996) *Rethinking Local Democracy*, Basingstoke, Macmillan.

Kingdom, J.E. (1986) 'Public Administration: Defining the Discipline', *Teaching Public Administration*, Vol. 6, No 1, pp. 1–13; No. 2, pp. 1–21.

Kingdom, J.E. (1991) *Local Government and Politics in Britain*, Hemel Hempstead, Philip Allen.

Kingdom, J.E. (1999) *Government and Politics in Britain*, 2nd edn, Oxford, Polity Press.

Laffin, M. (1986) *Professionalism and Policy: The Role of the Professionals in the Central-Local Relationship*, Aldershot, Gower.

Laffin, M. (1989) *Managing under Pressure: Industrial Relations in Local Government*, London, Macmillan.

Laffin, M. and Young, K. (1990) *Professionalism in Local Government*, Harlow, Longman.

Lagroye, J. and Wright, V. (eds) (1979) *Local Government in Britain and France*, London, George Allen and Unwin.

Lansley, S., Goss, S. and Wolmar, C. (1989) *Councils in Conflict: The Rise and Fall of the Municipal Left*, Basingstoke, Macmillan.

Layfield, F. (1976) *Report of the Committee of Enquiry into Local Government Finance*, Cmnd. 6453, London, HMSO.

Leach, S. (1998) *Local Government Reorganisation: The Review and its Aftermath*, London, Frank Cass.

Leach, S. and Stewart, J. (1985) 'The Politics and Management of Hung Authorities', *Public Administration*, Vol. 66, No. 1. pp. 35–56.

Leach, S. and Stewart, J. (1992) *The Politics of Hung Authorities*, London, Macmillan.

Leach, S., Stewart, J. and Walsh, K. (1994) *The Changing Organisation and Management of Local Government*, London, Macmillan.

Lee, J.M. (1963) *Social Leaders and Public Persons*, Oxford, Oxford University Press.

Lively, J. (1975) *Democracy*, Oxford, Basil Blackwell.

Llewellyn, A. (ed.) (1999) *The Guardian Local Authority Directory*, London, Alcourt Publishing.

Local Government Ombudsman (2000) *Annual Report 1999/2000*, London, HMSO.

Loughlin, J. (ed.) (1999) *Regional and Local Democracy in the European Union*, Luxembourg, Office for Official Publications of the European Union.

Lowndes, V. (1999) 'Management Change In Local Governance' in Stoker, G. (ed.) *The New Management of British Local Governance*, Basingstoke, Macmillan, pp. 22–39.

Lynd, R. and Lynd, H. (1929) *Middletown*, New York, Harcourt, Brace and World.

Machin, H. (1977) *The Prefect in French Public Administration*, London, Croom Helm.

Mallaby, G. (1967) *Report of the Committee on the Staffing of Local Government*, London, HMSO.

Maloney, W., Smith, G. and Stoker, G. (2000) 'Social Capital and Urban Governance: Adding a more Constitutional Top Down Perspective', *Political Studies*, Vol. . 48, No. 4, pp. 802–20.

Malpass, P. (2000), *Housing Associations and Housing Policy: A Historical Perspective*, Basingstoke, Macmillan.

Maud, J. (1967) *Committee on the Management of Local Government*, London, HMSO.

McKenzie, R.T. (1963) *British Political Parties*, 2nd edn, London, Mercury Books.

Michels, R. (1958) *Political Parties*, Glencoe, Free Press.

Midwinter, A. (1984) *The Politics of Local Spending*, Edinburgh, Mainstream.

Mill, J.S. (1975) *Considerations on Representative Government* in Mill, J.S. (1975) *Three Essays*, Oxford, Oxford, University Press.

Miller, W.L., Dickson, M. and Stoker, G. (2000) *Models of Local Governance: Political Opinion and Theory in Britain*, Basingstoke, Palgrave.

Moore, C. and Richardson, J.J. (1989) *Local Partnership and the Unemployment Crisis in Britain*, London, Unwin Hyman.

Municipal Year Book (1994–2000) *The Municipal Year Book*, London, The Municipal Journal Ltd.

Newton, K. (1976) *Second City Politics*, Oxford, Oxford University Press.

Newton, K. and Karran, T.J. (1985) *The Politics of Local Expenditure*, London, Macmillan.

Niskanen, W.A. (1973) *Bureaucracy and Representative Government*, New York, Aldine-Atherton.

Niskanen, W.A. (1973a) *Bureaucracy: Servant or Master*, London, Institute for Economic Affairs.

Norton, A. (1991) *The Role of the Chief Executive in British Local Government*, Birmingham, Institute of Local Government Studies.

Office for National Statistics (1999) *Annual Abstract of Statistics*, London, HMSO.

Office for National Statistics (2000a) *Annual Abstract of Statistics*, London, HMSO.

Office for National Statistics (2000b) *Financial Statistics*, London, HMSO.

Osborne, D. and Gaebler, T. (1992) *Reinventing Government*, Reading, MASS, Addison-Wesley.

Page, E.C. (1987) *Central and Local Government Relations: A Comparative Analysis of West European Unitary States*, London, Sage.

Parrott, L. (1999) *Social Work and Social Care*, Eastbourne, Gildredge Press.

Parry, G. (1969) *Political Elites*, London, George Allen and Unwin.

Phillips, A. (1994) *Local Democracy: The Terms of the Debate*, London, Commission for Local Democracy,

Pimlott, B. (1985) *Hugh Dalton*, London, Jonathan Cape.

Plant, R. (1974) *Community and Ideology*, London, Routledge and Kegan Paul.

Poole, K.P. (1978) *The Local Government Service in England and Wales*, London, George Allen and Unwin.

Pratchett, L. (ed.) (2000) *Renewing Local Democracy: The Modernisation Agenda in British Local Government*, London, Frank Cass.

Pratchett, L. and Wilson, D. (eds) (1996) *Local Government and Local Democracy*, Basingstoke, Macmillan.

Prior, D. (1995) 'Citizen's Charters' in Stewart, J. and Stoker, G. (eds) *Local Government in the 1990s*, Basingstoke, Macmillan, pp. 86–106.

Rallings, C. and Thrasher, M. (1994) *Local Elections in England and Wales*, Plymouth, Local Government Chronicle Election Centre.

Rallings, C. and Thrasher, M. (1996) *Participation in Local Election*, in Pratchett, L. and Wilson, D. (eds) *Local Government and Local Democracy*, Basingstoke, Macmillan.

Rallings, C. and Thrasher, M. (2000) *Local Elections in England and Wales*, Plymouth,

Local Government Chronicle Election Centre. http://www.lgcnet.com/pages/products/elections/turnout.htm

Rawlinson, D. and Tanner, B. (1990) *Financial Management in the 1990s*, Harlow, Longman.

Redcliffe-Maud, J. (1969) *Royal Commission on Local Government in England 1966–1969*, Cmnd. 4040, Vol. I and Vol. III, London, HMSO.

Redlich, J. and Hirst, F.W. (1958) *The History of Local Government in England*, ed. Keith-Lucas, B., London: Macmillan.

Redlich, J. and Hirst, F.W. (1970), *Local Government in England*, ed. Keith-Lucas, B. London, Macmillan.

Regan, D.E. (1977) *Local Government and Education*, London, George Allen and Unwin.

Rhodes, R.A.W. (1981) *Control and Power in Central-Local Government*, Farnborough, Gower.

Rhodes, R.A.W. (1986) *The National World of Local Government*, London, Allen and Unwin.

Rhodes, R.A.W. (1986a) 'Power Dependence: Theories of Central–Local Relations: A Critical Assessment' in Goldsmith, M. *New Research in Central-Local Relations*, Farnborough, Gower.

Rhodes, R.A.W. (1988) *Beyond Westminster and Whitehall*, London, Allen and Unwin.

Rhodes, R.A.W. (1991) 'Theory and Methods in British Public Administration: The view from Political Science', *Political Studies*, Vol. 39, No. 3, pp. 533–54.

Rhodes, R.A.W., Hardy, D. and Pudney, K. (1983) 'Corporate Bias' in *Central-Local Relations: A Case Study of the CCGLF*, Colchester, Department of Government, University, of Essex Occasional Paper.

Rhodes, R.A.W. and Marsh, D. (1992) 'Policy Networks in British Politics: A critique of Existing Approaches' in Marsh, D. and Rhodes, R.A.W. (eds) *Policy Networks in British Government*, Oxford, Oxford University Press, pp. 1–26.

Ridley, N. (1988) *The Local Right: Enabling not Providing*, London, Centre for Policy Studies.

Robinson, D. (1977) *Report of the Committee on the Remuneration of Councillors*, London, HMSO.

Robson, W.A. (1954) *The Development of Local Government*, 3rd edn, London, George Allen and Unwin.

Salmon, C.B. (1976) *Royal Commission on Standards in Public Life*, Cmnd. 6524, London, HMSO.

Saunders, P. (1979) *Urban Politics: A Sociological Interpretation*, London, Hutchinson.

Saunders, P. (1981) *Social Theory and the Urban Question*, London, Hutchinson.

Saunders, P. (1984) 'Rethinking Local Politics' in Boddy, M. and Fudge, C. *Local Socialism?*, London, Macmillan, pp. 22–48.

Schumpeter, J. (1947) *Capitalism, Socialism and Democracy*, London, George Allen and Unwin.

Seabrook, J. (1984) *The Idea of Neighbourhood*, London, Pluto Press.

Sharpe, L.J. (1970) 'Theories and Values in Local Government', *Political Studies*, Vol. 18, No. 2, pp. 153–74.

Sharpe, L.J. and Newton, K. (1984) *Does Politics Matter?*, Oxford, Oxford University Press.

Shaw, B. (1908) *The Commonsense of Municipal Trading*, London, A.C. Fifield.

Sheldrake, J. (1992) *Modern Local Government*, Aldershot, Dartmouth.

Smitham, K. (1991) 'The New Urban Right: A Study of Bradford City Council 1988–1990', BA Public Administration, Sheffield City Polytechnic.

Stanyer, J. (1976) *Understanding Local Government*, Oxford, Martin Robertson.

Stewart, J. (1971) *Management in Local Government*, London, Charles Knight.

Stewart, J. (1974) *The Responsive Local Authority*, London, Charles Knight.

Stewart, J. (1983) *Local Government: The Conditions of Local Choice*, London, Allen and Unwin.

Stewart, J. (1986) *The New Management of Local Government*, London, Allen and Unwin.

Stewart, J. (2000) *The Nature of British Local Government*, Basingstoke, Macmillan.

Stewart, J. and Stoker, G., (eds) (1995) *Local Government in the 1990s*, Basingstoke, Macmillan.

Stoker, G. (1989) 'Local Government in a Post-Fordist Society' in Stewart, J. and Stoker, G. *The Future of Local Government*, Basingstoke, Macmillan, pp. 140–70.

Stoker, G. (1991) *The Politics of Local Government*, 2nd edn, Basingstoke, Macmillan.

Stoker, G. (1994) *The Role and Purpose of Local Government*, London, Commission for Local Democracy.

Stoker, G. (1995) 'Intergovernmental Relations', *Public Administration*, Vol. 73, pp. 101–22.

Stoker, G. (ed.) (1999) *The New Management of British Local Governance*, Basingstoke, Macmillan.

Stoker, G. (ed.) (2000) *The New Politics of English Local Governance*, Basingstoke, Macmillan.

Stone, C. (1989) *Regime Politics: Governing Atlanta*, Lawrence, University of Kansas Press.

Taaffe, P. and Mulhearn, T. (1988) *Liverpool: A City that Dared to Fight*, London, Fortress.

Thomas, R. (1978) *The British Philosophy of Administration*, London, Longman.

Tiebout, C. (1956) 'A Pure Theory of Local Expenditures', *Journal of Political Economy*, Vol. 64, pp. 416–24.

Tocqueville de, A. (1946) *Democracy in America* (tr. Henry Reeve), (ed.) H.S. Commager, Oxford, Oxford University Press.

Travers, T. (1986) *The Politics of Local Government Finance*, London, George Allen and Unwin.

Travers, T. (1995) 'Finance' in Stewart, J. and Stoker, G. (eds) *Local Government in the 1990s*, Basingstoke, Macmillan, pp. 9–27.

Tree, D. (1989) 'A Critical Analysis of the Justifications for Decentralisation within Local Authority Service Departments with specific reference to East Sussex County Council', B.A. Public Administration Dissertation, Sheffield City Polytechnic.

Tullock, G. (1975) *The Vote Motive*, London, Institute for Economic Affairs.

Walker, D. (1983) *Municipal Empire: The Town Halls and their Beneficiaries*, London, Temple-Smith.

Waller, R. (1980) 'The 1979 Local and General Elections in England and Wales: Is there a Local/National Differential', *Political Studies*, Vol. 28, No. 3 pp. 443–50.

Walsh, K. (1995) *Public Services and Market Mechanisms*, London, Macmillan.

Webb, S. and Webb, B. (1920) *A Constitution for the Socialist Commonwealth of Great Britain*, Cambridge, Cambridge University Press.

Widdicombe, D. (1986) *The Conduct of Local Authority Business*, Cmnd. 9797, London, HMSO.

Williams, P. (1979) *Hugh Gaitskell*, London, Jonathon Cape.

Wilson, D. and Game, C. (1998) *Local Government in the United Kingdom*, 2nd edn, Basingstoke, Macmillan.

Wollmann, H. and Schroter, E. (2000) *Comparing Public Sector Reform in Britain and Germany*, Aldershot, Ashgate.

Wood, B. (1976) *The Process of Local Government Reform 1966–1974*, London, George Allen and Unwin.

Wood, R.C. (1961) *1400 Governments*, Cambridge, Mass, Harvard University Press.

Young, K. and Rao, N. (1997) *Local Government since 1945*, Oxford, Blackwell.

Index